The Aristotelian Ethics

The Aristotelian Ethics

A STUDY OF THE RELATIONSHIP
BETWEEN THE *EUDEMIAN* AND
NICOMACHEAN ETHICS OF ARISTOTLE

ANTHONY KENNY

CLARENDON PRESS · OXFORD
1978

Oxford University Press, Walton Street, Oxford OX2 6DP

OXFORD LONDON GLASGOW NEW YORK
TORONTO MELBOURNE WELLINGTON CAPE TOWN
IBADAN NAIROBI DAR ES SALAAM LUSAKA
KUALA LUMPUR SINGAPORE JAKARTA HONG KONG TOKYO
DELHI BOMBAY CALCUTTA MADRAS KARACHI

© *Oxford University Press 1978*

British Library Cataloging in Publication Data

Kenny, Anthony John Patrick
The Aristotelian ethics.
1. Aristotle—Ethics
I. Title
170   B491.E7   77-30640

ISBN 0-19-824554-8

*Printed in Great Britain by
William Clowes & Sons Ltd.
London, Beccles and Colchester*

PREFACE

THIS book is an attempt to solve a long-standing problem of Aristotelian scholarship on the basis of historical and philosophical arguments and a statistical study of features of style. To be fully qualified to undertake such a task a man must be a professional philosopher, classicist, and statistician. I can claim to be professionally qualified only as a philosopher: I am a very amateur classicist and a complete novice in statistics. My excuse for being undeterred by this is the fact that most of those working in the field of literary statistics are also, in one or other respect, novices, or, as they would no doubt prefer to put it, pioneers. When the statistical study of literary texts has grown into a systematically organized discipline, monographs such as the present will no doubt look very amateurish. But any discipline in its earliest days must depend upon the contributions of untaught and inexpert amateurs.

The amateur who ventures into a field on the borderline of several disciplines must, however, be more than usually conscious of the debt he owes to his colleagues in the adjacent fields in which he is himself unskilled. In writing the present work I have been at every step dependent on the learning and generosity of the philologists, historians, statisticians, and computer experts who have patiently striven to remove my misunderstandings and fill up the gaps in my knowledge. In a field so well trodden as that of Aristotelian studies it would no doubt be rash to claim even that my mistakes are original: but it is more than usually true to say that the errors which remain in the book are in no way the responsibility of the kind friends who have taken pains to see that others were expunged.

I must express my gratitude to my classical colleagues in Balliol who were often the immediate target for my brain-picking forays; in particular Dr. Oswyn Murray who gave me much useful historical information, and Mr. Jasper Griffin who read the whole book in typescript and tactfully deleted a number of solecisms. I am very much indebted to Mr. Paul Griffith, statistical officer at the Oxford Computing Laboratory, who checked the statistical argument of Chapter 4, to Mr. Frank Pettit, who first taught me how to use a computer, and to Mrs. Susan Hockey who taught me everything that I know about the use of the computer for literary studies. I wish also to thank Professor Thedore Brunner and the staff of the Thesaurus Linguae Graecae at Irvine, and Stephan Gruen who as a graduate student prepared for me a computer-readable text of the *Eudemian Ethics*, on which I carried out my preliminary studies before the tapes prepared by the Thesaurus Linguae Graecae became available.

Drafts of chapters of the book were read as papers to the Bs club in Cambridge, to the Philological Society in Oxford, to the American Philological Society in Washington, and to the Moral Sciences Club in Cambridge; and also to societies and seminars at King's College, London, at the University of Texas at Austin, at Swarthmore College, at the University of Pennsylvania, at the University of Michigan, and at Bristol University. I am most grateful to those who took part in the discussions at those places for many helpful suggestions and criticisms.

The Revd. Andrew Q. Morton of Culross, and Dr. Alan Jones of the Oriental Institute in Oxford were both extremely helpful and encouraging to me when first I became interested in the statistical study of classical texts. Professor Charles Kahn of the University of Pennsylvania and an anonymous reader for the Archiv für Geschichte der Philosophie made searching and valuable criticism of an early draft of the central argument of the book.

Dr. C. J. Rowe, whose study of the relationship between the *Eudemian* and *Nicomachean Ethics* in 1971 awoke my own interest in the problem, assisted me, in discussion and in correspondence, at every stage of my work—bent as I was on the destruction of the theory he had so ably defended—with the most admirable impartiality, generosity, and friendliness. Professor D. J. Allan— who has for decades stood out, almost alone in the republic of classical letters, against the universal acceptance of the fashions set by Werner Jaeger, and has given courage to others less learned than himself to do likewise—has placed me greatly in his debt by his constant encouragement and willingness to share with me the unparalleled store of learning he has acquired in more than twenty years' study of the *Eudemian Ethics*. To these and to the other Aristotelian scholars who have taken a friendly interest in my work I am most grateful, in particular to Professor J. L. Ackrill, Jonathan

Barnes, Professor G. E. L. Owen, Richard Sorabji, Pamela Huby, and Michael Woods.

Finally I must express my gratitude to four scholars whom I have never met but to whose writings I owe a great deal. Professor J. D. Monan's *Moral Knowledge and its Methodology in Aristotle* first made me aware of the flimsiness of the arguments on which the accepted chronology of Aristotle's ethical writings rested. The monumental commentaries of Gauthier and Jolif and of Dirlmeier are classical expressions of the theories which are the target of the present work: but I am aware that at every step I draw upon their erudition and industry for the very information on which my criticism of the reigning orthodoxy of Aristotelian scholarship is based.

I am indebted to the Trustees of the Craven Fund for a travel grant which enabled me to consult manuscripts of the *Ethics* and of Aspasius in Florence and in Rome.

CONTENTS

LIST OF TABLES

CHAPTER I

The Aristotelian *Ethics*
in Antiquity

FOR many centuries the *Nicomachean Ethics* have been regarded as *the Ethics* of Aristotle. From the Byzantine period twenty manuscripts of the *Nicomachean Ethics* survive; of the *Eudemian Ethics* only two (Harlfinger, 1971, 27). Since the Middle Ages commentaries on the *Nicomachean Ethics* have appeared about once a decade; the *Eudemian Ethics* has received only four commentaries in its whole history (Maurus, 1668; Fritzsche, 1851; Dirlmeier, 1969; von Fragstein, 1974). Nineteenth-century scholars, following the lead of Schleiermacher (1835) and Spengel (1841) almost unanimously regarded the *Eudemian Ethics* as spurious: they were so confident of its inauthenticity that Susemihl could print on the title-page of his still-indispensable edition of the text '*Eudemii Rhodii Ethica*'. Early in the present century scholarly opinion, in the wake of von der Mühll (1909), Kapp (1912), and above all Jaeger (1923) swung in favour of accepting the work as authentic; but it has never been accorded anything like parity of esteem with the Nicomachean treatise. Twentieth-century scholars have treated it as a product of the comparatively young Aristotle, still under the stiflingly metaphysical influence of Plato. Once again the most recent scholarly monograph on the topic (Rowe, 1971) comes to the conclusion that the *Nicomachean Ethics* is the definitive statement of Aristotle's ethical system, reorganizing an earlier excessively Academic draft in the *Eudemian*. The third of the traditional Aristotelian ethical treatises, the *Magna Moralia*, was rejected as post-Aristotelian by the school of Jaeger (Walzer, 1929; Brink, 1933). This rejection has been hotly contested (von Arnim, 1924, 1927, 1929; Gohlke, 1944; Dirlmeier, 1958; Düring, 1966; Cooper, 1973). Despite these defences it is still probably the case that most scholars continue to reject the *Magna Moralia*: but while Jaeger's position here has been under attack, his judgement on the

Eudemian Ethics has been so widely accepted and so little questioned (exeptions are Allan, 1958 and 1966; Monan, 1968) as to have become a dogma of Aristotelian scholarship. It is the purpose of the present work to attack, and, I hope, to demolish this dogma.

The arguments used to relegate the *Eudemian Ethics* to an inferior and provisional position in comparison with the *Nicomachean* have been predominantly based on internal evidence. Scholars have disagreed whether the *Eudemian Ethics* was the work of the immature Aristotle or of a posthumous admirer; but they have agreed that it was in various ways unworthy of the master in his years of greatness: it was too unworldly, too pious, too formalistic, too incoherent, too chaotic, too systematic. Evidence has been collected in the Eudemian books for a Platonic, purely theoretical, sense of the word *phronēsis*, for a Platonic view of ethical method, and a Platonic ideal of the philosophical life. Scholars have argued that in style and content the *Eudemian Ethics* is closer than the *Nicomachean Ethics* to the currently accepted reconstructions of the lost text of Aristotle's juvenile *Protrepticus*. Similarities of thought and vocabulary have been traced between the *Eudemian Ethics* and the Plato of the *Philebus* and the *Laws*.

The especial esteem of tradition for the *Nicomachean Ethics* is self-fortifying in a way which makes it difficult to examine the internal evidence with an impartial eye. Stock put the problem in a vivid if provincial light in his introduction to the Oxford translation of the *Magna Moralia* and of the *Eudemian Ethics* (1925, iii).

To an Oxford man . . . who has been nurtured on the *Nicomachean Ethics*, and to whom the treatise has become, mentally speaking, 'bone of his bone and flesh of his flesh' it seems too self-evident to require discussion that the *Nicomachean Ethics* is the substance of which the others are the shadow. But this confidence may be born of prejudice, and it is possible that, if the same person had had the *Eudemian Ethics* equally carefully instilled into him in youth, he might on making acquaintance with the *Nicomachean* find nothing more in that than a less literary rearrangement of the *Eudemians*.

More seriously, the impoverished manuscript tradition of the *Eudemian Ethics* means that when reading important parts of it we must struggle with a corrupt text which either does not make sense or does so only by benefit of editors' conjectures. These conjectures in their turn cannot help being influenced by the editors' over-all views of the nature of the treatise and its relationship to Aristotle's other works.

Despite this, the internal case for the priority and inferiority of the *Eudemian Ethics* crumbles on close inspection. Rowe, whose careful study supports the main lines of Jaeger's thesis, none the less admits 'The kernel of Jaeger's discussion of the ethics, his account of the history of the term *phronēsis* . . . has been shown conclusively to rest on a misinterpretation of the texts' (Rowe, 1971, 11). Criteria for tracing the development of Aristotle's thought that have been offered by scholars more recent and less panoramic than Jaeger—Nuyens's criterion of the gradual application of hylomorphic theory, and Owen's criterion of the growing realization of the power of the theory of focal meaning (Nuyens, 1948; Owen, 1960)—suggest if valid that the *Eudemian Ethics* is earlier than the *De Anima* and the developed position of Metaphysics *ΓEZ*, but they offer no clear grounds for assigning a chronological priority to one *Ethics* over the others.[1] Scholars have seen that in some respects—notably in placing happiness essentially in the activity of the separable *nous* rather than in the exercise of the virtues of man as a whole—the *Nicomachean Ethics* is closer to Platonic ideals than the *Eudemian* is (Monan, 1968). In particular the explicit criticisms of Plato in *EE* I.8 seem to be made from a greater distance than those of *NE* 1.6 (Cf. Verbeke, 1951). The non-ethical works of Aristotle which in virtue of their content stand closest to the *Eudemian Ethics* (*Metaphysics Λ* and the *Politics*, especially books 1, 7, and 8, cf. Bendixen, 1856) are themselves books whose dating is a matter of keen scholarly debate:[2] but they are both, as it happens, works whose early placing by Jaeger has been rejected by some recent scholars (cf. Monan, 1968; Nuyens, 1948). Finally, the reliability of our reconstructed texts of the *Protrepticus* has been seriously called into question (Rabinowitz, 1957). Until the criticisms of the reconstruction have been met, it seems unwise to rely on them for the dating of the *Eudemian Ethics*.

When we turn from the date to the quality of the *Eudemian Ethics* matters become yet more complicated. What counts as internal evidence for the superiority or inferiority of a work of philosophy naturally depends on the standards of evaluation within philosophy

1. Nuyens's system has been severely criticized by Hardie (1964) and Block (1961) and seems to be now generally rejected by writers in English, despite the magisterial endorsement of Gauthier and Jolif (1958, 1970).

2. Düring (1966, 333) places *EE* before Plato's death;,*Politics* 1, 7, 8 in the years of Aristotle's travels; *Met. Λ* very early, before *EE*; the rest of *Politics* in Aristotle's second sojourn in Athens.

itself. An analytical philosopher in the latter half of the twentieth century is not likely to have the same canons of philosophical value to apply to an ancient work as those applied in neo-Platonic Athens, Byzantine monasteries, or Hegelian or positivist German universities of a bygone age. As it happens, many of the features which scholars have noted as characteristic of the Eudemian books in contrast to the Nicomachean—a greater interest in the rigorous presentation of argument and a lesser interest in the dramatic portrayal of character; a preoccupation with the specific characteristics of practical reasoning which set it off from theoretical deduction; an identification of pleasure with pleasurable activity rather than with a supervenient phenomenon—these are features in which contemporary analytic fashion accords more closely with the interests and positions of the Eudemian than with the Nicomachean version of Aristotle's system. No conclusion, of course, can be drawn from this except that it is unwise to rely too heavily on philosophical value judgements as evidence for chronological conclusions.

Many of those who have attempted to assess the internal evidence for the relationship of the three Aristotelian Ethics seem to me to have made a serious methodological error. They have compared the undisputed Nicomachean books with the undisputed Eudemian books, and on the basis of pre-established criteria have attempted to settle the priority between them. They have then gone on—often almost as an afterthought—to discuss, on the basis of their results, the provenance of the three books which the manuscript tradition attributes to both the Nicomachean and Eudemian treatises. This is a mistaken procedure because, as I shall show, there is far more evidence both internal and external to establish the provenance of these disputed or common books than there is to enable us to decide by independent means the relationship between the two sets of undisputed books.[1] Thus, to tackle the question in the customary order is to reverse the correct procedure of approaching what is more dubious on the basis of what is more certain.

The greater part of the present work will consist of an attempt to settle in a definitive manner the original context of the disputed

---

1. The faulty method is most palpable in Jaeger, who having dated the *Eudemian Ethics* on the basis of a theory which takes for granted the Nicomachean origin of the disputed books, mentions the dispute itself only in a closing footnote (Jaeger, 1948, 258).

books. In order to have an untendentious mode of reference to the Aristotelian treatises, I shall use the abbreviation *NE* for the undisputed Nicomachean books, which I shall refer to by Arabic numerals; and I shall use, with Roman numerals, the abbreviation *EE* for the undisputed Eudemian books. For the common books I shall use the abbreviation *AE* (*Aristotelian Ethics*) and the letters A, B, and C. Thus AE A $= NE$ 5 $= EE$ IV; AE B $= NE$ 6 $= EE$ V; AE C $= NE$ 7 $= EE$ VI. Having, as I hope, established the provenance of the disputed books I shall then, in the light of my results, turn to the question of chronology and endeavour to show that the orthodox theory of Aristotle's ethical development is devoid of all support.

In the first part of the work I shall limit myself to a consideration of the external evidence for the relationship between the two ethics and the provenance of the disputed books. The evidence is scanty: a mere score of authors can be cited who discuss or explicitly utilize either of the treatises in the first five centuries after their composition. But what evidence there is points in a single, surprising, direction. Ancient authors up to the second century A.D. do not regard the *Nicomachean Ethics* as having that primacy over the *Eudemian Ethics* which has been taken for granted during the last millennium and more. It is the Eudemian treatise which is more likely to be used and quoted as canonical, as *the Ethics* of Aristotle. When we reach the period of Alexander of Aphrodisias, this situation has clearly come to an end. The turning-point appears to be the second-century commentary on Aristotle's ethical writing by Aspasius, which has come down to us only in fragmentary form. That commentary itself, as we shall see, contains material which rightly understood provides inescapable evidence of the original position of the disputed books in the Aristotelian corpus. The ancient *testimonia* to be discussed are, in order: Aristotle himself, two pseudo-Aristotelian writers, Theophrastus, Andronicus of Rhodes, Cicero, Arius Didymus, Xenarchus, Nicolaus of Damascus, Plutarch, Favorinus of Arles, Aspasius, Atticus, Diogenes Laertius, Alexander of Aphrodisias, Clement of Alexandria, the anonymous scholiast on *NE* 2–4, and the unknown authors of the oldest lists of Aristotle's surviving works.

ARISTOTLE

Aristotle's *Ethics* are quoted seven times in his other works: six times in the *Politics* and once in the *Metaphysics*. The majority of these quotations are from the common books of the *AE*. Thus, in *Metaphysics A* 1, 981ᵇ25 we read 'We have said in the *Ethics* what the difference is between art and science and the other kindred faculties'—a clear reference to *AE* B 3 (1139ᵇ15 ff.: the parallel passage in *MM* 1196ᵇ36 ff. makes a different distinction). Three passages in the *Politics* refer back to the *Ethics* in ways which make it most likely that the book on Justice (*AE* A) is meant. Thus *Politics B* 2, 1261ᵃ30 f. says 'Wherefore the principle of reciprocal proportion, as I have already remarked in the *Ethics*, is the salvation of states.' This seems to allude to *AE* A 8, 1132ᵇ31 ff.: 'In associations for exchange this sort of justice does hold men together—reciprocity in accordance with a proportion and not on the basis of precisely equal return. For it is by proportionate requital that the state holds together.'[1] Again, *Politics Γ* 9, 1280ᵃ16 ff., 'Justice implies a relation to persons as well as to things, and a just distribution, as I have already said in the *Ethics*, implies the same ratio between the persons and between the things.' This is a reference to *AE* A 5, 1131ᵃ14 ff.:

Since the equal is a mean, the just will be a mean. Now equality implies at least two things. The just, then, must be both a mean and equal and relative (i.e. for certain persons). And *qua* mean it must be between certain things (which are respectively greater and less); *qua* equal it involves two things; *qua* just it is for certain people. The just, therefore, involves at least four terms; for the persons for whom it is just are two, and the things in which it is manifested, the objects distributed, are two.[2]

Connected with this is the passage in *Politics Γ* 12, 1282ᵇ18 ff. 'All men think justice to be a sort of equality; and to a certain extent they agree in the philosophical distinctions which have been laid down by us about Ethics. For they admit that justice is a thing and

---

1. *Pol. B* 2, 1261ᵃ30–1: διόπερ τὸ ἴσον τὸ ἀντιπεπονθὸς σώζει τὰς πόλεις, ὥσπερ ἐν τοῖς Ἠθικοῖς εἴρηται προτερον. *NE* 5.8, 1132ᵇ31–3: ἀλλ' ἐν μὲν ταῖς κοινωνίαις ταῖς ἀλλακτικαῖς συνέχει τὸ τοιοῦτον δίκαιον, τὸ ἀντιπεπονθὸς κατ' ἀναλογίαν καὶ μὴ κατ' ἰσότητα. τῷ ἀντιποιεῖν γὰρ ἀνάλογον συμμένει ἡ πόλις. There is a prima-facie discrepancy here which is resolved by the context.
2. ἐπεὶ δὲ τὸ ἴσον μέσον, τὸ δίκαιον μέσον τι ἂν εἴη. ἔστι δὲ τὸ ἴσον ἐν ἐλαχίστοις δυσίν. ἀνάγκη τοίνυν τὸ δίκαιον μέσον τε καὶ ἴσον εἶναι καὶ πρός τι καὶ τισίν, καὶ ᾗ μὲν μέσον, τινῶν (ταῦτα δ'ἐστὶ πλεῖον καὶ ἔλαττον), ᾗ δ'ἴσον, δυοῖν, ᾗ δὲ δίκαιον, τισίν. ἀνάγκη ἄρα τὸ δίκαιον ἐν ἐλαχίστοις εἶναι τέτταρσιν· οἷς τε γὰρ δίκαιον τυγχάνει ὄν, δύο ἐστί, καὶ ἐν οἷς, τὰ πράγματα, δύο (*NE* 5.6, 1131ᵃ14–20). ὥστ' ἐπεὶ τὸ δίκαιον τισίν, καὶ διήρηται τὸν αὐτὸν τρόπον ἐπί τε τῶν πραγμάτων, καὶ οἷς, καθάπερ εἴρηται πρότερον ἐν τοῖς Ἠθικοῖς (*Pol. Γ* 9, 1280ᵃ16–18).

has a relation to persons, and that equals ought to have equality.'[1] The reference seems to be to the same passage in the *Ethics*, and in particular to the passages which immediately precede and succeed that just quoted.

The passages so far discussed, being references which fit with a greater or lesser degree of exactitude sections of the common books of the *AE*, do not help to settle any question of precedence between the *NE* and the *EE*. The remaining quotations from the *Politics* are more interesting. 'If what was said in the *Ethics* is true, that the happy life is the life according to virtue lived without impediment, and that virtue is a mean, then the life which is in a mean, and a mean attainable by every one, must be the best,' we are told in *Δ* 11, 1295ᵃ35 ff.[2] The expression 'without impediment' recalls *AE* C 13, 1153ᵇ9 ff. 'Perhaps it is even necessary, if each disposition has unimpeded activities, that whether the activity (if unimpeded) of all our dispositions, or that of some one of them is happiness, this should be the thing most worthy of choice.' The allusion is once again to a passage of the common books, but this time to a section of *AE* C which deals with pleasure, which even those who regard most of the disputed books as belonging to the Nicomachean version are prepared to assign to the Eudemian one. The idea that happiness is the exercise of virtues concerned with means is also closer to the Eudemian ideal of happiness as the exercise of *all* virtues than the Nicomachean one according to which happiness is essentially the exercise of an intellectual virtue which has nothing to do with a mean.

The final two quotations from the *Politics* are more decisively Eudemian. In chapter 13 of *Politics H* (1332ᵃ7 ff.) happiness is said to have been defined in the *Ethics* as 'the complete activity and use of virtue, not conditionally but absolutely'. Though the definition cannot be found in these precise terms in either *Ethics*, the notion of the 'use' of virtue is one which is characteristic of the Eudemian version, and the identification of happiness with the activity of

1. δοκεῖ δὲ πᾶσιν ἴσον τι τὸ δίκαιον εἶναι, καὶ μέχρι γέ τινος ὁμολογοῦσι τοῖς κατὰ φιλοσοφίαν λόγοις, ἐν οἷς διώρισται περὶ τῶν ἠθικῶν (τί γὰρ καὶ τισὶ τὸ δίκαιον, καὶ δεῖν τοῖς ἴσοις ἴσον εἶναί φασιν).

2. εἰ γὰρ καλῶς ἐν τοῖς Ἠθικοῖς εἴρηται τὸ τὸν εὐδαίμονα βίον εἶναι τὸν κατ' ἀρετὴν ἀνεμπόδιστον, μεσότητα δὲ τὴν ἀρετήν, τὸν μέσον ἀναγκαῖον εἶναι βίον βέλτιστον (*Pol. Δ* 11, 1295ᵃ35–8). ἴσως δὲ καὶ ἀναγκαῖον, εἴπερ ἑκάστης ἕξεώς εἰσιν ἐνέργειαι ἀνεμπόδιστοι, εἴθ' ἡ πασῶν ἐνέργειά ἐστιν εὐδαιμονία εἴτε ἥ τινος αὐτῶν, ἂν ᾖ ἀνεμπόδιστος, αἱρετωτάτην εἶναι (*NE* 7.13, 1153ᵇ9–12).

virtue (as opposed to 'activity of the soul in accordance with virtue') is likewise Eudemian.[1] Later in the same chapter of the *Politics* we read: 'This definition too was given in our ethical writings—that a good man is the sort of man for whom, on account of his virtue, the things that are good in the abstract are good.' This is the clearest of the Eudemian references, to the final book (1248^b26 f.): 'a good man is the sort of man for whom things good by nature are good'.[2]

Of the seven references to the *Ethics*, then, in Aristotle's other works, five are to the common books of the *AE*, one is undoubtedly to the *EE*, and the remaining one, while fitting neither exactly, is closer to the Eudemian than to the Nicomachean version.

PSEUDO-ARISTOTLE: THE PROBLEMS

Books 27–30 of the Aristotelian *Problems* deal with topics covered in the *Ethics*: courage, temperance, justice, and wisdom respectively. The following passage comes in the treatment of temperance:

> Why are those who exceed in the pleasures of touch and taste called incontinent? For those who exceed in sexual lust and in the enjoyment of food are called intemperate. In some of the enjoyments connected with food the pleasure is in the tongue, in others in the throat; that is why Philoxenus prayed to have the throat of a crane. But those whose pleasures are in sight and hearing are not so described. Is it because the pleasures from those senses are common to us and the other animals?[3]

The restriction of the scope of intemperance to the pleasures of taste and of touch, and indeed in the case of taste to the tactile pleasures of the gourmand, is made both in the *EE* (1230^b36–1231^a37) and in the *NE* (1118^a1 ff.). But if this passage in

1. φαμὲν δὲ (καὶ διωρίσμεθα ἐν τοῖς Ἠθικοῖς, εἴ τι τῶν λόγων ἐκείνων ὄφελος) ἐνέργειαν εἶναι [sc. τὴν εὐδαιμονίαν] καὶ χρῆσιν ἀρετῆς τελείαν, καὶ ταύτην οὐκ ἐξ ὑποθέσεως ἀλλ' ἁπλῶς (*Pol. H* 13, 1332^a7–10); δῆλον ... τὴν τῆς ἀρετῆς ἐνέργειαν τῆς ψυχῆς ἄριστον εἶναι. ἦν δὲ καὶ ἡ εὐδαιμονία τὸ ἄριστον (*EE* II.1, 1219^a28–34). On the 'use' of virtue see *EE* II.1, 1219^a18, *EE* VIII.1, *passim*, and below, p. 68. On the difficulty of fitting the definition to any Nicomachean text, see Newman, 1891, 341, and 575.

2. καὶ γὰρ τοῦτο διώρισται κατὰ τοὺς ἠθικοὺς λόγους, ὅτι τοιοῦτός ἐστιν ὁ σπουδαῖος, ᾧ διὰ τὴν ἀρετὴν [τὰ] ἀγαθά ἐστι τὰ ἁπλῶς ἀγαθά (*Pol. H* 13, 1332^a21–3); ἀγαθὸς μὲν οὖν ἐστιν ᾧ τὰ φύσει ἀγαθά ἐστιν ἀγαθά (*EE* VIII.3, 1248^b26–7); τὰ φύσει ἀγαθά = τὰ ἁπλῶς ἀγαθά (1249^a1–12).

3. διὰ τί οἱ κατὰ τὴν τῆς ἁφῆς ἢ γεύσεως ἡδονήν, οὗ ἂν ὑπερβάλλωσι ἀκρατεῖς λέγονται; οἵ τε γὰρ περὶ τὰ ἀφροδίσια ἀκόλαστοι, οἵ τε περὶ τὰς τῆς τροφῆς ἀπολαύσεις. τῶν δὲ κατὰ τὴν τροφὴν ἀπ' ἐνίων μὲν ἐν τῇ γλώττῃ τὸ ἡδύ, ἀπ' ἐνίων δὲ ἐν τῷ λάρυγγι, διὸ καὶ Φιλόξενος γεράνου φάρυγγα εὔχετο ἔχειν. κτλ (950^a1–7).

Problems is not by Aristotle himself but by a follower who is drawing on his work, it is clear from a number of points that the work he is drawing on is the *Eudemian* and not the *Nicomachean Ethics*. Only the *EE* draws the distinction between the pleasures of the tongue and the pleasures of the throat; and only the *EE* gives us the name of the man who prayed to have the throat of a crane.[1]

PSEUDO-ARISTOTLE: THE *MAGNA MORALIA*

It has been recognized since the time of Schleiermacher that the *MM* and the *EE* are much closer to each other than either of them is to the *NE*. For the nineteenth-century scholars who held the *Eudemian Ethics* to be the work of Aristotle's discipline Eudemus this presented no problem: the *Magna Moralia* merely represented a further stage in the decline of the Peripatos from the standards set by the master. In the twentieth century, however, the *MM* set a problem for the reigning orthodoxy. According to Jaeger the chronological order of the three treatises was *Eudemian, Nicomachean, Magna Moralia*: it was strange that the earliest and the latest ethics should resemble each other more than either of them resembled the intermediate one. This point gave support to the partisans of von Arnim (who shared with the Jaegerians the unquestioning acceptance of the priority of the *EE* to the *NE*). The order offered by von Arnim—*Magna Moralia, Eudemian, Nicomachean*—was, in its way, as logical as that of Spengel and Fritzsche in the nineteenth century. In support of Jaeger, Brink (1933) attempted to show that despite appearances the *Magna Moralia*, in its deep structure, was closer to the *Nicomachean* than to the *Eudemian Ethics*. This, the theme of the second half of his monograph, did not win that scholarly support which has been commanded by the first half in which he studied the peculiarities of the style of the *MM*.[2] Festugière, in his monograph on Aristotle's theory of pleasure, reached a conclusion which, though based on a particular study of the sections of the *Ethics* devoted to this topic, is true in general of almost the whole of the *MM*: 'The common

1. In *Problems* 30.5, 955^b 37 science is described as an 'instrument of the understanding' in a manner paralleled in the works of Aristotle only by *EE* VIII.2, 1248^{a}29. I am indebted to Professor D. J. Allan for drawing my attention to this further point of contact between the *Problems* and the *EE*.
2. Brink's claim that the *NE* was the model for the *MM* depended on a serious misunderstanding of the structure of *EE* I. The real structure of that book has been made clear by Allan (1961) and Rowe (1971) and is discussed below at pp. 191–8.

model of the *MM* is the *EE*: the borrowings from the *NE* are
entirely secondary. . . . In our section too the *EE* is the author's
textbook; he treats the *NE* simply as a kind of commentary.'[1]

The verdict of Festugière seems the only possible one for those
who do not regard the *MM* as being the work of Aristotle himself.
In my opinion the arguments of Jaeger, Walzer, and Brink for the
inauthenticity of the treatise have not been overthrown by the
counterattacks of von Arnim, Dirlmeier, Düring, and Cooper.
Whether the Jaegerians were right to assign the work to a post-
Aristotelian date is another matter, which we shall investigate in the
final chapter of this book. The weakness of the view that the *MM* is
an *early* work of Aristotle himself (the view of von Arnim's
followers, though not of von Arnim himself) is shown above all by
the need felt by partisans of this theory to postulate a double
redaction of the work—a manifestly *ad hoc* device to escape the
evidence for a comparatively late *terminus post quem* given by the
historical allusions. This is a question to which we shall return. For
the moment there is no need to enter into the question of the date of
the composition of the *MM*: what is significant for our present
purpose is that the author, whoever he was and for whatever
purpose he compiled his treatise, regarded the *Eudemian Ethics*, and
not the *Nicomachean*, as the appropriate Aristotelian work on which
to base his own.[2]

This is significant because the author undoubtedly knew the
Nicomachean Ethics and from time to time makes use of parts of it.
D. J. Allan has recently drawn attention to a cento of quotations
from the *NE* occurring in the fifth to the ninth chapters of the first
book, beginning with a citation which is introduced by the words
'this can be seen from the *Ethics*' (1185[b]15).[3] As Allan says, this use

---

1. . . . le modèle ordinaire de la *G.M.* est l'*Éth. Eud.* Les emprunts à l'*Éth. Nic.* sont tous
secondaires. En ce qui regarde notre section, le phénomène est manifeste et bien
significatif . . . l'*Éth. Eud.* demeure, ici encore, son *textbook*. Et il ne voit en l'*Éth. Nic.* qu'une
sorte de commentaire destiné à expliciter, ou, parfois, à corriger le livre qui lui sert de base'
(Festugière, 1946, lvi).

2. Theiler, 1934, says that it leaps to the eye that *MM* is closer to *EE*; to save the Jaegerian
position he postulates a lost Middle Ethics (*ME*) between *EE* and *NE*, from which *MM* is
derived. Among those who deny the authenticity of the *MM* opinions as to its date vary from
the Theophrastean peripatos to the early first century B.C.: there is a neat summary of
positions in Allan, 1957.

3. Allan, 1957, 1966. Most scholars have refused to see these words as a citation. τοῦτ'
ἰδεῖν ἔστιν ἐκ τῶν 'Ηθικῶν is an unusual way of quoting, but the text is most naturally
interpreted in Allan's way, as witness the scholars who have felt obliged to emend the text to
avoid having so to interpret it (e.g. Cooper, 1973).

of the *NE* is unparalleled elsewhere in the *MM*. There is little if any verbatim quotation of the *EE*: but its ideas and structure are all-pervasive. If scholars had not been so obstinately convinced that the *NE* is later than the *EE*, they might have been struck by the fact that the Nicomachean cento occurs in the *MM* at a point in the argument where the *EE* itself, in a mysterious phrase which has become a notorious crux, makes reference to an appendix.[1] If the Eudemian treatment were later than the Nicomachean it might well have carried with it an appendix of Nicomachean material: in that case, the *MM* by incorporating it at the point suggested by the *EE* would be following rather than violating its usual practice. But at the present stage of the argument, that is a piece of premature speculation.

What is not speculation is the general closeness of the *MM* to the *EE*. The Nicomachean cento is one of half a dozen places where the *MM* deviates from the *EE* as a model, as can be seen from Table 1.1.

TABLE 1.1 *Parallels to the* Magna Moralia *in the* NE *and* EE

MM book and chapter	Bekker pages*	Closest Aristotelian parallel
A 1ᵃ (Introduction)	1181ᵇ–1182ᵇ (2)	None
A 1ᵇ (Idea of Good)	1182ᵇ–1183ᵇ (3)	*EE*
A 2 (Divisions of 'Good')	1184ᵃ (1)	None
A 3–4 (Happiness)	1184ᵇ–1185ᵇ (2)	*EE*
A 5–9 (Virtue)	1185ᵇ–1187ᵃ (4)	*NE* (the Allan cento)†
A 10–32 (Will, Virtues)	1187ᵃ–1193ᵇ (12)	*EE*
A 33 (Justice)	1193ᵇ–1196ᵇ (6)	*AE*
A 34–B 3 (Wisdom)	1196ᵇ–1199ᵃ (5)	*AE*
B 3 (5 *Aporiai*)	1199ᵃ–1200ᵃ (2)	None
B 4–7 (*Akrasia*, Pleasure)	1200ᵇ–1206ᵇ (12)	*AE*
B 7–10 (Topics of *EE* VIII)	1206ᵇ–1208ᵇ (4)	*EE*
B 11–12 (Friendship)	1208ᵇ–1212ᵃ (9)	*EE*
B 13–14 (Self-love)	1212ᵃ–1212ᵇ (2)	*NE*
B 15–17 (Friendship)	1212ᵇ–1213ᵇ (2)	*EE*

* The number in brackets is the approximate number of Bekker columns involved.

† Even within this section, there are passages where the *MM* is dependent rather on the *EE*: e.g. 1186ᵃ20–ᵇ4.

---

1. ἐν τοῖς ἀπηλλαγμένοις, 1220ᵇ11. See Dirlmeier, 1962; Allan, 1966.

It will be seen that the *MM* is closer to the *EE* for approximately thirty-two Bekker columns, and closer to the *NE* for only six. Spengel summed up the situation thus:

At the beginning the *MM* looks back to both, and contributes a certain amount of its own material. But from the tenth chapter of the first book until the thirty-fourth there is a manifest attachment to the *EE*, although here too individual expressions can be found which can only have been taken from the *NE*. . . . From A 34 until B 7 the *MM* follows the *NE*, and immediately afterwards goes back to the *EE* (1841, 515).

By saying that from A 34 until B 7 the *MM* follows the *NE* and then returns to the *EE* what of course Spengel really meant was that from A 34 until B 7 the *MM* followed the common books of the *AE*: he took it for granted that the disputed books belonged to the *NE* because he regarded the *EE* as spurious. But surely it is on the face of it unlikely that the author of the *MM*, having followed the structure of the *EE* faithfully from 1187^a to 1193^b, should switch for twenty-five Bekker columns to following the *NE*, and then switch back, by an extraordinary coincidence, just when the disputed books end, to follow once again the lead of the *EE*. If the disputed books are taken as belonging with the *EE*, then everything runs more smoothly: for twenty-four Bekker pages the *MM* lets itself be guided, with minor variations in order and occasional small interruptions, by the *EE*. The structure of the *MM* is itself, then, substantial evidence of a Eudemian origin for the disputed books. And its over-all fondness for the *EE*, despite its acquaintance with parts at least of the *NE*, is a striking indication of the relative standing of the two treatises in peripatetic circles at whatever time it was written. The whole topic will occupy us further in our final chapter.

THEOPHRASTUS

There have survived two quotations of the *Ethics* by Theophrastus. One occurs in a passage of Stobaeus' anthology taken by scholars as part of Arius Didymus' summary of peripatetic thought.

The mean with regard to us is best; as, for instance, Theophrastus says, one man spends a lot of time in idle chatter, another says very little and not even what is essential, while a third chooses the right time to say just what he ought. This mean is a mean with regard to us, because it is fixed by us by reasoning. Thus virtue is a disposition for choice placed in a mean with respect to us, determined by reasoning and the way that the wise man would determine it. Then, setting out a number of triads in the footsteps of his master, examining each in turn he endeavoured to complete an induction as follows: for the sake of example the following were chosen: temperance, intemperance, insensibility; gentleness, irascibility, insensitivity; courage, rashness, cowardice; justice; liberality, prodigality, meanness; magnanimity, pusillanimity, vanity; magnificence, shabbiness, extravagance. Of these dispositions some are bad because they are excessive or deficient with regard to the passions; others are good, clearly because they are means.[1]

The passage then proceeds to a consideration of each of the triads in turn. Scholars disagree about the extent and the degree of literalness of the quotation from Theophrastus. Von Arnim, who first focused the attention of the learned world on the importance of the passage, regarded it as an extensive, verbatim quotation. He pointed out (1924, 124–41) that the table of virtues and vices given here corresponds in several respects to the one given in the *EE* (1220^b38–1221^a12) rather than to the one mentioned in the *NE* (1107^a34) in so far as the latter can be reconstructed from the text. (For example: the two lists are introduced by the same phrase; they both give the defect corresponding to gentleness as insensitivity rather than spiritlessness; both mention justice with the major moral virtues.)[2] Some details of the subsequent development of the discussion, likewise, recall the Eudemian discussion of the table:

1. Τὸ οὖν πρὸς ἡμᾶς μέσον ἄριστον, οἷον, φησὶν ὁ Θεόφραστος, ἐν ταῖς ἐντυχίαις ὁδὶ μὲν πολλὰ διελθὼν καὶ μακρῶς ἀδολεσχήσας, ὁδὶ δ' ὀλίγα καὶ οὐδὲ τἀναγκαῖα, οὗτος δὲ αὐτὰ ἃ ἔδει μόνα τὸν καιρὸν ἔλαβεν. Αὕτη ⟨ἡ⟩ μεσότης πρὸς ἡμᾶς ⟨ἀρίστη⟩, αὕτη γὰρ ὑφ' ἡμῶν ὥρισται τῷ λόγῳ. Διὸ ἔστιν ἡ ἀρετὴ 'ἕξις προαιρετική, ἐν μεσότητι οὖσα τῇ πρὸς ἡμᾶς, ὡρισμένη λόγῳ καὶ ὡς ἂν ὁ φρόνιμος ὁρίσειεν'. εἶτα παραθέμενος τινὰς συζυγίας, ἀκολούθως τῷ ὑφηγητῇ σκοπῶν ἔπειτα καθ' ἕκαστα ἐπάγειν ἐπειράθη τὸν τρόπον τοῦτον· ἐλήφθησαν δὲ παραδειγμάτων χάριν αἵδε· σωφροσύνη, ἀκολασία, ἀναισθησία· πραότης, ὀργιλότης, ἀναλγησία· ἀνδρεία, θρασύτης, δειλία· δικαιοσύνη *** ἐλευθεριότης, ἀσωτία, ἀνελευθερία· μεγαλοψυχία, μικροψυχία, χαυνότης· μεγαλοπρέπεια, μικροπρέπεια, σαλακωνία. Τούτων δὴ τῶν ἕξεων αἱ μὲν τῷ ὑπερβάλλειν ἢ ἐλλείπειν περὶ πάθη φαῦλαί εἰσιν, αἱ δὲ σπουδαῖαι, τῷ μεσότητες εἶναι δηλονότι (Wachsmuth, ii.140 6 ff.).
2. [Theophrastus?]: ἐλήφθησαν δὲ παραδειγμάτων χάριν αἵδε. EE: εἰλήφθω δὴ παραδείγματος χάριν. EE and Theophrastus have ἀναλγησία where NE has ἀοργησία. Some of von Arnim's conclusions perhaps need qualification. On the order of the list, see below, p. 23.

for instance, the comparison of the insensible man to a stone (Stob. ii.141.7, *EE* 1221[a]23).[1]

It is difficult to settle with any certainty the boundaries between the nested quotations from Arius, Theophrastus, and Aristotle. Von Arnim thought all the passage set out above was from Theophrastus except the words 'Theophrastus says' and 'Then, setting out a number of triads . . . as follows'. This would include in the Theophrastean passage a verbatim quotation of the definition of virtue from the *NE* (1107[a]1), and the words 'for the sake of example the following were chosen', which would thus lead into a verbatim quotation by Theophrastus from Aristotle. More recently Moraux has argued convincingly that the Nicomachean quotation, important features of which are irrelevant to the context, cannot be part of the Theophrastean passage; he is inclined to think that the quotation from Theophrastus is interrupted by a number of remarks by Areios (who is certainly the spokesman in the sentence about setting out triads in the footsteps of his master) and is not resumed until the triads themselves are set out.[2] The most natural way of reading the passage is to see the quotation as being resumed immediately after 'as follows' (*ton tropon touton*); it is then difficult not to agree with von Arnim that the clause 'for the sake of example the following were chosen' is a quotation by Theophrastus of the familiar *EE* passage beginning 'for the sake of example let there be chosen . . .' and continuing with the list of triads. Having set forth the *EE* text, Theophrastus then goes on to comment on it: there is no reason to be surprised that not everything in the commentary

1. Cf. Von der Mühll, 1909, 28. Not everything in the discussion of the table can be traced to the *EE*: von Arnim concludes that it was the *MM* Theophrastus had before him. But the *MM* neither contains nor mentions a table of virtues, and von Arnim is obliged to suppose a lacuna at the crucial point. Mansion's judgement is surely sound: 'Pour affirmer qu'il dépend du passage correspondant du *MM* que nous ne possédons plus, on en est reduit en somme à se baser sur le contenu conjectural d'un texte perdu. C'est bien peu de chose' (1927, 449).

2. Moraux 1973, 383 ff. Moraux concludes that the quotation must be very free: 'Er zitiert nicht wörtlich, sondern gibt in grossen Zügen das Wesentliche aus Theophrasts Ausführungen wieder. Wenn es sich so verhält, so verlieren die gelegentlichen Berührungen mit *EE* oder *MM* beträchtlich an Bedeutung, denn es ist nicht sicher, ob sie bereits in Theophrasts Originalschrift gestanden haben oder von deren Epitomator herrühren' (390). I do not see why Areios' method of quoting Theophrastus should differ from his method of quoting Aristotle when he does so at first hand: i.e. not verbatim, throughout, but preserving many of the actual turns of phrase of the original. If the quotation of Theophrastus is of this sort, then quite enough turns of phrase and features of structure are preserved to make it clear that what Theophrastus was commenting on was the table of virtues in the *EE*. If von Arnim exaggerates the amount of information to be obtained from this text, Moraux undervalues it to an equal degree.

can be traced to the *EE* itself; commentaries would be superfluous if nothing was contained in a commentary *on* a text except material *from* the text. Aspasius' commentary on Aristotle's *Ethics* (*CAG* xix.156.17) preserves another fragment in which Theophrastus made a literal quotation from Aristotle's *Ethics*: this is the sentence 'any pleasure, whether it happens to be the contrary of the pain involved or not, has the effect, provided it be strong enough, of driving out that pain.' This comes from the section of *AE* C devoted to pleasure. The anonymous scholiast on *AE* A tells us that the quotation from Theognis occurring at *AE* A, 1129ᵇ30 is used also twice by Theophrastus, though attributed by him to Phocylides.[1]

CICERO[2]

A passage in *De Finibus* V.12 (*c.* 45 B.C.) is often quoted as the earliest evidence for the title of the *Nicomachean Ethics*. Cicero

1. On Theophrastus' use of the *Ethics*, see also Regenbogen, *RE* Suppl. vii, 1354 ff.; Wehrli, 1972, 490 ff.
2. The reader may be surprised to find no section devoted to Epicurus' use of Aristotle. The reason for the omission is that I am unconvinced that we have any evidence that Epicurus knew any of Aristotle's surviving ethical treatises at first hand: the negative, if not the positive, side of the thesis of Bignone (1936) seems to me to have survived the criticism of later scholars. Certainly, Epicurus during his Athenian studies had the opportunity to become familiar with Aristotle's doctrines, and two of his major interests—pleasure and the relation between freedom and necessity—are discussed at length in the *NE* and the *EE*; but nothing survives to show first-hand knowledge of the relevant texts. Merlan (1960, 1–37) has made an interesting comparison between the two treatments of pleasure in the *NE* and *AE* and the theory of Epicurus; but he attempts no textual *rapprochement*. Furley (1967, 161–236) compares the treatment of voluntary action in Aristotle and Epicurus. He begins with the candid admission: 'I have not made a systematic attempt to prove that Epicurus could have read or did read Aristotle's school treatises'; he simply assumes in Epicurus familiarity with the *NE*. But if one is to assume without proof acquaintance with Aristotle's *Ethics*, the *EE* is at least as likely, on the basis of Furley's comparison, to have been Epicurus' Aristotelian source. The closest textual comparison he offers is between *NE* 3.5, 1113ᵇ17 ff. and Epicurus referring to voluntary agents as internally caused agents—ἔχοντας καὶ ἐν ἑαυτοῖς τὴν αἰτίαν (*On Nature* 31.27.3–9, Arringhetti). Equally good parallels would be *EE* II.6, 1222ᵇ15–23ᵃ20, and 8, 1224ᵇ2–29. On voluntariness Furley writes: 'The relation between Aristotle's two *Ethics* on this problem is particularly interesting but a thorough examination of it would take too long now. My own view is that the treatment in the *Eudemian Ethics* is consistent with its being intermediate between Plato's views and that of the *Nicomachean Ethics*, and that the *Nicomachean Ethics* (including the controversial books E–H) rather than the *Eudemian Ethics* is likely to have influenced Epicurus' (p. 225). It is unfortunate that Furley did not have time to give reasons for this judgement: in fact he goes on to assert that on the principal point—offering a positive rather than a negative criterion of voluntariness—the *EE* is more explicit. Rist (1970, 101–2) argues that the distinctions drawn in *AE* C 11–15 'form at least part of the background' for Epicurus' distinctions between

complains that Theophrastus in his treatise on the happy life made happiness too dependent on good fortune. 'Let us therefore follow Aristotle and his son Nicomachus, whose carefully written books on ethics are said to be the work of Aristotle, though I do not see why the son could not have been similar to the father.'[1] It is commonly taken that Cicero is referring here exclusively to the *Nicomachean Ethics*: his attribution of the work to Nicomachus is taken not very seriously, as a mere conjecture based on the title. But the natural way to read the passage is that Cicero is here referring to *two* authorities: first, an unnamed but undisputed work of Aristotle's, and secondly an ethics with the title 'Nicomachean' which is attributed to the father but which Cicero is prepared to attribute to the son.[2] The important point is that the ethical work which Cicero regards as undoubtedly Aristotle's is *not* the *Nicomachean Ethics*.[3] Given the authority which Theophrastus and the author of the *Magna Moralia* attach to the *Eudemian Ethics*, it is tempting to see here a reference to that treatise; but we cannot be certain that Cicero is not referring to the *Magna Moralia* or an exoteric work like the *Protrepticus*.[4] It has often been pointed out that the doctrine Cicero here attributes to Aristotle and Nicomachus—that virtue and wisdom suffice for happiness without fortune—does not fit the teaching of the *NE*; but the *Eudemian Ethics* also teaches, less insistently, that gifts of fortune are a *sine qua non* of happiness, and the common books of the *AE* include an attack on the thesis that the just man is happy on the rack.[5]

Cicero twice makes reference to Aristotle's comparison of the life

katastematic and kinetic pleasures. Such highly qualified phrases seem to me the appropriate ones for expressing the relationships between Aristotle's doctrines and those of Epicurus. On the alleged use of Aristotle's *Ethics* by Menander and the comic poets, see the judicious remarks of Bodéus, 1973, 463–4.

1. 'Quare teneamus Aristotelem et eius filium Nicomachum, cuius accurate scripti de moribus libri dicuntur illi quidem esse Aristoteli, sed non video, cur non potuerit patri similis esse filius.'

2. If only one work were in question here, Cicero should surely have written 'Aristotelem v e l eius filium Nicomachum'.

3. Of all the commentators I have read on this passage, only Titze (1826, 38 f.) has seen this important point: he concludes the reference is to the *EE*.

4. On the other hand it is possible that the work he attributes to Nicomachus is the *MM* and not the *NE*: we know from Elias (*CAG* xviii, 32) that the *Magna Moralia* was known in antiquity as the 'Great *Nicomachean* Ethics', the *NE* as the 'Lesser Nicomachean Ethics'.

5. See e.g. *EE* I, 1214^{b}16; VIII, 1249^{a}14; *AE* C, 1153^{b}19.

of a Sardanapallus to that of a bull,[1] which occurs in *EE* (I.5, 1216ᵃ1-16) and not in *NE*. But he does so in a way which makes it probable that he is drawing on a different source, which may or may not have been, as Jaeger conjectured, the *Protrepticus*.[2]

In *De Finibus* II.6 Cicero attributes to Aristotle a definition of happiness as the exercise of virtue accompanied by the prosperity of a complete life. This definition is perhaps closer to the one given in the *Magna Moralia* than to anything in either of the authentic *Ethics*.[3]

Cicero, then, is a witness that in his time the *NE* did not yet enjoy that primacy as the canonical expression of Aristotle's ethical thought which it held for later generations: but it is unclear whether his own knowledge of Aristotle's ethical teaching, in so far as it depends at all on first-hand acquaintance with his writings, derives from the *EE*, the *MM*, or the exoteric writings.[4]

THE EDITION OF ANDRONICUS

Some time in the first century B.C.[5] Andronicus of Rhodes undertook an edition of Aristotle's works: he grouped and ordered the treatises, it appears, in the form which the manuscript tradition was later to hand them down to us. He drew up a *pinax*, or *catalogue raisonné*, of Aristotle's works. This has not survived, but scholars believe that it can be reconstructed from the list of Aristotle's works found in the *Life* of Aristotle by Ptolemy—which is known only from late Arabic sources: Ibn al-Qifti (12th–13th cent.) and Ibn Abi Usaibia (13th cent.) both of whom offer closely resembling lists of the writings of the Aristotelian corpus which they attribute to a

---

1. *Tusculan Disputations*, v.35.101; *De Finibus* ii.32.106.

2. Jaeger, 1948, 254–5. On Cicero's possible use of the *Protrepticus* in his lost *Hortensius*, see Diels, 1888; Chroust, 1973, 98 ff.; Rabinowitz, 1957.

3. 'Virtutis usum cum vitae perfectae prosperitate'. Cf. *MM* A 3–4, 1184ᵇ15–39. Closer than any Aristotelian source is the version in Areios Didymos, ap. Stobaeus ii.51.12 Wachsmuth: χρῆσις ἀρετῆς τελείας ἐν βίῳ τελείῳ προηγουμένη.

4. Cicero himself makes the distinction between Aristotle's exoteric writings and those written in a more austere professional style (*limatius*). He could have found the distinction in the *NE* (1102ᵃ27) the *AE* (1140ᵃ3), and most clearly in the *EE* (1217ᵇ22), though it is also to be found in the *Politics*. Dirlmeier (1969, 116) is surely correct in thinking that Düring (1957, 442) goes too far in saying that this passage proves knowledge of the *EE*. Elsewhere (1957, 428) Düring himself is more cautious on the same topic.

5. Scholars disagree on the date of Andronicus' edition: Düring (1968, 195) places his activity between 40 and 20 B.C.; Moraux, accepting the tradition of Elias (*CAG* xviii.113), thinks he became head of the peripatetic school *c.* 80–78 (1973, 58).

18   *The Aristotelian Ethics*

Ptolemy-el-Garib.[1] Clearly, a reconstruction of Andronicus' catalogue based on a tradition passing through so many intermediaries (Ptolemy, his Arabic translator, and the two medieval writers) cannot be treated with complete confidence. None the less, it is of great interest that our best evidence for the contents of the edition of Andronicus suggests unequivocally that it did not contain the *Nicomachean Ethics*. The only ethical entries in the list are:

35, a book entitled *Major treatises on ethics*, in Greek *ēthikōn megalōn*, two books;

36, a book entitled *Minor treatises on ethics*, which he dedicated to Eudemus, in Greek *ēthikōn Eudēmeiōn*, eight books.[2]

Not only is the omission of the *NE* significant: so also is the fact that the *EE* is listed as having eight books. This means, if the list in the Arabic sources really goes back to Andronicus' *pinax*, that the disputed books were included in his edition with the *EE*. As has been said, the complicated history of the transmission of the *pinax* makes it difficult to be certain of its content: but changes made by editors in the course of its transmission would surely be likely to be in the direction of making it accord with the state of the Aristotelian corpus at the time of editing. It is, then, very striking that during a period of centuries during which the *NE* became regarded as the *Ethics par excellence*, and during which the disputed books were commented on as part of the Nicomachean treatise, this evidence for a deutero-canonical status of the *NE* and for a Eudemian provenance of the disputed books should have been so faithfully preserved.

---

1. No one has succeeded in identifying, or even dating within a century or two, this Ptolemy to the satisfaction of other scholars. See Moraux, 1951, 289–94; Düring, 1968, 168. Düring regards it as probable that he is identical with the fourth-century Platonist, cited by Iamblichus and Proclus.

2. The translation is that of Düring, 1957, 224. Many commentators cannot believe their eyes at this point, and emend the text (e.g. Moraux, 1951, 138). A recent example of such incredulity is Bodéus, who having decided that the omission of the *NE* is 'un accident dans la transmission' goes on to conclude—on the sole ground that Andronicus and Eudemus both hailed from Rhodes—that it was Andronicus who put together the *EE* 'parachevant son édition en la baptisant sur le modèle dé l'*Éthique à Nicomaque*' (1973, 462). 'L'attitude d'Andronicus', he continues, 'éditant sur cette base un nouveau *cursus* revenait, en somme, à épingler l'*Éthique à Nicomaque* en modèle; les commentateurs de l'ère chrétienne ont respecté cette échelle des valeurs, en négligeant à son profit l'*Éthique à Eudème* et les *Grandes Morales*.' It would be difficult to find—even among Aristotelian scholars—a case of such weighty conclusions being drawn from a non-existent piece of evidence.

XENARCHUS

During the latter part of the first century B.C. the scholarch of the Peripatos was Xenarchus. Simplicius has preserved, in his commentary on Aristotle's *De Caelo* (*CAG* vii.55.25–31) a fragment of his writing. Discussing the principle that everything has one and only one contrary or opposite, he observes that Xenarchus gave as a counter-example the fact that every virtue has two opposites. 'In our ethical writings,' he says, 'we say that to each of the virtues there are two contraries: for instance wisdom has the two contraries cunning and stupidity, courage has the two contraries rashness and cowardice, and so in other cases.'[1] The examples show that the writings he is alluding to were following the *EE*, not the *NE*: the listing of wisdom as a mean between cunning and stupidity occurs only in the table of virtues in *EE* II.3, 1221ª12.[2] No passage in the *NE* suggests anything of the kind, and it would be hard to pick a single brief quote from the *EE* which would more clearly betray its source.[3]

ARIUS DIDYMUS

It is commonly agreed among scholars that the outline of peripatetic ethics preserved in the second book of Stobaeus' anthology is one prepared by Arius Didymus, the court philosopher of the emperor Augustus. The outline, which occupies some thirty-six pages of Wachsmuth's edition Stobaeus (116–49), is entitled 'The opinions of Aristotle and the other Peripatetics about Ethics'. It does not profess, therefore, to be a summary of Aristotle's views: and in part it bears apparent marks of Stoic influence. Von Arnim, the author of the most extended twentieth-century study of the work (1926), strove to show that the Stoic influence was no more than apparent, and that the non-Aristotelian elements need not derive from any source substantially later than

---

1. λέγομεν δέ, φησί [Ξενάρχος] καὶ ἐν τοῖς περὶ τῶν ἠθῶν λόγοις, ἑκάστῃ τῶν ἀρετῶν δύο εἶναι τὰ ἐναντία, ὡς φρονήσει μὲν πανουργίαν καὶ εὐήθειαν, ἀνδρείᾳ δέ θρασύτητα τε καὶ δειλίαν καὶ ἐπὶ τῶν ἄλλων ὁμοίως.

2. Even in the *EE* the appearance of wisdom as a mean is surprising, with the apparent corollary that wisdom is a moral virtue. For this reason some scholars, without manuscript warrant, have excised 1221ª12 (von Arnim, 1924, 127). See below, pp. 213–14.

3. See Moraux, 1973, i.208. Of Xenarchus' date, Moraux says: '...werden wir kaum fehlgehen, wenn sir sein Leben zwischen 80/75 v. Chr. und der Zeitwende ansetzen' (ibid. 197).

Theophrastus. His thesis has not secured universal assent;[1] for our present purposes it is fortunately not necessary to decide whether the non-Aristotelian parts of the epitome derive from Theophrastus or from later sources. What is important, and what is established beyond doubt by von Arnim's extensive and painstaking examination, is that in its Aristotelian sections it is much closer to the *Eudemian Ethics* and to the *Magna Moralia* than it is to the *Nicomachean Ethics*—as indeed is apparent to anyone who looks up the parallels marked in the footnotes to Wachsmuth's edition.[2] The reader is referred to von Arnim for the detailed comparison: but here are a few parallel texts by way of illustration.

Arius, 128.11 ff.: Excellence is the name of the best disposition, of the disposition which makes its possessor in the best condition. This is clear from induction: for excellence in a shoemaker is the condition which makes him best able to make a good shoe. . . .

EE II.1, 1218ᵇ37–19ᵃ1: Let it be assumed as to excellence that it is the best disposition or state or power of each thing that has a use or output. This is clear from induction . . . (1219ᵃ19–23) . . . we say that something is the output of a thing and its excellence, though not in the same way; as a shoe is the output of the act of shoemaking and of the art of shoemaking; so that if there is an excellence of shoemaking and of the good shoemaker, its output is a good shoe.[3]

Arius, 147.22: The virtue which is a synthesis of all the moral virtues is called *kalokagathia*, and it is perfect excellence; it makes expedient goods into noble goods, and chooses noble things for their own sake.[4]

In most respects, this passage could hardly be bettered as a summary of the first part of the final chapter of the *EE*, the key passage dealing with the union of all excellence in an all-round virtue of *kalokagathia*—a notion quite lacking in the *NE*.

1. For a recent study and a bibliography, see Mingay, 1973.
2. So too the most recent account, Moraux, 1973, 435: '. . . dabei sind die Berührungen mit den *MM* und auch die der *EE* enger und zahlreicher als mit der *NE*.'
3. ἀρετὴν δ' ὠνομάσθαι τὴν ἀρίστην διάθεσιν ἢ καθ' ἣν ἄριστα διάκειται τὸ ἔχον. τοῦτο δ' ἐκ τῆς ἐπαγωγῆς δῆλον· σκυτοτόμου γὰρ ἀρετὴν λέγεσθαι καθ' ἣν ἀποτελεῖν ἄριστον ὑπόδημα δύναται (Areios, 128.11 ff.). ταῦτα δὴ οὕτως ὑποκείσθω καὶ περὶ ἀρετῆς, ὅτι ἐστὶν ἡ βελτίστη διάθεσις ἢ ἕξις ἢ δύναμις ἑκάστων, ὅσων ἐστί τις χρῆσις ἢ ἔργον. δῆλον δ' ἐκ τῆς ἐπαγωγῆς . . . λέγομεν ὅτι τὸ ἔργον τοῦ πράγματος καὶ τῆς ἀρετῆς, ἀλλ' οὐχ ὡσαύτως. οἷον σκυτοτομικῆς καὶ σκυτεύσεως ὑπόδημα· εἰ δή τίς ἐστιν ἀρετὴ σκυτικῆς καὶ σπουδαίου σκυτέως, τὸ ἔργον ἐστὶ σπουδαῖον ὑπόδημα (*EE* II.1, 1218ᵇ 37 ff.).
4. τὴν δὲ ἐκ πασῶν τῶν ἠθικῶν ἀρετὴν συνεστηκυῖαν λέγεσθαι μὲν καλοκαγαθ-ίαν, τελείαν δ' ἀρετὴν εἶναι, τά τε ἀγαθὰ ὠφέλιμα καὶ καλὰ ποιοῦσαν τά τε καλὰ δι' αὐτὰ αἱρουμένην.

I have chosen these two passages because they illustrate dependences on the *EE* which must be direct and not mediated via the *MM*. The similarities with that work are even more striking than the similarities with the *EE*: for instance the thirteen main moral excellences are listed in exactly the same order in Arius (p. 146) as they are in *MM* A 20–34, 1190^{b}9–1196^{b}3. Almost certainly Arius knew also the *NE*, since a number of points to be found in his outline occur only in that work and not in the *EE* or *MM*.[1] This makes it the more significant that he should prefer to follow the structure of the *EE* and *MM* and that on a number of points where the *EE* and *NE* diverge he should follow the Eudemian version.[2]

In Stobaeus' anthology, prior to the outline of Stoic and peripatetic philosophy, there occurs a section of prolegomena. This passage contains the following remark: 'Aristotle in the tenth book of the *Nicomachean Ethics* thinks that the astronomer Eudoxus held the doctrine that the end is pleasure' (Wachsmuth 52.10).[3] Are these prolegomena, as many scholars assume, drawn from the epitome of Arius? If they are, then the passage just quoted is of great importance: it becomes the earliest unambiguous evidence for the existence of the *Nicomachean Ethics*— for an *Ethics*, moreover, in ten books, which must therefore have included the disputed books. But is the statement really by Arius?

The reason for believing that the summary of peripatetic ethics in Stobaeus is by Arius is that the anonymous epitome contains a passage (129.19–130.12) which appears also in the fourth volume of the anthology (918.16–919.6) with the rubric 'from the epitome of Didymus'.[4] This makes it likely that the whole epitome also belongs to Arius, and it is a reasonable assumption that so too does the preceding epitome of Stoic philosophy constructed on the same

1. e.g. the expression ἐν βίῳ τελείῳ on p. 130; the parallel to *NE* 8.12 at 148.15; the reference to the proverb about one swallow not making a summer at 132.5; the description of the good man in adversity (132.10); the definition of virtue discussed above, p. 14.

2. The following are among the points on which Arius follows Eudemian by preference to Nicomachean doctrine: the identification of the blessed and the happy (132.11); the restriction of happiness to those who are awake (the divergence here—133.11—is one of terminology rather than of substance, cf. von Arnim 1926, 41); the triple sense of 'The Good' (Areios 134.8 ff. = *EE* I, 1217^{b}1 ff.); the attitude to riches (cf. von Arnim, 60); the theory of natural virtue (von Arnim, 71); the presence of *kalokagathia*, as illustrated in the passage cited, and the absence of an account of theoretical happiness on the model of *NE* 10.

3. Ἀριστοτέλης ἐν τῷ δεκάτῳ τῶν Νικομαχείων Εὔδοξον τὸν ἀστρόλογον οἴεται τέλος δογματίζειν τὴν ἡδονήν.

4. This was first pointed out by Meinecke (1859); his interpretation has won general acceptance especially since Diels, 1879, 71 ff.

model. But it provides no grounds for believing that every reference to peripatetic philosophy in Stobaeus is a direct quotation from Arius. The passage which refers to *NE* 10 is preceded by a discussion of Aristotle's definition of happiness (50.11–51.17) and of possible goals (51.18–52.9); a passage marked by an obsession with triads, which in part duplicates and in part conflicts with the treatment of Aristotle's views on happiness presented in the epitome itself.[1] The explicit quotation of, and reference to, book 10 of the *NE* is totally without parallel in the epitome and is quite unlike Arius' manner of utilizing his texts.[2] Altogether, it is much more likely that the reference to the Eudoxus passage is by Stobaeus himself, and dates therefore from the fifth rather than the first century A.D.

NICOLAUS OF DAMASCUS

Some twenty years ago there was discovered in a mosque at Fez an Arabic manuscript containing, along with an Arabian version of parts of the *Nicomachean Ethics*, a translation of a Greek ethical treatise attributed by the copyist to one Nicolaus. Scholars conjectured that it might be the work of Nicolaus of Damascus, the adviser and court historian of Herod the Great, who wrote a number of peripatetic treatises. This attribution was endorsed by R. Walzer in *The Encyclopedia of Islam.*[3]

Unless the treatise has been very heavily interpolated it cannot in fact be the work of Nicolaus, because it refers to Plotinus and mentions other proper names from late antiquity. However, the central section of the treatise, which breaks the continuity of the work as a whole, may well be of earlier date than the surrounding material: it is a summary of Aristotelian ethics which follows sources in Aristotle very closely. The only indication of its date is a critical reference to the Christians. Scholars have suggested that

---

1. Several of these divergencies are noted by Moraux (1973, 274) who concludes 'Daran geht deutlich hervor, dass Areios aus zwei verschieden Quellen, die eine jeweils anderer Deutung desselben Definition bote, geschöpft hat.' It is surely Stobaeus, not Arius, who is using two incompatible sources.

2. This too is noticed by Moraux. From Arius' general method of using his sources, Moraux concludes that he may well not have read them at first hand; it is the more astonishing that he should ascribe this precisely located reference to Arius rather than Stobaeus. (Compare Moraux, 1973, 313 and 436.)

3. On the Fez manuscript see Arberry, 1955; Lyons, *Oriens*, 13.55; Paret, 1959/60.

though not the work of Nicolaus this central section may well be the oldest surviving commentary on the *Aristotelian Ethics*.[1]

It is regrettable that the date of the treatise is so uncertain because in the context of the relationship between the *NE* and the *EE* its interest is considerable. A large part of the discussion is devoted to the ethical virtues, and both in general structure and in detail the treatment follows the *EE* and the *MM* more closely than it follows the *NE*, although from time to time Nicomachean material is utilized.

The order in which the major moral virtues are treated is closer to the *EE* and *MM* than to the *NE*. (No great importance can be attached to the order of treatment: but it may be of interest to set

TABLE 1.2 *The Ordering of the Virtues in Peripatetic Ethical Treatises*

Virtue	NE 2.7	NE 3-4	EE list	EE 2.3	EE 3	MM	Theo.	Arius	Fez
Courage	1	1	2	2	1	1	3	1	1
Temperance	2	2	4	3	2	2	1	2	2
Liberality	3	3	7	10	4	4	5	4	4
Magnificence	4	4	13	11	6	6	7	6	5
Magnanimity	5	5	12	9	5	5	6	5	6
(Ambition)*	6	6	—	—	—	—	—	—	—
Gentleness	7	7	1	1	3	3	2	3	3
Candour	8	9	8	5	11	12	—	12	9
Wittiness	9	10	—	—	12	10	—	10	12
Friendliness	10	(8)*	9	6	9	11	—	11	7
Dignity	—	—	10	7	10	8	—	8	8
Shame	11	11	3	—	8	9	—	9	11
Nemesis	12	5	5	13	7	7	—	7	10
Justice	13	12	6	4	13	13	4	13	13
Hardiness	—	—	11	8	—	—	—	—	—
Wisdom	—	—	14	12	—	—	—	—	—

* Here this virtue is unnamed.

1. See Moraux, 1973, 442. Partly because of the anti-Christian remarks Lyons suggests that the Nicolaus of the treatise may be Nicolaus of Laodicea, a contemporary of Julian the Apostate. But there is nothing in the central section which is incompatible with a considerably earlier date. It is known that Nicolaus of Damascus *did* write an introduction to the *Ethics*: it is quoted by the twelfth-century Arabic philosopher Ibn Al-Matran (Peters, *Aristotle and the Arabs*, 270). The surviving genuine works of Nicolaus make use of Aristotelian ethical ideas (e.g. that man is an ἀρχὴ πράξεως) but not in a manner which enables one to tell which treatise is being drawn upon. See Drossaart Lulofs, 1969.

out the ordering of the virtues in the treatises we have so far considered (Table 1.2).) More important, the inclusions and exclusions in the list agree with the *EE* and *MM* against the *NE*. The principal differences between the treatment of the virtues in *NE* 3–4 and that in *EE* III is that the *NE* contains seven major virtues and three minor ones (the distinction between the two is drawn at 1108ᵃ9) whereas the *EE* contains six virtues and six 'means of passion' (the distinction between the two being drawn at 1234ᵃ24–34). The six virtues of the *EE* are the seven virtues listed as major in the *NE*, less the unnamed one which is a proper degree of ambition; the six passional means of the *EE* are the three minor virtues of the *NE*, plus shame, *nemesis*, and dignity. (The first two of these are mentioned in the *NE* in the preliminary discussion in book 2 of means of passion, but only one, shame, is actually discussed in the full treatment in book 4; dignity is not mentioned in the *NE* at all.) In these respects the Fez manuscript, like the *MM* and Areios, follows the *EE* and not the *NE*: it does not include the unnamed mean of ambition and therefore has six and not seven major virtues; it includes dignity in its list, and it has a discussion of *nemesis* or righteous indignation which is based on the *EE* text. To be sure, in these respects the Fez manuscript resembles the *MM* also; but a number of details indicate direct dependence on the *EE*: for instance, the naming of the gourmand who wanted a crane's gullet as the son of Eryxis (cf. *EE* III, 1231ᵃ18). In the discussions of the particular virtues the text is sometimes closer to the Eudemian version (as in accounts of courage[1] and temperance) and sometimes closer to the Nicomachean (e.g. in the distinction between possession and use in the treatment of liberality, and in the attribution of wittiness to Socrates as at *NE* 1127ᵇ5).

PHILO OF ALEXANDRIA

Philo (d. A.D. 45) shows acquaintance with a number of Aristotelian ethical themes, such as the doctrine of the mean and the peripatetic definition of happiness. The way in which Philo applies the doctrine of the mean to particular virtues makes it more likely, if he is drawing on Aristotle directly, that he was acquainted with the Eudemian than the Nicomachean version of the doctrine;[2] but the

---

1. Especially in the accounts of the five types of unreal courage.
2. While most of the virtues and vices to which Philo applies the doctrine of the mean occur in both the *EE* and *NE* lists (e.g. ἀλαζονεία, θρασύτης, δειλία, ἀνδρεία,

freedom with which he applies it—e.g. to the triad impiety–piety–superstition (*Immut.* xxxiv.163)—leaves it open that he is improvising upon a theme known to him at second hand. Philo divides virtues into those that are inborn, those that are acquired by training, and those that come by treaching, in a way which has reminded some scholars of *NE* 10, 1179^{b}20; but it is equally reminiscent of Plato's *Meno* (70^{a}1 ff.) as is his frequent use of the concept of divine destiny.[1] Philo frequently uses the threefold division of goods into external goods, goods of the body and goods of the soul: this division is to be found in *NE* 1, 1098^{b}12 and other Aristotelian contexts, but it is also very frequent in Plato.[2] Philo defines happiness as the use of complete virtue in a complete life: this is close to the *EE* definition, but closer to the *MM* and closer still to the epitome of Areios Didymus.[3] Like the *AE*, Philo regards happiness as a combination of learning and wisdom; but unlike the *AE* he regards learning as being concerned with the service of God (*Praem.* xiv.81). The service of God, he says, in a phrase which echoes the final section of the *EE*, is the beginning and end of happiness: God is the standard (*horos*) of happiness (*De Spec. Leg.*, ed. Cohn, v.594). Philo's use of Aristotelian ethical material is too free for us to be able to say that he actually quotes the ethical treatises, or to decide with confidence which of them he is using: we can only say he is in general slightly closer to the *EE* than to the *NE*.[4] Certainly there is no passage which conclusively proves first-hand knowledge of any Aristotelian ethical treatise.[5]

δαπανηρία, σωφροσύνη—see *Migr.* xxvi.147 and *Immut.* xxiv.163-4) φρόνησις and πανουργία occur only in the Eudemian treatment.

1. See e.g. *Somn.* i.xxvii.164; on θεία μοῖρα see Wolfson, 1962, 165 ff.

2. The relevant texts in Plato are collected in Gauthier and Jolif, 1959, 62; for Philo see Cohn's edition i.259, v.325, etc.

3. Philo, ed. Cohn, i.272; see p. 17 above. Philo regards happiness as a combination of practical and theoretical life, like *EE* and the *Politics*, but he uses this division in a way somewhat different from Aristotle (*Praem.* 2.11).

4. Wolfson, 1962, 165 ff., collects together all the texts in which he thinks Philo is following Aristotle: none of them amounts to a verbatim quotation.

5. The same observation holds for Seneca, some years later than Philo. Some scholars have thought that the *clementia* of Seneca is a Romanization of Aristotle's ἐπιείκεια. Griffin (1976, 159 ff.) has shown this opinion to be without foundation, and Murray, who once (1965, 176 ff.) discussed whether the Aristotelian theory of equity gained widespread acceptance towards the end of the Roman republic, has decided that it did not (1967, 355 f.). Even if Seneca was acquainted with Aristotle's notion of equity, he can have derived his knowledge of it from a reading of the *Rhetoric* (1374^{a}26 ff.), a work with which the *De Ira* suggests familiarity.

PLUTARCH

A moralist as voluminous as Plutarch might be expected to have had ample occasion to quote from Aristotle's ethical writings. A glance at Helmbold and O'Neill's index *Plutarch's Quotations* seems to confirm this expectation, for it lists seventeen reminiscences or quotations to the *NE* and three to the *EE*. Inspection of the three *EE* passages mentioned show that the corresponding passages in Plutarch are simply common quotations of third parties (Herodotus and Bion) and so not any evidence of knowledge of the *EE*. This fact, plus the prima facie striking fact that not one of the seventeen passages of the *NE* listed in the index is from the *AE*, might seem to lend support to the hypothesis that the *NE* did not originally contain them: for the hypothesis would explain why Plutarch, apparently a keen *NE*-quoter and a non-*EE*-quoter, makes no use of them. But, alas, close inspection shows that of the seventeen 'reminiscences' of the *NE* all except one are souvenirs so faint as to amount to no more than the common employment of a commonplace. The single passage in which Aristotle is explicitly quoted is at 704 E, where Plutarch criticizes him for saying that there is no incontinence in respect of the pleasures of sight and hearing on the grounds that these are peculiar to humans.[1] The reference could be either to the *NE* or the *EE*; if it has to be to one or other, the *EE* is the more likely source because of details of language. But more likely than either as a source for Plutarch is the passage of the *Problems* considered earlier.[2] Only there is the question of the sharing of pleasures with animals brought into conjunction with the topic of incontinence rather than intemperance.

FAVORINUS OF ARLES

In the *Life of Aristotle* by Diogenes Laertius there is a list of Aristotle's sayings which concludes thus: 'Favorinus in the second book of his *Memorabilia* mentions as one of his habitual sayings "He who has many friends has no friend". This can be found also in the seventh book of the *Ethics*.'[3] Though the sentiment quoted by

---

1. δοκεῖ δέ μοι μηδ' Ἀριστοτέλης αἰτίᾳ δικαίᾳ τὰς περὶ θέαν καὶ ἀκρόασιν εὐπαθείας ἀπολύειν ἀκρασίας, ὡς μόνας ἀνθρωπίνας οὔσας, ταῖς δ' ἄλλαις καὶ τὰ θηρία φύσιν ἔχοντα χρῆσθαι καὶ κοινωνεῖν.

2. p. 8.

3. φησὶ δὲ Φαβωρῖνος ἐν τῷ δευτέρῳ τῶν Ἀπομνημονευμάτων ὡς ἑκάστοτε λέγοι, 'ᾧ φίλοι, οὐδεὶς φίλος'. ἀλλὰ καὶ ἐν τῷ ἑβδόμῳ τῶν Ἠθικῶν ἐστι.

Favorinus can be traced in both *Ethics*, in the epigrammatic form quoted it occurs only in the *EE* (VII.12, 1245^{b}21).[1] This is made explicit in the attached comment, which must be a reference to the Eudemian version since the corresponding passage in the *NE* (1171^{a}15–17) occurs in the *ninth* book.[2] The comment is evidence also that the version of the *EE* referred to must have contained the disputed books of the *AE*; otherwise the book on friendship would be the fourth and not the seventh book.[3] It is striking that the *EE* is cited so firmly as *the Ethics* of Aristotle.

It would be pleasant to know for certain who was responsible for the citation. It is possible, though hardly likely, that it was attached to the epigram by Favorinus. It may be by Diogenes himself, or by some earlier writer from whom he has drawn the collection of Aristotelian sayings. Other scholars have thought that the citation was attached to the epigram *before* Favorinus and originated in some source of his. Once the edition of Andronicus had established the *Nicomachean Ethics* in a position of pre-eminence, argued von der Mühll (1909, 26), no one could refer to the *EE* as 'the *Ethics*'; therefore the quotation must be by some writer of the Ptolemaic era who included a list of apophthegms in a life of Aristotle.[4] Düring went so far as to identify this ancient source as Hermippus.[5]

In fact, as we have seen, there is no reason to believe that Andronicus' edition even included the *Nicomachean Ethics*, let alone that it conferred on it a pre-eminent status. The allusion to the *EE* as Aristotle's *Ethics* is consistent with all the ancient allusions we have so far considered. To whatever date prior to

1. οὐθεὶς φίλος ᾧ πολλοὶ φίλοι.
2. οἱ δὲ πολύφιλοι καὶ πᾶσιν οἰκείως ἐντυγχάνοντες οὐδενὶ δοκοῦσιν εἶναι φίλοι, πλὴν πολιτικῶς.
3. Consequently those who have, implausibly, maintained that the *EE* is complete in five books have had to explain away this passage in Diogenes as a late gloss (e.g. Titze: see Rowe, 1971, 80).
4. 'Ut Diogenem vel Favorinum, quem Diogenes excerpsit, Eudemia perlegisse putem, vix mihi persuadebis, praesertim cum editione Androniaca pervulgata Nicomachea talia dignitati Eudemiis praecellerent, ut *Ēthikōn* vocabulo semper ad Nicomachea usus scriptorum revocaret. Itaque laudationem illam neque Diogenis neque Favorini sapientiae thesauros suppeditasse apparet, sed Ptolemaeorum saeculo a viro docto in vita Aristotelis cum apophthegmate collocata est, unde Favorinus eam recepit.'
5. His comment on the passage is puzzling, seeming to support two inconsistent interpretations: 'Then follows . . . a note from Phavorinus, including an annotation from Diogenes himself "this is found in the seventh book of the *Ethics*, too". This note proves that Hermippus (or the unknown author) had access to or knew an edition of the *Eudemian Ethics* which included the books which it has in common with the *Nicomachean Ethics*.' If the note is by Diogenes, it surely proves nothing about Hermippus' library (Düring, 1957, 67).

Diogenes we assign the present passage, we have further evidence for the ancient preference of the *EE* over the *NE*.

DIOGENES LAERTIUS

In addition to the apophthegm from Favorinus the *Life of Aristotle* contains other material relevant to our problem. Diogenes' summary of the philosopher's doctrines contains a section (v.31–52) on his ethical teaching. P. Moraux (1949) made a detailed study of this summary, along with the rest of the outline in Diogenes, with a view to establishing its immediate sources. After comparing it with the Aristotelian texts he came to the conclusion that it must have been written by an unknown author between the time of Andronicus and that of Diogenes. But there is no reason to believe that in constructing his ethical summary Diogenes looked anywhere else than to the epitome of Arius Didymus. In structure and in detail of vocabulary Diogenes' summary follows Arius[1] and in its whole length there is nothing which demands any different source except for three insignificant details. These details will not help us to decide whether Diogenes (or any source he had other than Arius) followed by preference the *NE* or the *EE*: for they are details which occur in none of the treatises of the Aristotelian corpus.[2]

---

1. I will illustrate this from Diogenes' first sentence:

Diogenes	Arius
τέλος δὲ ἐν ἐξέθετο χρῆσιν ἀρετῆς ἐν βίῳ τελείῳ. ἔφη δὲ καὶ τὴν εὐδαιμονίαν συμπλήρωμα ἐκ τριῶν ἀγαθῶν εἶναι· τῶν περὶ ψυχήν, ἃ δὴ καὶ πρῶτα τῇ δυνάμει καλεῖ· ἐκ δευτέρων δὲ τῶν περὶ σῶμα, ὑγιείας καὶ ἰσχύος καὶ κάλλους καὶ τῶν παραπλησίων· ἐκ τρίτων δὲ τῶν ἐκτός, πλούτου καὶ εὐγενείας καὶ δόξης καὶ τῶν ὁμοίων.	εὐδαιμονίαν δ'ἔναι χρῆσιν ἀρετῆς τελείας ἐν βίῳ τελείῳ (130, 19). It is a whole whose parts are συμπληρωτικά (130.9). ἔτι τῶν ἀγαθῶν τὰ μὲν εἶναι περὶ ψυχήν, τὰ δὲ περὶ σῶμα, τὰ δ' ἐκτός. περὶ ψυχὴν μέν, οἷον εὐφυΐαν τε καὶ τέχνην καὶ ἀρετὴν καὶ σοφίαν καὶ φρόνησιν καὶ ἡδονήν· περὶ σῶμα δὲ ὑγίειαν καὶ εὐαισθησίαν καὶ κάλλος καὶ ἰσχὺν καὶ ἀρτιότητα καὶ πάντα τὰ μόρια σὺν ταῖς δυνάμεσι καὶ ἐνεργείαις· ἐκτὸς δὲ πλοῦτον καὶ δόξαν καὶ εὐγένειαν καὶ δυναστείαν καὶ φίλους καὶ συγγενεῖς καὶ πατρίδα. (136.9–16).

2. The three points are (1) the statement that the goods of the soul are πρῶτα τῇ δυνάμει, (2) the definition of friendship as equality of reciprocal goodwill (ἰσότητα εὐνοίας ἀντιστρόφου), (3) the statement that the virtues are not mutually interdependent, which is in plain contradition to *AE* C, 1144[b]30 ff.

Two other points elsewhere in Diogenes are more indicative. Among Aristotle's sayings he gives the definition of friendship as a single soul dwelling in two bodies.[1] Like the saying in Favorinus, this too seems to be an allusion to the *EE*. The *NE* does not figure, in the same way, in the *Life* of Aristotle. Indeed, Diogenes, like Cicero, seems to have believed that the *Nicomachean Ethics* was the work of Aristotle's son: for in his *Life* of Eudoxus (viii.88) we read 'Nicomachus, the son of Aristotle, states that he declared pleasure to be the good';[2] a reference to *NE* 10.2, 1172^b9 ff.

Diogenes' most valuable service is his preservation of the ancient list of Aristotle's writings. This, which raises more problems about the *Ethics* than it clearly solves, will be considered later on its own.

ASPASIUS

From the study we have so far undertaken of twelve ancient writers, the following conclusions emerge. Every writer, from Aristotle himself until the second century A.D., who shows a first-hand knowledge of the Aristotelian ethical writings also shows a preference for the *EE* over the *NE*: either in the sense that he refers to it as *The Ethics*, sans phrase, or that he quotes it exclusively, or that he prefers its doctrine, or its terminology, or its systematic structure. No author (with the exception of the author of the *Magna Moralia*) quotes the *Nicomachean Ethics* as 'The Ethics'; and the only two authors who show awareness of an *Ethics* with that title both regard it as the work of Aristotle's son.

The comparative silence of antiquity about the *NE* comes to an end with Aspasius, the author of a line-by-line commentary on the *Ethics* which is the earliest of all the surviving Aristotelian commentaries.[3] In Aspasius' writing we find the situation with which we have been familiar for centuries: the *Nicomachean Ethics* is the undoubted treatise of Aristotle, the *Eudemian Ethics* is the problematic treatise whose attribution fluctuates, regarded now as authentic Aristotle, now as the work of his disciple Eudemus. But if Aspasius departs from the earlier tradition in his ranking of the two

1. μία ψυχὴ δύο σώμασιν ἐνοικοῦσα (cf. *EE* 1240ᵇ2; see Düring, 1957, 67).
2. φησὶ δ' αὐτὸν Νικόμαχος ὁ 'Αριστοτέλους τὴν ἡδονὴν λέγειν τὸ ἀγαθόν.
3. The date of Aspasius is uncertain: his *floruit* is generally placed in the first half of the second century. It may well be that his commentary is earlier in date than the passages from Diogenes cited above, p. 28. Diogenes himself, according to R. D. Hicks (1925, xvi) 'has been variously dated in every century A.D. from the first to the fourth'.

Ethics, he is at one with it—as we shall see—in regarding the disputed books as belonging essentially to the Eudemian version.

Unfortunately, all that survives of Aspasius' writing is commentaries on *NE* 1–4, part of *AE* C, and part of *NE* 8. These commentaries are, of course, in our editions treated as commentaries on books 1–4, 7, and 8 of the *Nicomachean Ethics*: but we cannot be certain without further ado of the original context of his commentary on C. If the disputed books belonged originally with the *Eudemian Ethics*, we cannot rule out in advance the possibility that Aspasius' commentary covered both ethical treatises, and that we have four and a half books surving of his commentary on the *NE*, and half a book surviving from his commentary on the *EE*. That is, indeed, the hypothesis that some of the evidence from his commentary would suggest, though it may not be the one which, taking the evidence as a whole, is the most plausible over-all explanation. Let us examine the evidence in detail.

The most important evidence is contained in Aspasius' commentary on the following well-known passage in *AE* C.

If certain pleasures are bad, that does not prevent the chief good from being some pleasure, just as the chief good may be some form of knowledge though certain kinds of knowledge are bad. Perhaps it is even necessary, if each disposition has unimpeded activities, that, whether the activity (if unimpeded) of all of our dispositions or that of some one of them is happiness, this should be the thing most worthy of our choice; and this activity is pleasure. Thus the chief good would be some pleasure, though most pleasures might perhaps be bad without qualification. (1153^b7–13, trans. Ross)

Commenting on the second of these sentences, Aspasius writes:

These words make it look as if he was proving that the good and pleasure are one and the same; but that is not so: what he is doing is—in a dialectical manner against those who say that pleasure is a process or that some pleasures are bad and draw the conclusion that it is not the good—to try to show that it is possible to say that it is the supreme good. For in the *Nicomachean Ethics* it is discussed, and there Aristotle says clearly about pleasure that it is not the same thing as happiness but accompanies it like the bloom on the cheek of youth. It is a sign that the present passage is not by Aristotle but by Eudemus that in the . . . . . . he talks about pleasure as if it had not yet been discussed; but whether this text is by Eudemus or by Aristotle, what is said is dialectical; the reason that the greatest good is said to be pleasure is that pleasure goes with the greatest good and cannot be separated from it. (*CAG* xix.151.18–27)[1]

This important passage has many puzzling features. It is commonly taken as showing that Aspasius is in doubt whether the passage he is commenting on—and, by implication, the disputed books in general—belong to the Eudemian or to the Nicomachean version. And this is certainly suggested by his reference to the fact that in the tenth book of the *NE* Aristotle talks of pleasure as if he were discussing it for the first time: this is a premiss which many people since Aspasius have reasonably used as evidence that book seven is Eudemian. But a closer reading of the text suggests that his doubt is not whether the present book belongs to the *Eudemian Ethics*, but whether the *Eudemian Ethics*, to which in his view the present book belongs, is by Aristotle or by Eudemus.[2] When he says that Aristotle discussed pleasure 'in the *Nicomachean Ethics*' it is barely credible that he takes himself to be at that moment commenting on a book of the *Nicomachean Ethics*; if he did so, surely he would have to say 'in the tenth book' or 'later'. Aspasius is obviously embarrassed by what Aristotle here says about pleasure, and is torn between several ways of dealing with it and resolving the apparent discrepancy between the present passage and the passage that we know as the tenth book of the *NE*. One solution he investigates is that there is no real inconsistency because the present passage is

1. διὰ μὲν οὖν τούτων δοκεῖ ταὐτὸν ἀποφαίνεσθαι τἀγαθὸν καὶ τὴν ἡδονήν· οὐ μὴν οὕτως ἔχει, ἀλλὰ πρὸς τοὺς λέγοντας γένεσιν εἶναι ἢ φαύλας τινὰς τῶν ἡδονῶν, οἷς καὶ δι' αὐτὸ τὸ μὴ εἶναι αὐτὴν τὸ ἀγαθὸν ἐπιγίνεται[καὶ], ἐπιχειρεῖ ἐνδόξως ὡς ἐνὸν αὐτὴν τὸ ἄριστον λέγειν, ἐπεὶ ἔν γε τοῖς Νικομαχείοις, ἔνθα διείληπται καὶ περὶ ἡδονῆς 'Αριστοτέλης σαφῶς εἴρηκεν αὐτὴν μὴ ταὐτὸν εἶναι τῇ εὐδαιμονίᾳ ἀλλὰ παρακολουθεῖν 'ὥσπερ τοῖς ἀκμαίοις τὴν ὥραν'. σημεῖον δὲ τοῦ μὴ εἶναι τοῦτ' 'Αριστοτέλους ἀλλ' Εὐδήμου τὸ ἐν τῷ . . . . . . λέγειν περὶ ἡδονῆς ὡς οὐδέπω περὶ αὐτῆς διειλεγμένου· πλὴν εἴτε Εὐδήμου ταῦτά ἐστιν εἴτε 'Αριστοτέλους, ἐνδόξως εἴρηται· διὰ τοῦτο λέγεται τὸ ἄριστον ἡδονή, ὅτι σὺν τῷ ἀρίστῳ καὶ ἀχώριστον αὐτοῦ. The lacuna of approximately six letters where one would expect the number of the *NE* book which treats of pleasure is interesting. The number which we would expect, and which a later tradition and Heylbut obviously did expect, is 'tenth'. The lacuna may mean that the number which was actually in the manuscripts was not this: which would support the thesis that the original place of the disputed books was not in the context of the *NE*.

2. Of course the 'τοῦτ'' which he is prepared to consider as being not by Aristotle but by Eudemus need not be the whole disputed books of the *AE*, but a more limited context of the quotation: e.g. the treatment of pleasure. But (a) within the text of Aspasius himself there is no indication of a break between the treatment of pleasure and the rest of *AE* book C; (b) there is no indication, independent of the present passage, of a Eudemian origin for the treatment of pleasure here other than the fact that the whole of the *AE* is by the manuscript tradition regarded as belonging also to a work which some scholars have regarded as written by Eudemus rather than by Aristotle.

only dialectical; another is that the inconsistency is not surprising because one treatment is by Aristotle and the other is by Eudemius. But having offered the fact that the two treatments of pleasure ignore each other as independent evidence that the current one is by Eudemus he then goes on to say that even if it is by Eudemus it is consistent with the Aristotelian treatment because it is only dialectical.

If we reject as incredible the traditional suggestion that Aspasius, at the moment when he talks of 'the *Nicomachean Ethics*' as a different work, was commenting on a text of the *NE* which included the disputed books, there are two solutions which can be offerred of the problems set by this difficult passage. One possibility is that Aspasius commented on both the *Nicomachean* and *Eudemian Ethics*, and that the partial commentary on book seven is a fragment of his commentary on the *EE* just as his partial commentary on book eight is a fragment of his commentary on the *NE*. The weak point of this hypothesis is the following: if Aspasius regarded the two treatments of pleasure as clearly belonging to two different works, why should he be surprised to find no cross-reference? Other parallel treatments of topics in the two *Ethics* are not signalized in either *Ethics*, so why should the absence of a reference here be taken as an argument that the *EE* is by Eudemus?

There is another solution which seems to me the more plausible one. That is, that Aspasius was writing a commentary on a text of the *NE* which did not contain the disputed books, but which contained, as our texts of *NE* 1–4 do, forward references to treatments of topics such as justice, wisdom, and continence. There existed in his time—as is surely most likely from the whole history we have hitherto investigated—texts of the *Eudemian Ethics* containing the common books; but their title gave Aspasius some reason to believe that they were not by Aristotle but by Eudemus, just as the title of the *Nicomachean Ethics* gave Diogenes and perhaps Cicero reason to believe that the *NE* was not by Aristotle but by Nicomachus. I conjecture that in these circumstances Aspasius, having commented on books 1–4 of the *NE*, proceeded to comment on books IV–VI of the *Eudemian Ethics*, in order to have a full commentary on Aristotle's ethical system, in spite of the lacuna in the Nicomachean version.

This can be no more than a conjecture: but it would explain all the features of the puzzling passage of Aspasius in a very simple manner. First, it explains why he refers to the *NE* as if it was a different work from the one he is currently commenting on. Second, it explains why, in spite of this, he comments on the lack of cross-reference between the two treatments of pleasure as surprising. For if the only books of the *EE* he commented on were the disputed books, the passage about pleasure, being the only clear doublet with the *NE* books, would be the most obvious place to remark on the fact that the *NE* and *EE* apparently make no cross-references to each other. This is indeed surprising, given the general frequency in Aristotle of cross-references to treatments of similar topics in other works (e.g. to the *Analytics*);[1] it is indeed something from which a scholar might be tempted to draw conclusions about the authenticity or spuriousness of a work.

Obiously, this is no more than conjecture, as has been said. If Aspasius deliberately moved the three disputed books into the *Nicomachean Ethics* from the *Eudemian* for purposes of commenting on a unified and comprehensive treatment of Aristotle's ethics, the place where he would have to announce this would be the beginning of his commentary on the first disputed book, *NE* 5 = *EE* IV.[2] But his commentary on book 5 is unfortunately lost. But there are several other features of the surviving parts of the commentary which go some way to confirm our conjecture.

First, a passage in the commentary on *NE* 8 places it beyond doubt that Aspasius regarded the *NE* as containing a lacuna that needed filling. Aristotle is critizing those who argue that there is only one kind of friendship on the ground that friendship admits of degrees. 'Things different in kind also admit of degrees,' he says, 'But these matters have been discussed before' (1135^b13-16).

1. It has been fashionable to treat the cross-references as untrustworthy and possibly interpolated. Düring (1968, 191) is rightly critical of this fashion: 'Die zahlreichen Vor-, Querund Rüchverweise in seinen Schriften stimmen erstaunlich gut; höchstens ein Zehntel der Verweise sind problematisch. Ein später Redaktor hätte nie ein so feinmaschiges Netz von Verbindungen zwischen den einzelnen Schriften herstellen können.'

2. Earlier scholars who attributed the *AE* to Eudemus thought they could detect the suture in Aristotle's own text. Grant regarded as spurious the last two sentences of *NE* 4. ('Continence is not a virtue either, but an intermediate state: This will be explained later. We must now discuss justice.') 'Aristotle's MS. of the fourth book having ended abruptly at the word ἐπιεικές Nicomachus, or the editor, whoever he was, in all probability added these clauses in order to give the book a seeming unity with the three Eudemian books which were now to be grafted on' (1885, ii.94). Aspasius' commentary on *NE* 4 ends a column earlier at 1128^a33; the anonymous second-century commentary has a curious comment at this point (*CAG* xix.126, xx.204; see below, p. 37). But there is no manuscript support for the excision.

Aspasius comments: '"They have been discussed" he says "before". It looks as if they have been discussed in the lost parts of the *Nicomachean Ethics*' (*CAG* xix.161).[1] Now of course we cannot be certain that by 'the lost parts of the *Nicomachean Ethics*' Aspasius means the lacuna it displays if it is deprived of the common books. But such is certainly the simplest explanation of his remark: that lacuna is the only lacuna for which there is independent evidence in the anomalous nature of the manuscript tradition.[2] If this is the lacuna that Aspasius means, we cannot tell whether he knew as a fact that there were once other Nicomachean books where the *AE* books now stand, or whether he merely conjectured that there must have been because of the forward and backward references in the *NE* itself.

Secondly, an examination of Aspasius' method of citation from one part of the *Ethics* to another suggests that he regarded the *AE* as forming a block separate from that of the undisputed *NE*. When he makes a forward or back reference within a single book, or from one undisputed *NE* book to another, he uses an expression such as 'as was said before' or 'later'.[3] So too when he refers, within his commentary on book C, to the disputed books.[4] But when he quotes the disputed books from the commentary on the *NE*, he uses different modes of expression: 'in the book on justice' (160.11) 'elsewhere' (178.22, a reference to book A; 18.6, a reference to a number of texts including book B as well as *NE* 1).[5] Similarly, when referring from the disputed book C to the undisputed Nicomachean books, Aspasius says 'elsewhere' (138.22, reference to *NE* 4) 'in the *Nicomachean Ethics*' (151.22).[6] The discrepancy is sufficiently systematic to suggest that it is deliberate.[7] 'Elsewhere', the

1. εἴρηται δέ, φησί, περὶ αὐτῶν ἔμπροσθεν, ἔοικε δὲ εἰρῆσθαι ἐν τοῖς ἐκπεπτω-κόσι τῶν Νικομαχέων.

2. I agree in this, against Rose (1871, 107), with Moraux and Harlfinger (Harlfinger, 1972, 45–7).

3. πρότερον is used thus at 19.25; 121.15; 119.27; 83.4; 88.2; 116.3; 86.9; 105.14; 53.4; 101.8; 106.15; 168.4; 174.2. ὕστερον is used in a similar way at 19.2; 23.29.

4. So for references within book C, and in the two references back from C to B, 136.31 and 140.2 and 30.

5. ἐν ἄλλοις (178.22; 18.6); ἐν τοῖς περὶ δικαιοσύνης (160.11).

6. ἐν ἄλλοις (138.22) ἐν τοῖς Νικομαχείοις (151.22).

7. Of thirty-odd cross-references in Aspasius I have found only one that is a real exception to the rule that internal citations are introduced differently from citations across the *NE–AE* boundary. That is 8.30, where, discussing an *aporia* in book *NE* 1 Aspasius says that Aristotle solves it προϊών. The reference appears to be to a passage in B (1145ᵃ 10). This, unlike the other cross-references in Aspasius, suggests that he read B as part of a text continuous with the *NE*.

expression used to refer across the boundary between the disputed books and the rest of the *NE*, is also used in a case where, from the commentary on the *NE*, Aspasius refers to the *EE*.[1]

Thirdly, with regard to both the *AE* and the *EE* Aspasius is undecided whether to ascribe authorship to Aristotle or to Eudemus. In the case of the *AE* we have already looked at the famous passage in which he assigns at least the section on pleasure to Eudemus; at 2.24 on the other hand Aristotle is given credit for the definition of *technē* in *AE* A and at 18.6 the psychology of book B (and elsewhere) is attributed to Aristotle, and at 178.22 in the commentary on *NE* 8 Aristotle is referred to as the author of the treatise on justice, which is presumably *AE* A.[2] Similarly, there is vacillation about the authorship of the *Eudemian Ethics*. At 11.5 Aristotle is cited as the author of the Eudemian view of riches, and at 132.3 (in a section of C where Aristotle is treated without question as the author) the Eudemian account of the insensible man is quoted.[3] But in the commentary on *NE* 8 a quotation from the seventh book of the *EE* is attributed to Eudemus.[4]

To summarize, therefore, the evidence of Aspasius. It seems clear that Aspasius regarded the disputed books as belonging to the *EE* for the following reasons: (1) In his commentary on C he refers to the *NE* as a different work. (2) He is certain that the *NE* is by Aristotle, but is prepared to consider the possibility that C is by Eudemus, just as he is unsure whether the *EE* is by Aristotle or Eudemus. (3) With one exception, he quotes the *AE* when commenting on the *NE*, and the *NE* when commenting on the *AE*,

---

1. At 11.5 Aspasius says that the remark in the *NE* that riches are desirable ἄλλου χάριν does not fit his remarks ἐν ἄλλοις that they are good in themselves. This appears to be a reference to the *EE*, where several times (1214ᵇ8, 1217ᵃ37, 1227ᵃ14, 1232ᵇ10, 1248ᵇ28) riches are given as an example of an ultimate end.

2. And of course throughout the text of C itself is attributed to Aristotle (133.30; 136.7; 138.19; 150.5).

3. ὁ δὲ ἐλλείπων περὶ τὰς ἡδονὰς καὶ μὴ ταῖς ἀναγκαίαις χρώμενος ὁ ἀντικείμενος τῷ ἀκολάστῳ, ὃν ἐν τοῖς κατ' ἀρχὰς λόγοις ἀναίσθητον ἔλεγε. This reference is clearly to *EE* III.2, 1231ᵃ26 ff.: ἀναίσθητος μὲν οὖν . . . ὁ οὕτως ἔχων ὥστε καὶ ἐλλείπειν ὅσων ἀνάγκη κοινωνεῖν ὡς ἐπὶ τὸ πολὺ πάντας καὶ χαίρειν. The *NE* does not link the insensible man with the notion of necessary pleasures, and is indeed sceptical of his very existence (1107ᵇ28; 1114ᵃ10). This quotation is very interesting, for it is introduced in C by the expression ἐν τοῖς κατ' ἀρχὰς λόγοις which is used by Aspasius (162.3) and by Aristotle (1104ᵃ2; 1149ᵇ27) to refer to earlier parts of the *same* work. It is thus another piece of evidence that Aspasius regarded the *AE* as belonging to the *EE*.

4. λέγει δὲ καὶ Εὔδημος καὶ Θεόφραστος, ὅτι καὶ αἱ καθ' ὑπεροχὴν φιλίαι ἐν τοῖς αὐτοῖς γίνονται, ἢ δι' ἡδονὴν ἢ διὰ τὸ χρήσιμον ἢ δι' ἀρετήν. The reference is to *EE* VII.4, 1239ᵃ1 ff. (*CAG* xix.178.3).

with the style of quotation he uses for introducing quotations from other works, rather than that which he uses for forward and backward references in the same work. (4) From the *AE* he quotes the *EE* with a form of words he uses for backward reference in the same work. (5) He speaks of the existence of a lacuna in the *NE* as a familiar fact.

We shall see that after the time of Aspasius the common books are normally taken with the *NE*: the earlier tradition leaves as its only trace—other than the presence of the *AE* in the manuscripts of the *EE*—a continuing confusion about the numbering of the books of the *NE*. If we are right in our conjecture that the Aspasian evidence is best explained by postulating that he commented on the three *EE*-books in the Nicomachean context in order to fill a lacuna in the *NE*, then it may very well have been Aspasius' own activity as a commentator which inaugurated the tradition of counting the disputed books with the Nicomachean treatise. If that is so, the *Nicomachean Ethics* as we know them—*NE* plus *AE*—might be more aptly termed the 'Aspasian Ethics'.

ATTICUS

Eusebius (*Praeparatio Evangelica* XV.4) quotes a comment by the Platonist Atticus on the worthlessness of Aristotle's three ethical treatises: the *Eudemian*, *Nicomachean*, and *Great Ethics*.[1] Atticus was active in the time of Marcus Aurelius (161–80): he is thus the earliest testimony to the three traditional titles of the treatises of the Aristotelian corpus. He is also useful in the present context as determining the date of the anonymous scholia on books 2–5 of the *NE*, which we shall next consider.

THE SCHOLIAST

The scholiast on book 5 of the *Nicomachean Ethics* (*CAG* xx. 248.24–6) is discussing the idea that some things are indifferent (*adiaphora*): he mentions its proponents 'among whom previously Aristonymus belonged, but now even some who pretend to be Platonists, while surreptitiously introducing this doctrine, among whom also Atticus appears to belong'. This passage, noticed by

1. αἱ γοῦν Ἀριστοτέλους περὶ ταῦτα πραγματεῖαι Εὐδήμειοί τε καὶ Νικομάχειοι καὶ Μεγάλων Ἠθικῶν ἐπιγραφόμεναι μικρόν τι καὶ ταπεινὸν καὶ δημῶδες περὶ ἀρετῆς φρονοῦσι.

Mercken,[1] indicates that the writer of the scholia was a contemporary of Atticus and should therefore be assigned to the second half of the second century. The commentary on *NE* 5 appears continuous with those on *NE* 2–4 and is written in very much the same style: the writer clearly regarded *NE* 5 as belonging with *NE* 1–4, and refers in the first line of his commentary on 5 to the discussions of *akribeia* preceding in the *NE*. He refers forward to B from an earlier book, and cites it by its Nicomachean number (*CAG* xx.125.30); on the other hand, at the end of book 4 he appears to promise a discussion of continence by Aristotle in the book after next, rather than as we would expect after two intervening books.[2] In general, this writer witnesses to the Nicomachean tradition as familiar in later centuries.[3]

ALEXANDER OF APHRODISIAS

In the writings of Alexander, who began lecturing at Athens *c.* 198, there is no doubt of the existence of the ten-book *Nicomachean Ethics* with which we are familiar. Alexander did not write a line-by-line commentary like Aspasius; but both in his commentary on the *Metaphysics* and in his minor ethical writings he refers to the disputed books at belonging to the *Nicomachean Ethics*.[4]

1. 1973, 15*.
2. ὕστερον δὲ ἐπὶ πλέον ἐρεῖ περὶ ἐγκρατείας καὶ καρτερίας καὶ μαλακίας μετὰ τὸ ἑξῆς βιβλίον (*CAG* xx.204).
3. We can make a guess at the identity of this scholiast. We know from Athenaeus (XV.673 e) that Adrastus of Aphrodisias wrote five books on Theophrastus' ethics and six (or a sixth) on Aristotle's. Six books must have been the extent of the second-century scholia on the *NE*, since the popular composite medieval commentary published in *CAG* xx appears to have been built up on the basis of the scholiast's work, replacing particular books by works of more prestigious Christian writers as these became available, as in the case of Eustratius for book 1. (The trumping process can actually be observed in the New College manuscript of the commentaries in which both the anonymous scholia on *AE* A and the preferred commentary of Michael of Ephesus have been preserved.) The composite commentary, however, has to rely on a late anonymous author for book 7, suggesting that the original scholiast had here neither commented nor been trumped. Some may find it too much of a coincidence to have both a second-century six-book commentator on the *Ethics* whose commentary has been lost and a second-century six-book commentary on the *Ethics* whose author has disappeared. In addition to the reference to Atticus the internal evidence of the scholia suggests a second-century date. The latest author quoted is Lucian; there is no evidence of Christian interest with the possible exception of the three words οὕτως καὶ 'Αβεσαλώμ (229.22) at the end of the story in book 5 of Phoenix's affair with his father's concubine. Mercken (1973, 15*) is probably right to see these words as a late gloss, added at the very end of a paragraph.
4. In his commentary on the *Prior Analytics* (*CAG* ii.1.8.31) he refers to book 1 of the *NE* and then refers to there being ten books in that work. In commenting on the *Metaphysics*

CLEMENT OF ALEXANDRIA

In his 'miscellanies', which are commonly dated to the very earliest years of the third century, Clement draws freely on both the *Eudemian* and the *Nicomachean Ethics*, quoting the *Eudemians* without hesitation as Aristotle's work. His method of utilizing his sources makes it difficult to draw any conclusions about the position of the disputed books in the texts available to him.[1]

LATER COMMENTATORS

No commentary on Aristotle's *Ethics* survives from the period between Alexander and the Byzantine renaissance. In the second half of the third century Porphyry wrote a commentary which is known only through Arabic sources. Scholars assume that it was a commentary on the *Nicomachean Ethics*, but there is no decisive evidence for this; all we know is that the commentary was on a twelve-book ethics (or was itself in twelve books).[2]

A study of citations of the *Ethics* by commentators on Aristotle

(*CAG* i.7.13) he refers to B as book 6 of the *Nicomachean Ethics*; the commentary on the *Sophistici Elenchi* in his name (II.3.172.20) refers to A as book 5 of the *NE*. In his commentary on the *Topics* he quotes the *NE* a dozen times, but without specific citations. He does not appear to have quoted the *EE*. The *Ethical Questions* attributed to him on doubtful authority discuss passages of the *NE* at length, and refer twice (Suppl. Ar. II.127.29; 134.30) to book C as *NE* 7. The picture is not entirely clear, however, for in Alexander's second treatise *De Anima* there are two passages which suggest an eleven-book *Nicomachean Ethics* (Suppl. Ar. II). At 151.11 a reference to *NE* 8 is described as occurring ἐν τῷ ἐνατῷ, nine lines further on a reference to *NE* 9 is described as ἐν τῷ δεκατῷ, and in 153.14 a quotation of *EE* 10.3, 1175ᵃ10 is introduced with the words λέγει δὲ ἐν τῷ κ τῶν Νικομαχείων. This work may be however considerably later than Alexander (see Gauthier, 1970, 101).

1. Thus he makes use of the quotation which introduces the *EE* and occurs later in the *NE*, at Strom. 7.12; he refers to the etymology of σωφροσύνη from the common book B at 7.3, and the reference to the stubbornness of mere belief in book C at 7.16. There is a long development, without explicit acknowledgement of Aristotle, of the passage in *NE* 3 concerning ignorance of circumstances.

A quotation from the *EE* is introduced with an explicit mention of Aristotle in the following passage: κᾂν ὁ Ἀριστοτέλης ἀναλογῇ, τὸ μὲν ποιεῖν καὶ ἐπὶ τῶν ἀλόγων ζῴων τάσσεσθαι καὶ ἐπὶ ἀψύχων διδάσκων, τὸ δὲ πράττειν ἀνθρώπων εἶναι μόνων (cf. *EE* 2.6, 1222ᵇ20; 2.8, 1224ᵃ28).

2. Porphyry's commentary is mentioned by the Arab bibliographer Ibn al-Nadim (A.D. 987); see Müller, 1873, and Walzer, *Greek into Arabic*, 220 ff., 240. The commentary certainly included discussions of *NE* 1 and *NE* 10, as we know from the quotations in other Arabic writers: see Ghourab, in Stern, Hourani, and Brown, 1972, 78, on al'Amiri. From al'Amiri we know also that Themistius, the secretary of Julian the Apostate, commented on the passages on practical reasoning in book B of the *AE* (ibid. 83–7).

between the third and tenth centuries yields rather inconclusive results.[1]

A late witness to the uncertainty about the authorship and content of the *Nicomachean Ethics* is contained in the entry in the Suda on Nicomachus, which is said to be likely to derive from Hesychius (*c.* 5th cent.). There we are told that Nicomachus wrote six books of *Ethics* as well as a commentary on his father's *Physics*. Some commentators regard this as a confusion between Nicomachus and Eudemus, who did write a commentary on the *Physics*, and whose name is associated with the *EE* (some manuscripts of which lump books VII and VIII together). Possibly so: but equally possibly the six-book *Ethics* might be the *Nicomachean Ethics* less the disputed books; there is one book short in either case.[2]

THE CATALOGUES OF ARISTOTLE'S WRITINGS

Three ancient lists of Aristotle's works have come down to us. The first, in the *Life* by Diogenes Laertius (v.22–7) is commonly held to have been made by Hermippus, librarian of the library of Alexandria, who wrote a life of Aristotle in about 200 B.C. The second is in the *Life* of Aristotle by Hesychius (the *Vita Menagiana*) of the fifth century. The third is the list of Ptolemy which is preserved in two Arabic versions in the *Lives* of Aristotle by al-Qifti (d. 1248) and by Usaibia (d. 1270).[3] We have already referred to the third list in discussing Andronicus: we must now consider the other two.

THE LIST OF HERMIPPUS

The thirty-eighth item in the Hermippus list is an *Ethics* in five books; no other *Ethics* is listed. Many scholars have seen this five-

1. Philoponus in the fifth century quotes both the *NE* (*CAG* xvi.3.19) and the *EE* (*CAG* xvi.237.26, 335.22) as simply 'the *Ethics*'. He quotes 1139ᵃ8, from *AE* B, as being from the *Nicomachean Ethics* (xiv.3.84.15). Simplicus in the sixth century quotes the *NE* and *EE* both by name (viii.4.27, 6.14, 12.8, 170.6). At one point he attributes to the *NE* a distinction made only in the *EE* in our manuscripts (x.303.32 ff.).

2. ἔγραψεν Ἠθικῶν βιβλία ϛ´ καὶ περὶ τῆς φυσικῆς ἀκροάσεως τοῦ πατρὸς αὐτοῦ. The passage is printed in Düring, 1957, 265, who conjectures that it has been transferred from a notice of Eudemus.

3. Moraux attributes the list in Diogenes to Ariston, scholarch of the Peripatos in the last quarter of the second century (1951, 237); but this attribution has not been generally accepted: see Düring, 1956, 11–21; Kearney, 1972. The list of Hesychius is printed in Düring, 1957, 83–9; the most accessible reproduction of the Ptolemy list is likewise in Düring, 221–31; see also Moraux, 1951, 289–321.

book *Ethics* as being the *EE* without the disputed books.[1] It may be so, and if it is so, it is further confirmation of the general thesis that the *EE*, during the centuries immediately succeeding Aristotle's death, was better known than the *NE*. It would, however, suggest that the disputed books did not belong with the *EE*, and this would clash with the evidence we have seen and the evidence to be presented later in this book. Other scholars have stressed that the division of the *Ethics* into books may well be later than the catalogue of Hermippus, so that the five books may not correspond to any of our present books. Thus Margueritte, reviewing Jaeger in 1930 (p. 104) suggested that the title in the catalogue represented the complete *Eudemian Ethics* in five books made up from *EE* I (1), *EE* II and III (2), *AE* A (3), *AE* B and C and *EE VIII (4)*, *EE* VII (5): the topics of the five books being happiness, virtue, justice, wisdom, friendship respectively.[2]

A close inspection of Diogenes' list permits a conjecture about the five-book *Ethics* which is simpler than Margueritte's, and which is more in accord with the evidence of Aspasius, and the internal evidence we shall shortly examine, than the common opinion which sees in Diogenes' list a reference to the *EE* without the disputed books.

Before proposing it, I must draw attention to some features of the ordering of the titles in the list.[3] The list begins with some two dozen popular and Platonic works. There follow about four dozen mainly logical and dialectical works. Next come sixteen works on practical philosophy (politics, rhetoric, poetry). Then, twenty works on physics (including ten on the history of physics) and on biology, plus half a dozen works on mathematical topics including optics and musical theory. The remaining thirty titles are 'hypomnematic' works, collectanea, letters, and poetry. The most interesting feature of the ordering, in the present context, is that the

---

1. Thus Jaeger, 1948; Ross, 1923; Moraux, 1951. Düring, in the apparatus to his edition of the list (1957, 43) says: 'Potest esse editio Ethicae Eudemeae, sine libris DEZ et cum libro H in duos libros (1–5, 6–15) distributo, sed mera coniectura est.' Titze, 1825, thought that the five-book *Ethics* was the first five books of the *NE*; he sought the remaining books of that *Ethics* under other titles, and located the *EE* as items 20 (περὶ τἀγαθοῦ α΄β΄γ΄) and item 24 (περὶ φιλίας, ά) of Diogenes' list.

2. In support of this Margueritte appeals to 'l'annonce que fait l'*EE* au début du Livre I des deux principaux sujets à traiter, l'ἀρετή et le φρόνησις, et aux références ou aux transitions que nous lisons ailleurs' (1930, 104).

3. On the ordering of the list, see Moraux 1951, 190, and Düring 1957, 68–9.

Ethical works appear to be misplaced. One would expect them to be gathered together in the section devoted to practical philosophy, immediately before the political works, say between items 73 and 74 of the list. In fact they are scattered among the logical and dialectical works in pairs, so that the first part of the list presents the following appearance:

1–22 Popular and Platonic works
23   *Economicus*
24   *On Friendship*, one book
25–36 Logical and dialectical works
37   *On the passions of anger*, one book
38   *Ethics*, five books
39–52 Logical and dialectical works
53   *On what is better*, one book
54   *On the idea (of the good)*, one book
55–67 Logical and dialectical works
68   *On the voluntary*, one book
69   *On the noble*, one book
70–3 Dialectical works[1]

From 74 the practical works begin, and the disturbed pattern ends. The fact that the ethical works occur thus spaced in pairs, at more or less regular intervals (from the beginning the intervals are 2 × 11 titles; 12 titles; 13 titles; 12 titles) suggests that they originally belonged together and have been misplaced either owing to an accident in the manuscript tradition or to some feature of the library whose catalogue is most likely at the basis of Hermippus' list.[2]

If this is so, then *inter alia* the three titles 'On friendship', 'On the passions of anger', and 'Ethics, five books' may be taken together.

---

1. The Greek titles of the Ethical works are: Οἰκονομικὸς ᾱ, περὶ φιλίας ᾱ, περὶ παθῶν ὀργῆς ᾱ, 'Ηθικῶν ᾱβ̄γ̄δ̄ε̄, περὶ τοῦ βελτίονος ᾱ, περὶ τῆς ἰδέας ᾱ, περὶ ἑκουσίου ᾱ, περὶ καλοῦ ᾱ. Several points in my list call for comment. (1) I have not counted 34—προτάσεις περὶ ἀρετῆς ᾱβ̄—as an ethical title, because προτάσεις on all topics seem to be regarded by the compiler as dialectical (see 45–7, 66–7). (2) In counting I have followed Düring (1957, 44–5) in regarding 45–6 and 66–7 as making a single title. (3) I assume that the Idea mentioned in 54 is the idea of the Good. What other idea deserves the title of '*The* Idea'? (So Titze, 1825, 38.) (4) It is not clear whether the practical section of the list should be regarded as commencing at 68 (περὶ ἑκουσίου) or at 74 (πολιτικά β̄). The reason is that 70–3 are all θέσεις and therefore dialectical; but are, in at least three of the cases, about more or less ethical topics. See below, p. 45.

2. Moraux observed that the ethical titles 24, 37, and 38 were out of place (1951, 190); he has an ingenious reconstruction of the *pinax* to explain this and other displacements.

In the light of this, I conjecture that the five-book *Ethics* is neither the truncated *EE* minus the *AE*, nor the hypothetically reconstructed *Eudemian Ethics* of Margueritte, but the first five books of the *Eudemians* as they are in the manuscript tradition, i.e. *EE* I–III followed by *AE* A and *AE* B. These books read as a consecutive whole, each leading naturally into the next and forming as a totality a treatise on the virtues. Book C of the common books makes a fresh start and applies a new scheme for the classification of character to the material discussed in earlier books. While its doctrine is consistent with, and is at many points linked with, the earlier Eudemian books, it is capable of being studied separately as a treatise on continence and incontinence and pleasure, and in general the influence of passion on action. Book VII of the *EE* (with or without the chapters which in some manuscripts are treated as a separate book VIII) is also capable of standing alone as a treatise on friendship.

If we are right to see the five-book *Ethics* as *EE* I–V, it is natural to look for signs of *EE* VI and VII elsewhere in the list.[1] Next to it in the list is the title 'On the passions of anger'. The plural 'passions' is very strange, and all editors emend the text. Rose altered the text to 'On the passions or on anger'; Düring thought that two titles 'On the passions' and 'on anger' had been telescoped together.[2] A much simpler emendation than either of these is possible. The change of a single letter in the Greek would make the title 'On the influence of the passions'.[3] This would be an appropriate title for *EE* VI (the common book C) which is mainly devoted to incontinence.[4] Next to this title, if the ethical works were originally grouped together without the intervening dialectical dozens, we read 'On friendship'—the obvious title for *EE* VII. Thus, these three adjacent titles would yield our *Eudemian Ethics* complete. Next to them is the *Economicus*. If this is the first book of our *Oeconomica*, as many scholars believe, it would go naturally with the *EE* as a link

---

1. The several books of the *Topics* apparently appear scattered in the list under separate titles; cf. Moraux, 1951, 54 ff.
2. Rose: περὶ παθῶν ⟨ἢ περὶ⟩ ὀργῆς; Düring: περὶ παθῶν ⟨ᾱ περὶ⟩ ὀργῆς ᾱ.
3. περὶ παθῶν ὁρμῆς.
4. I am not of course suggesting that the title is Aristotle's own (though ὁρμή, 1102^b21, 1116^b30, is a word he uses in this sort of context) nor that he did not himself regard the *EE* as a complete and unified whole. I see from Bodéus (1974, 459) that Masellis (1956, 348) also identifies this work with *AE* C. Not having had direct access to Masellis's article I do not know whether he supports his conjecture with a similar emendation.

between that work and the eight books of our *Politics*, listed at 75 in the portion of the list succeeding the disturbance of the order. All this of course is conjecture. I make no claim for it other than the exceedingly modest claim that it is as plausible as most of the conjectures which are current about the titles in the Hermippus list. Certainly it accords with all the ancient external evidence as well as with the internal contents of the treatises we possess. But some of its more unexpected features can be further confirmed, as we shall now see.

THE LIST OF HESYCHIUS

Hesychius' list contains 197 titles. The first 139 of these form a group which resembles so closely the list of Diogenes that no scholar doubts that in some manner it originates from the same source. The remaining titles form an appendix, in four separate parts. Both the main text and the appendix throw light on our concerns.

The thirty-ninth title is an *Ethics* in ten books. Most scholars naturally enough identify this with the *Nicomachean Ethics*; but they do not agree what value to place on the testimony. Moraux regards the list as having been transcribed from the same original catalogue as Diogenes' list, but as having undergone a process of correction designed to eliminate apparent duplicates and to bring the list into accord with the works of Aristotle extant in the Christian era. Moraux agrees with Düring that Diogenes and Hesychius independently used the same original, and that in some small and rather unimportant details Hesychius has preserved the original better than Diogenes.[1] He thinks, accordingly, that the figure '10' is a comparatively late alteration to the original list. If so, it cannot be relied on as giving independent evidence of a ten-book *Nicomachean Ethics* prior to Aspasius.

It is possible, however, that the list in Hesychius is not so much a defective copy of the Hermippus list, as an independent inventory of the same library. A comparison of the two lists yields a number of features which suggest this. For instance, though the titles listed largely correspond, there is a great deal of random variation in the order in which they occur. However, no title travels very far from its original position. It is hard to see what reason a copyist would have

---

1. Moraux, 1951, 195–209; Düring, 1957, 91.

had to make so many tiny pointless changes in order: but it is easy enough to imagine books being replaced on shelves erratically, and catalogued at different times in different orders.[1]

Once again, though, the ethical titles are scattered among the Logical and dialectical books. But this time, instead of being distributed in pairs, with roughly a dozen books between each pair, we find them in approximately the same order,[2] but singly, with roughly half a dozen books between each one. The list goes thus:[3]

1–16   Platonic and popular works
17   *Oeconomicus*
18–23 Platonic and popular works (6)
24   *On friendship*, three books
25–9   Logical and dialectical works (5)
30   *On the passion of anger*

---

1. This impression is particularly strong in the case of the group beginning at no. 6 in each catalogue (nos. 1–5 coincide).

Diogenes	Hesychius
6. *Nerinthus*, one book	6. *Nerinthus*, one book
7. *The Sophist*, one book	7. *On wealth*, one book
8. *Menexenus*, one book	8. *The Sophist*, one book
9. *Concerning love*, one book	9. *On prayer*, one book
10. *Symposium*, one book	10. *Menexenus*, one book
11. *On wealth*, one book	11. *On noble birth*, one book
12. *Protrepticus*, one book	12. *Concerning love*, one book
13. *On the soul*, one book	13. *On the soul*, one book
14. *On prayer*, one book	14. *Protrepticus*, one book
15. *On noble birth*, one book	

It will be seen that in this section the titles contained are exactly the same, except that the *Symposium* has gone missing in the second list. However, the order is varied in such a way that the first four titles of Hermippus' list appear as even-numbered titles in Hesychius' list, and the last three titles of Hermippus' list appear as odd-numbered titles in Hesychius' list. It is hard to see what motive a copyist could have for such a switch; but if we imagine the books arranged thus in the library, it is easy to see how the two lists could arise:

Nerinthus	*On Wealth*
Sophist	*On prayer*
Menexenus	*On noble birth*
Concerning love	*On the soul*
Symposium	*Protrepticus*

If one man catalogued in columns, and the other read the titles across, the first man would produce a list very like Hermippus', and the second a list very like Hesychius': the differences would be explained by the loss of one book, and the slight reordering of two others, between one cataloguing and the next.

2. The order is identical except for the reversal of the two titles 'On the Idea' and 'On what is better'.

3. The numbers in brackets give the total of intervening titles.

31–8   Logical and dialectical works (8)
39   *Ethics*, ten books
40–4   Logical and dialectical books (5)
45   *On the idea (of the good)*
46–9   Logical and dialectical books (7)
50   *On what is better*
51–7   Logical and dialectical books (7)
58   *On the voluntary*
59–62 Logical and dialectical books (4)
63   *On the noble*
64   Political works and *theseis*

Probably it is idle to speculate on the cause of this striking relationship between the two lists. Certainly, it confirms the hypothesis of Moraux that a displacement of the ethical titles has taken place: and surely whatever explains the original misplacement will also explain why the titles occur in one list in pairs separated by a dozen titles, and in the other list in singletons separated by half a dozen titles.[1]

Most likely, the relationship between the two lists is to be explained by a combination of displacements of books in the library whose inventories are their basis, and emendations of the texts of the lists between the time of Hermippus and Hesychius. Moraux's explanation of the ten-book *Ethics* on the latter basis has already been mentioned. An explanation on the former basis is also possible. Suppose that our earlier supposition, that the library of Hermippus contained a five-book *EE*, plus two separately listed books making up the traditional *Eudemian Ethics*, is correct.

1. It is not difficult to imagine circumstances which would explain these features of the lists. Suppose, for instance, that a section of the library was, for some reason, arranged as follows, with the ethical works forming a separate, vertical group:

Half a dozen Platonic works	*Oeconomicus*
Half a dozen logical works	*On Friendship*
Half a dozen logical works	*On the passions*
Half a dozen logical works	*Ethics* in five books
Half a dozen logical works	*On the idea*
Half a dozen logical works	*On the better*
Half a dozen logical works	*On the voluntary*
Half a dozen logical works	*On the noble*

If Hesychius' cataloguer went from left to right along each shelf in turn, from bin to bin, he would get the order we find in Hesychius' list; if a cataloguer went zig-zag, reading alternate shelves from left to right and then from right to left, he would get the order in Hermippus' list.

Suppose further that between the time of Hermippus and the inventory which is the basis for Hesychius the remaining Nicomachean books had found their way into the library. Unless we suppose that at the same time the Eudemian books had got lost, the ten books of *Ethics* now listed must be the original five Eudemian ones plus five of the Nicomachean books, presumably *NE* 1–4 and 10 (*NE* 5 and 6 being already among the five-book *Ethics*, and *NE* 7 being the book on the influence of the passions[1]). That would leave the two Nicomachean books on friendship. These would presumably be placed with the original Eudemian book on friendship, making now a total of three books. And that is exactly what we do find. In the place where the Hermippus list has 'On friendship: one book' the Hesychian list has 'On friendship: three books'.

In the *Appendix Hesychiana* we find, under no. 174, the entry 'On the Nicomachean Ethics'. Moraux thinks this is the *NE* itself. To do so, he has to postulate some very botched editing by a compiler who (a) did not recognize the *NE* intended, on Moraux's view, by the correction in 39; and (b) quite misunderstood the work's title, inserting an 'about'. Surely this is more likely to be a work, not of Aristotle, but of some scholar of the period between Hermippus and Hesychius, concerning the *Ethics*. Such a work would be more likely to be included in a catalogue if it were itself a fragment of a *catalogue raisonné*, discussing perhaps the troubled history of the transmission of the *NE* to which the present study has borne witness.

THE MANUSCRIPT TRADITION

The manuscript tradition of the *EE* is very inferior to that of the *NE*. The oldest manuscript of the *NE* is the tenth-century Laurentianus 81, 11 (Bekker's K[b]); the *EE* does not survive in any manuscript earlier than the thirteenth century, from the end of which date the MS. Vat. gr. 1342 (P[b]) and the Cambridge MS. Cant. Ii 5.44 (C[c]). Altogether twenty-one manuscripts of the *EE* survive, the great majority from the fifteenth century. In a masterly study Dieter Harlfinger has shown how they can be grouped into two main classes: the *Recensio Messanensis*, of Southern Italian origin, whose earliest representatives are P[b] and C[c] (=Susemihl's

---

1. The title being, in our manuscripts of Hesychius' list, now further corrupted, a well-meaning scribe having corrected περὶ παθῶν ὀργῆς into περὶ πάθους ὀργῆς.

family Π^1), and the *Recensio Constantinopolitana*, of Byzantine origin, of which the archetype is the MS. Laurentianus 81, 15 of the 1420s (L).[1]

Since the time of Bekker it has been customary to say that the manuscripts of the *EE* do not include the text of the common books of the *AE*, but merely refer the reader to the text of the *NE*.[2] In fact, as Harlfinger has shown, eleven of our twenty-one manuscripts, all deriving from the *Recensio Constantinopolitana* and dependent on L, set out the text of the *AE* in full within the context of the *EE*. It is only in manuscripts in which the text of the *NE* precedes that of the *EE* that copyists, to save themselves from a duplication of labour, have contented themselves with a backward reference to the fifth, sixth, and seventh Nicomachean books. No argument, therefore, to an original Nicomachean home for the disputed books can be drawn from the failure of a number of manuscripts to set them out in full in their Eudemian context.

One might hope, however, that a stemmatological study of the manuscript traditions of the books of the *AE* might throw light on the problem. If, for instance, the Eudemian tradition of these books turned out to be independent of, and superior to, the Nicomachean tradition, that might support the hypothesis that the books belonged originally in a Eudemian context. In a long and patient study Harlfinger has shown that this hope is delusory. In fact, he inclines to think that the *EE* tradition of the disputed books, represented by L and its descendants, takes its origin from a point somewhere in the genealogy of *NE* manuscripts close to the vetustissimus K^b.[3] This, in turn, does not show that the *NE* is the original home of the common books, as Harlfinger is at pains to point out. For it may be

---

1. Harlfinger, 1971, 1–49.
2. Such was the case in the unrepresentative manuscripts which Bekker collated. Thus Marcianus 200 (Q) and 213 (M^b) at the end of *EE* III carried this remark: σημείωσαι ὅτι τὸ δ καὶ ε καὶ ϛ´ τῶν Εὐδημίων ἠθικῶν ἐνταῦθα παρεῖνται διὰ τὸ τὸ μὲν δ τῷ ε τῶν Νικομαχείων, τὸ δὲ ε τῷ ζ, τὸ δὲ ϛ´ τῷ η τῶν Νικομαχείων ἐν πᾶσι καὶ κατὰ λέξιν ὅμοια εἶναι. P^b contained merely the *incipit*s of books IV–VI of the *EE*.
3. On the basis of collations of ten Bekker columns in the *AE* Harlfinger concludes: 'Das in Detailfragen mit gewissem Vorbehalt, in der allgemeinen Tendez aber als ziemlich gesichert zu betrachtende Ergebnis ist folgendes: Der Text unseres Laur. 81, 15 (L) ist sehr eng mit dem des Laur. 81, 11 (K^b), jenes berühmten vetustissimus der *EN* und der *Magna Moralia*, verwandt. . . . Damit ist natürlich erwiesen, dass der Text der kontroversen Bücher, wie er uns in L vorliegt, aus einem Kodex der *EN* stammt, der im Stemma dieser Ethik irgendwo diesseits des Archetypus in der Nähe, aber nicht in der Deszendenz des höchstens eine von mindestens zwei voneinander unabhängigen Familien repräsentierenden Laur. 81, 11 (K^b) angesiedelt werden muss' (1971, 43).

that whereas the earliest *EE* manuscripts (those available; for instance, to Aspasius) contained the disputed books, there came a time when the only surviving manuscripts were ones in which the *EE* followed the *NE* and the common books were therefore represented in the *EE* context only by their *incipits* or by a back-reference. Then, at a stage later than that represented by the K^b manuscript of the *NE*, a scribe wishing to have a complete text of the *Eudemian Ethics* would need to obtain his text of the common books from an existing Nicomachean version. Harlfinger concludes that the manuscript evidence does not permit us to settle the question of the original context of the disputed books.

Students of the text of the *NE* differ in their valuations of its most important manuscripts; and their relative value appears to vary from book to book. Bekker based his edition principally on four manuscripts: in addition to K^b he used L^b (Parisiensis 1854, 12th cent.), M^b (Marcianus 213, 15th cent.), and O^b (Riccardianus 46, 14th cent.). Bonitz and Susemihl regarded M^b, in spite of its late date, as being second in importance to K^b. Jackson's edition of book A of the *AE* was based on a wider collation than previous ones: for that book he regarded L^b as the most trustworthy, though he conceded that K^b was the richest in preserving good readings elsewhere lost. Bywater, whose edition is the one most familiar to English readers of the *NE*, accorded an enormous primacy to K^b, while at the same time attaching perhaps undue importance to the readings of the medieval Latin version, which he regarded as 'almost as good as a Greek manuscript to us'.[1]

The oldest witness to the text of the *Ethics* is a single papyrus of the second century.[2] It contains only two small fragments, from the common book B (1142^b11-17 and 1144^z6-11); in two places it supports the readings of L^b against K^b, to that extent corroborating Jackson's judgement against Bywater's. By comparing the text of this papyrus with that of the best *NE* manuscripts on the one hand, and that of the Eudemian tradition represented by L on the other, one might hope to confirm or discredit Harlfinger's tentative conclusion that the text of the *AE*, as it stands in our Eudemian manuscripts, is not independent but derives from the Nicomachean stemma. The comparison goes some way to confirm Harlfinger's

1. On the manuscripts of the *NE* see Bywater, 1892; Jackson, 1879, ix–xii; Gauthier, 1970, 301–14.

2. Oxyrhynchus Papyrus no. 2402; Lobel, Roberts, Turner, and Barns, 1957, 124–6.

view of the dependent nature of the Eudemian tradition. There are six places in which there are discrepancies between the papyrus and the manuscripts. In four of these the papyrus agrees with K^b against L.[1] In two it agrees with L^b against L.[2] In no case does it agree with L against K^b. The tradition which—in these passages—the readings of L approach most closely to is that represented by M^b.[3]

1. Three of these are simple errors in L ($a\check{v}\xi\eta\sigma\iota s$ for $a\check{v}\tau\eta$ in 1142^b13; $o\check{v}$ omitted in line $^b14$; $\mu ov\lambda\epsilon v\acute{o}\mu\epsilon vos$ for $\beta ov\lambda\epsilon v\acute{o}\mu\epsilon vos$ in $^b14$). The fourth is the reading $\delta\iota\acute{\omega}\rho\iota\sigma\tau a\iota$ at 1142^b11 in which L agrees with Mb.

2. The readings $\acute{\epsilon}\acute{a}v\ \tau\epsilon$ instead of $\acute{\epsilon}\acute{a}v\ \tau\epsilon\ \kappa a\grave{\iota}$ at 1142^b15, and the reading $\epsilon\mathring{v}\delta a\iota\mu ov\acute{\iota}av$ at the well-known crux in 1144^b6.

3. In the two readings mentioned in the previous footnote, and the one non-trivial reading mentioned in n. 1, L is in agreement with M^b; it agrees with K^b only where the latter agrees with M^b. Since, according to Gauthier (1970, 311) M^b derives from a tradition independent of K^b and L^b, this tiny sample of readings does not accord with the results of Harlfinger's much more extensive survey.

CHAPTER 2

Cross-references in the
Ethics

HAVING examined the external evidence for the relationship between the *Eudemian* and *Nicomachean Ethics* I turn henceforth to the internal evidence concerning the original context of the disputed middle books. For, as I observed earlier, this is the question which should be raised and answered before any attempt is made on internal grounds to settle anything about the systematic or chronological relationship between the two *Ethics*. For if this is not first settled, then that *Ethics* to which the disputed books rightfully belong—whichever it may be—is being unfairly judged on the basis of an unnecessarily fragmentary text; and in any case, as we shall see, there is very much more internal evidence available to indicate the true home of the disputed books than there is to indicate which of the two treatises, as a whole, is chronologically prior. Failure to observe these obvious methodological points led in the case of scholars as gifted in different ways as Schleiermacher and Jaeger to fallacious and indeed circular argumentation.[1]

In such an inquiry the first essential though unexciting task is to examine the cross-references internal to each of the ethical treatises to see whether those in the undisputed Nicomachean books fit the content of the controverted books better or worse than those in the undisputed Eudemian books. In the present chapter I will examine the forward-looking references in the first five Nicomachean books, and the first four Eudemian books—excluding those which find their fulfilment clearly within those books themselves—and compare them with the disputed books.

1. Jaeger argued that the disputed books must belong to the *NE* because they contained a view of *phronēsis* which suited the *NE* not the *EE*; but *AE* B is itself the main evidence for attributing such a concept to the *NE* (cf. above, p. 4). Schleiermacher argued that the *NE* could not be by Aristotle because of the inconsistency between the view of virtue in the early books and in book 6; and then went on to attribute the disputed books to the *EE* (Schleiermacher, 1835).

The early Nicomachean books are not rich in forward-looking references.[1] When the three lives are introduced in 1.5 the consideration of the life of contemplation is postponed until later (1096^a7); and a little further on we are told that the element of self-sufficiency in happiness needs to be looked at again (1097^b14). Both of these promises seem to be kept within the undisputed Nicomachean books, the latter in chapters 9 and 10 of book 9, the former in the second half of book 10. But after the introduction of the Mean in book 2 we read, at the end of the preliminary list of mean states: 'About these there will be another occasion to speak; but with regard to justice, since the term is used in more than one sense, we will later distinguish between them and show how the two kinds are severally mean states; and similarly with regard to the rational virtues' (1108^b6 ff.). The 'other occasion' to speak about the listed virtues is presumably the detailed treatment of them in books 3 and 4. The reference to justice will fit well the treatment in *AE* A: there he does indeed distinguish between two forms of (particular) justice, namely distributive and corrective, and argues that each of them is concerned with a mean (1131^a17 ff. and 1132^a19 ff.). However, the final remark about 'the rational virtues' does not seem to fit the content of the disputed books: at no point in them does Aristotle attempt to show that the intellectual virtues are mean states.[2]

A more apt foreshadowing of the content of *AE* B comes earlier in book 2 where virtue is provisionally described as acting in accordance with right reasoning: 'There will be a discussion of this later, and of what right reasoning is, and what is its relation to the other virtues' (1103^b32–4). Right reasoning on the topics appropriate to the virtues, we are told at 1144^a24 in *AE* B, is wisdom; and there follows immediately a discussion of the relation between wisdom and the other virtues. (The points made here about the relation between wisdom and the virtues are also made in *NE* 10, 1178^a16, but too briefly to be the fulfilment of the promise of *NE* 2.)[3]

---

1. Examinations of the cross-references can be found in Spengel (1841, 489 ff.), Fritzsche (1851, xxxiv ff.), Grant (1885, 47 ff.), Festugière (1936, xxx–xliv), Fragstein (1974, 398 ff.).

2. For this reason, and because the expression λογικαὶ ἀρεταί does not occur elsewhere in Aristotle, most commentators regard the clause as an interpolation. However, the reading is attested by Aspasius, and at *EE* 1221^a12 Aristotle lists wisdom as a mean between cunning and simplicity.

3. Though Aristotle's words fit *AE* B well, Aspasius' commentary at this point does not:

Finally, at the end of book 4 we read: 'Neither is continence a virtue, but something intermediate; it will be discussed later; now let us talk about justice.' Grant thought that these words had been added by an editor, after an abrupt and interrupted ending to book 4, 'to give the book a seeming union with the three Eudemian books which were now to be grafted on' (Grant, 1885, 94). If there are independent grounds for regarding the middle books as Eudemian, then there may be reason for regarding the present passage as an interpolation; but at the present stage of the argument it would be a *petitio principii* to do so.[1]

Taking the text of *NE* 1–4 as it stands, therefore, we can say that it leads us to expect a later treatment of justice as a mean, in two parts; of right reasoning as a virtue; and of continence. This fits well enough the content of the disputed books: if one could not learn their detailed contents from these slender allusions, equally one cannot claim that they contain anything that contradicts them, except for the reference to intellectual virtues as means.

The references foward in the early books of the *Eudemian Ethics* are very much fuller.

(1) *EE* 1.5, 1216ᵃ37:

δείξει δὲ ὅτι ὁ ὀρθὸς λόγος ἐστὶν ἡ φρόνησις, ἔχει δὲ πρὸς τὰς ἄλλας ἀρετὰς ἡ φρόνησις ὡς ἡγεμονική τις. δηλωθήσεται δὲ περὶ τούτου, ὅταν καὶ αὐτὸς λέγῃ. ἐκεῖνο δὲ ὑπομνηστέον, ὅτι τὸ κατὰ τὸν ὀρθὸν λόγον πράττειν οὐ μόνον τοῖς ἔχουσι τὰς τελείας ἀρετὰς προσνέμει, ἀλλὰ καὶ τοῖς μὴ ἔχουσι τὰς τελείας. πράττουσι γὰρ οὗτοι, ὡς ἂν ὁ ὀρθὸς λόγος ὑπαγορεύσειεν, οὐ μὴν ἔχοντες τὸν λόγον ἀποδεικτικὸν ἀλλὰ τὸν δοξαστικόν, ὅτι τοῦτο μὲν πρακτέον, τοῦτο δὲ οὐ πρακτέον. There are several striking differences between Aspasius' remarks here and *AE* B. First, in Aristotle there is no suggestion of any hegemony of wisdom over the other virtues: there is rather a partnership. Secondly, though Aristotle does distinguish (1144ᵇ27) between those who act κατὰ τὸν ὀρθὸν λόγον and those who act μετὰ τοῦ ὀρθοῦ λόγου he does not connect this at all with a distinction between perfect and non-perfect virtue (the terms are used in *AE* to draw a different distinction: 1129ᵇ21); nor would Aristotle agree with the distinction between the apodeictic and doxastic *logoi*; for him, wisdom is the virtue of the doxastic faculty (1144ᵇ14). This passage perhaps suggests that the *NE* on which Aspasius commented did have a discussion of wisdom rather than the complete lacuna conjectured earlier (p. 33), but it shows also that it is not the one which we have as *AE* B. Unless we are to say that he took the forward reference to be merely to later passages in *NE* 2 (e.g. 1107ᵃI) and that the un-Aristotelian remarks are his own unprompted additions.

1. A possible trace of disorder in the *NE* text is found in the commentary of the anonymous scholiast on this passage: ὕστερον δὲ ἐπὶ πλέον ἐρεῖ περὶ ἐγκρατείας καὶ καρτερίας καὶ μαλακίας, μετὰ τὸ ἑξῆς βιβλίον; see above, p. 37. The singular is odd, suggesting that *AE* C succeeded *AE* A in his text. But this in turn is contradicted by the same scholiast's commentary on the text discussed above, 1103ᵇ33, which reads: ῥηθήσεται δ᾽ ὕστερον περὶ αὐτοῦ, ἐν τῷ ἕκτῳ ὅπου περὶ φρονήσεως λέγει.

It is clear that all relate happiness to three lives, the life of the politician, of the philospher, and of the hedonist. Now of these the pleasure which is concerned with the body and its enjoyments[1] is no difficult matter to decide what and what kind of thing it is and how it is produced; what we need to inquire about them is not what they are, but whether they contribute to happiness or not, and in what way they contribute, and whether some pleasures should be attached to living a noble life, and if so whether these should; or whether these should be partaken of in some other way while there are some other pleasures in accordance with which the happy man may reasonably be said to live a life of pleasure and not merely a life free from pain. But these matters must be investigated later.

It has been shown by Festugière that this passage admirably fits the discussion of pleasure at the end of the third disputed book. Though the end of that discussion is described as having dealt with the question what pleasure is, the discussion is far less concerned with the nature of pleasure than the corresponding one in *NE* 10 and is almost wholly devoted to the question of the relationship between pleasure and the supreme good.

All the questions asked here are answered in *AE* C: bodily pleasures contribute to happiness because the happy man needs bodily goods so that his characteristic activities may not be impeded ($1153^{b}17$); there is a right way of enjoying food and wine and sex, and it is only excess in them that is blamable ($1154^{a}16$); the happy life is one of pleasure, not just of freedom from pain ($1153^{a}28$), but the pleasure which constitutes happiness and indeed the greatest good is not bodily pleasure but is the unimpeded exercise of virtue ($1153^{b}13$).

(2) The passage of *EE* I continues thus: 'First we must consider virtue and wisdom, what the nature of each is, and whether they, or the actions which arise from them, are part of the good life.' This is an accurate prediction of the structure of the *EE* including the disputed books: the account of pleasure promised comes after the treatment of virtue (*EE* II and III and IV) and of wisdom (*EE* V = *AE* B). The relation between the moral virtues and the parts of happiness is stated in *AE* A at $1129^{b}18$, where it is said that legal justice, which combines the virtues of courage, temperance, meekness, etc., is concerned with the things that produce and

---

1. Professor D. J. Allan has pointed out to me that if Stewart's emendation (1892, 220) τὰς σωματικὰς ἀπολαύσεις is read at this point, there is a striking coincidence of expression with *AE* C, $1148^{a}5$.

preserve happiness and its parts. The intellectual virtues of practical and philosophical wisdom are described in *AE* B as producing happiness, the latter as 'a part of total virtue' (1144^a5). While the promise of *EE* I is fulfilled to the letter in the disputed books, it is impossible to see a fulfilment for it within the undisputed Eudemian books; those therefore, like Schächer, who maintain that the *EE* never contained more than five books, have to regard the whole passage as a false start (Schächer, 1940, 66).

(3) At 1218^b12 we are told that the good which is the final end of things achievable by man is the good which is the object of the discipline or disposition which governs all others. 'This', Aristotle goes on, 'is politics and economics and wisdom. For these dispositions differ from others in being of this kind; whether they differ at all from each other will be explained later.'[1]

The later explanation is given, as promised, at 1141^b23 in *AE* B. Wisdom, politics, and economics are all the same disposition, but they connote different exercises of that disposition, concerned with different subject matters. 'Wisdom' in the broad sense is the general name for the disposition: it may be exercised about an individual's own affairs (that is wisdom in the narrow sense) or it may be concerned with a wider scope. If it concerns his household, then it is economics; if it concerns the state, then it is politics. Any exercise of wisdom concerning the state is politics in the broad sense; but the exercise of wisdom in this way may be expressed in legislative, executive, or judicial decisions; only in the two latter cases can it be called 'political' in the narrower sense.[2]

(4) The *EE*, like the *NE*, after introducing the notion of right reasoning into the concept of virtue, promises a further consideration of its nature. 'What right reasoning is, and what is the mark to which we must look in order to specify the mean, must be examined later' we are told at 1222^b8.[3] As with the *NE* reference, the promise to examine what right reasoning is is fulfilled in the examination of wisdom in *AE* B; but the second question about the

1. ὥστε τοῦτ' ἂν εἴη αὐτὸ τὸ ἀγαθὸν τὸ τέλος τῶν ἀνθρώπῳ πρακτῶν. τοῦτο δ'ἐστὶ τὸ ὑπὸ τὴν κυρίαν πασῶν. αὕτη δ'ἐστὶ πολιτικὴ καὶ οἰκονομικὴ καὶ φρόνησις. διαφέρουσι γὰρ αὗται αἱ ἕξεις πρὸς τὰς ἄλλας τῷ τοιαῦται εἶναι· πρὸς δ'ἀλλήλας εἴ τι διαφερουσιν, ὕστερον λεκτέον.

2. A schematic tree of the different branches of wisdom is given by von Fragstein (1974, 232 f.).

3. τίς δ' ὁ ὀρθὸς λόγος, καὶ πρὸς τίνα δεῖ ὅρον ἀποβλέποντας λέγειν τὸ μέσον, ὕστερον ἐπισκεπτέον.

mark which specifies the mean is merely repeated, but not answered, in book B (1138^b22). For an answer we have to wait until *EE* VIII. (The question is not raised in the undisputed *NE* books.)

(7) In his discussion of voluntariness Aristotle commends the legal distinction of events into voluntary, involuntary, and premeditated; even if the distinction is not exact, he says, they do grasp the truth in a certain manner. 'But we will speak about these matters in our inquiry into justice' (1227^a2). This promise is kept when in chapter 8 of *AE* A a detailed treatment of voluntariness replaces the simple threefold legal division with a many-branched schema which preserves its main lines while allowing for more complicated cases. The exactness of this forward reference is striking: it is by no means something to be taken for granted that a treatise on justice will contain a discussion of the various degrees of *mens rea*.

(8) In the last chapter of *EE* II Aristotle asks whether what virtue does is to safeguard one's choice of end or one's reasoning. Some people, he says, think the latter 'but what does this is continence: it is this which keeps the reasoning uncorrupt. Virtue and continence are different. We must speak later about them, because this is the reason why those who do so regard virtue as that which makes the reasoning right' (1227^b15 ff.). It is not difficult to find in the disputed books a treatment of the difference between continence and virtue—that is one of the major themes of *AE* C— but it is not at first obvious how what is here said about the relation between continence and reasoning fits what is said later. On the one hand, we are told in *AE* B that it is temperance which preserves the wisdom which is identical with right reasoning (1140^b12; 1144^b28); yet temperance is the virtue which in *AE* C is distinguished from continence (1152^a1-3). On the other hand, correctness of reasoning seems to extend beyond the bounds of virtue not merely to the boundary between continence and incontinence, but to the boundary between incontinence and vice; for we are told in *AE* C that the incontinent man has a good *prohairesis* (1152^a17) which must include right reasoning (1139^a24); and indeed the incontinent man is often described precisely as the man who does not stick to his reasoning (1151^a20, $^a32$, $^b25$).

The inconsistency between the *EE* and the *AE* is only an apparent one: indeed, if it were a genuine inconsistency it would be internal to the *AE* itself. It is true that there are incontinent men whose reasoning is perfectly correct: but besides these weak incontinents there are the headstrong incontinents whose passions are so strong that they are lead astray by passion without deliberating at all (1150^b19 ff.). Consequently it is only of the continent that it can be said without exception that their reasoning is safe. On the other hand the difference between the continent man and the temperate man is not a matter of reasoning but of feeling: the continent man has unruly desires, but unlike the incontinent he is not led astray by them; whereas the temperate man does not feel unruly desires at all (1152^a1). None the less continence resembles temperance, and can be called temperance by analogy (1151^b32); and it is surely that which Aristotle was doing when, in reporting a popular etymology of the Greek word for 'temperance' (*sophrosynē*) he said that it was what preserves wisdom (*sōzei tēn phronēsin*). The imprecision of this passage is corrected by the later distinction: what the temperate man is here contrasted with is not the continent man but the man 'corrupted by pleasure and pain'—the intemperate man whose first principles are perverted (1140^b20).

(9) At the conclusion of the discussion of intemperance in *EE* III Aristotle promises to treat with greater exactitude 'of the class of pleasures' when he comes to deal with continence and incontinence. *AE* C of course contains a detailed treatment of pleasure in conjunction with a treatment of continence and incontinence: but some scholars have complained that despite the full discussion the class of pleasures with which intemperance is concerned (those of touch, of a certain kind) is no more precisely defined than in *EE* III (1230^b25–1231^a25). But though the class of pleasures was precisely defined in *EE* III, *AE* C shows in chapter 4 how this class can be viewed as a species of various genera of pleasures according to particular classifications, in chapter 5 how the class itself is a genus of which natural and perverse pleasures are species, and in chapter 7 how even in the case of natural and necessary pleasures one must distinguish between excessive and defective instances. These passages come not in the section of *AE* C devoted exclusively to pleasure, but, as the preannouncement stated, in the section devoted to continence and incontinence.[1]

---

1. The objection, first made by Spengel, was forcefully taken up again by Kapp (1912, 23). The best treatment of the passage is by Festugière (1946, xxiv–ix, lxx), who shows that the subdivisions of objects of pleasure in *AE* C 7 give three classes: (a) necessary, bodily pleasures which provide the field of temperance and intemperance (1147^b24 ff.) = the

(10) At 1234^a28 Aristotle says that 'as will be said later, every virtue is found in one way by nature and in another way with wisdom'. This fits admirably the account of natural virtue in *AE* B (1144^b1-17) which concludes 'in the part of the soul concerned with character there are two kinds of virtue, natural virtue and full-blooded virtue, and full-blooded virtue does not come about without wisdom'.

(11) Like *NE* 4, *EE* IV ends with an announcement of a treatment of justice (1234^b14).

All these eleven forward-looking allusions, then, fit without difficulty the disputed books; but there are other passages which are not so easy to locate as correspondences to previous announcements. This was pointed out by Spengel (1841, 489 ff.): Aristotle, having said that beasts cannot be called happy at 1217^a26, goes on: 'Nor can anything else whose name does not indicate that it shares in its nature in something divine; it is by some other mode of participation in goods that some of them have better lives than others. But that this is so must be considered later.' Dirlmeier may be right to say that Aristotle here allows for the possession of happiness by divine and superhuman entities like the aether (1969, 191); but it is not this that he promises to consider later. It is more naturally taken to be the applicability of happiness, or sharing goodness, to animals. That is how von Fragstein takes it (1974, 31) and refers forward to *AE* C, 1148^b15 ff.: 'some things are pleasant by nature, and of these some . . . in accordance with the species of animals and men.' But a passage which is more obviously concerned with the relation between animals and the supreme good is *AE* C, 1153^b25 ff.

And indeed the fact that all things, both brutes and men, pursue pleasure is an indication of its being somehow the chief good. . . . But since no one nature or state either is or is thought the best for all, neither do all pursue the same pleasure; yet all pursue pleasure. And perhaps they actually

intermediate pleasures of 1148^a25; (b) the pleasure-making things that are choiceworthy in themselves (1147^b25) but admit of excess = the naturally choiceworthy pleasures (1148^a24), namely honour, victory, riches; and (c) the things naturally unchoiceworthy (1148^a24), not naturally pleasant but only pleasant through innate or acquired corruption (1148^a16 ff.). This seems the best interpretation of a difficult passage. Cf. also D. J. Allan, 1971. These divisions are necessary to complete the account of the relationship between temperance and bodily pleasures: because the vice of intemperance concerns only excesses of natural pleasures, the disposition corresponding to unnatural pleasures of touch and taste is not vice but bestiality ($1148^b25-1149^a1$).

pursue not the pleasure they think they pursue nor that which they would say they pursue, but the same pleasure; for all things have by nature something divine in them.

This mysterious passage shows, I think, that Aristotle again has in mind the topic raised in the passage from *EE* I; but it seems to indicate a slightly different point of view. He agrees in both passages that only things which have something divine in them can enjoy the supreme good; but in the *AE* passage he seems to be willing, as he was not in the *EE* passage, to countenance the idea that animals lower than man have something divine in them. But of course not even in the *AE* passage does he suggest that the animals' pursuit of pleasure, which may be a pleasure in some sense identical with the pleasure which is the supreme good, entitles them to be described as happy.

In this case, then, we have an echo rather than an answer to the question postponed for discussion in book one. But from the other eleven passages considered in the *EE* we could form quite a detailed picture of what is to follow the treatment of the ethical virtues in *EE* I–III. There is to be a treatment of justice containing a detailed discussion of the relation between the voluntary, the involuntary, and the premeditated, with special reference to legal terminology; there is to be a discussion of the nature of right reasoning, and a treatment of the relationship between wisdom and on the one hand political and economic skill and on the other hand natural virtue; the place of wisdom in over-all happiness is to be settled. There is to be a treatise on continence and incontinence, which will draw a precise distinction between continence and virtue, and which will contain a detailed classification of pleasures. There is to be a treatise on pleasure which will settle which are the pleasures which constitute happiness, and what contribution to happiness is made by bodily pleasures in particular.

The picture which is presented fits admirably the disputed books as we have them; and it is an incomparably fuller picture than that which emerged from the brief allusions in the *Nicomachean Ethics*. At the very least we can say this: from the forward-looking references in the early books of the *EE* we can be certain that Aristotle planned to include in the *EE* a treatment of the topics which are dealt with in the *AE*; that the *AE* as we have it fits perfectly the description of that treatment as planned; and that if the *EE* was ever concluded by Aristotle according to his plan, and did not contain the *AE* as we have them, then it must have contained something very similar indeed.

CHAPTER 3

The Style of the
Treatise on Justice

THE first of the disputed books is in some respects more self-contained than either of the others, and it has consequently sometimes been treated as a separate unit. Fischer and von Fritzsche, for instance, who presented an array of arguments to show that *AE* B and *AE* C belonged to the *Eudemian Ethics*, thought that *AE* A was a Nicomachean book in the main, and pointed to the apparently purposeless repetition in chapter 11 as an indication that the end of the book alone was a Eudemian fragment (Fischer 1847, 12; von Fritzsche, 1851, xlvi–xlvii). On the other hand, even within the first ten chapters there are often difficulties in following the argument which have led many commentators to suspect doublets and dislocations in the text: so much so that Jackson in his commentary of 1879 printed a substantially rearranged text. Recently, Rowe (1971, 100–7) has argued that the unevenness of the text is to be explained by postulating two strata, an earlier *EE* version having been overlaid with new *NE* material. Most recently von Fragstein (1974, 162–214) has urged that the text is substantially in order, has offered frequently convincing accounts of the purpose of the apparent repetitions, and has assigned the whole book to the *EE*.

In the present chapter I shall go through the first chapter of the book as a sample of the whole and consider what evidence is to be gathered from vocabulary, style, and method of argumentation as to the original provenance of the book. We shall find that even a single chapter is rich in clues to its origin.

We may notice first that the transition from *EE* III to the treatise on justice is smoother than that from *NE* 4. Indeed there is some indication that *NE* 4 is incomplete. The list of mean states which Aristotle in book 2 ($1107^a28–1108^b10$) promises to deal with before treating of justice concludes with shame and righteous indignation (*nemesis*). But book 4 ends with the treatment of shame, followed by the abrupt forward references to treatments of continence and justice already quoted. Aristotle's failure to keep his promise to discuss righteous indignation has been noticed since antiquity, and variously explained.[1] There is no similar gap left in the transition from *EE* III to *AE* A.

The first chapter of A concerns the distinction between legal or general justice, or obedience to law as a whole, which is the same state of character as virtue as a whole, but considered in relation to others; and particular justice which has its own field of operation just as courage and temperance have. The argumentation of the chapter presents no difficulties of substance, and the doctrine is consistent with both *EE* and *NE*. For indications of its provenance we have to look at details of terminology and method: and of these there is no lack.

Consider, for instance, the first paragraph.

With regard to justice and injustice we must consider (1) what sort of actions they are concerned with (2) what sort of a mean state justice is (3) when something is just what are the extremes it is a mean between. Let our investigation follow the method of the previous discussion. We see that all men mean by justice that state of character which makes people capable of doing what is just and makes them act justly and wish for justice; and similarly by injustice that state which makes them act unjustly and wish for injustice. Let us too then lay this down at the start as a general basis. (*AE* 1129ᵃ3-11)

The practice of asking, concerning a state of character, 'what things it is concerned with' is common to both *NE* and *EE* (e.g. *NE* 1115ᵃ5, 1117ᵇ25, 1119ᵇ23, etc.; *EE* 1228ᵃ27, 1230ᵃ34, 1231ᵃ39, etc.). In speaking of justice as concerned with *actions* (*praxeis*) Aristotle might seem here to be closer to the *NE* (which said that virtue concerns passion and action, *pathē kai praxeis*, 1109ᵇ30) than to the *EE* (in which the fullest definition of virtue describes it as being concerned with pleasures and pains 1227ᵇ7). But in the *EE* too virtues are described as having particular types of *prāxis* for their province (e.g. 1233ᵃ32)—a formulation which is not

---

1. The anonymous scholiast comments on the lack of a discussion of *nemesis* (*CAG* xx, 204), and there is a lengthy discussion of Aristotle's reason for omitting it in Albertus Magnus. There is no discussion of the topic in the manuscripts of Aspasius because they do not preserve the whole of his commentary on book 4, breaking off at 1228ᵃ33.

incompatible with the idea that virtue is concerned with *pleasure* in a particular type of action (ibid. 1233ᵃ38).

The reference to previous methodological considerations (1129ᵃ5) fits the *EE* better than the *NE*. The methodological considerations of the *NE* concern the impossibility of exactness in moral science and the importance of beginning with things better known to us (*NE* 1.3, 1094ᵇ11 ff.) and it is to this that, according to the anonymous scholiast (*CAG* xx.205), Aristotle is here referring. But what he goes on immediately to do is to make reference to a universally held opinion, and lay it down as a hypothesis. It is the *EE* which, in its methodological chapter 1.6, 1216ᵇ26 ff., states that the opinions—preferably universal—of men are to be taken as evidences and examples.¹

Finally, the laying down of hypotheses is an activity characteristic of the *EE* rather than of the *NE*. The Greek word corresponding to 'lay down' is used in this technical sense only once in the *NE* (1104ᵇ27); it is used nine times in the *EE* and once in the *AE* (1139ᵃ6) in addition to the present passage.² The word 'hypothesis' in its technical sense is not used in the *NE*; in the *EE* (122ᵇ28, 1235ᵇ30) it is, and the use of hypotheses in mathematics is often compared to the role of the goal in practical reasoning (1227ᵃ9, ᵇ29) as it is in the *AE* (1151ᵃ17; cf. 1144ᵃ24).

After this introduction, two preliminary points are made: a state of character is not like a science, which can lead to opposite results; instead, it has a contrasting opposite, the study of which may throw light on itself. So in this case, from a plurality of senses of 'injustice' we can conclude to a plurality of senses of 'justice'. To illustrate these points, medical analogies are used: health is not like a science either (1229ᵃ15–17); studying bad bodily condition will tell us about good bodily condition (1229ᵃ19–23). The close use of medical analogies for ethical topics in this way is particularly characteristic of the *EE* and *AE*. Medical analogies of course occur so frequently

---

1. Burnet, ad loc., recognizes that the reference must be to the use of ἔνδοξα. Others take τὴν αὐτὴν μέθοδον τοῖς προειρημένοις to mean not 'the method described in the previous discussion' but 'the method used in the previous discussion'. The difference is not of great importance: the introduction of justice here parallels the introduction of courage at 1228ᵃ28 in the *EE* just as it fits the description of method in the *EE*. When *EE* I says that we must use the evidence of the φαινόμενα it means of course the opinions of others, not 'the facts'; see Owen, 1961.

2. In the *EE* ὑποκείσθω and ὑπόκειται are used in the technical sense at 1218ᵇ37; 1219ᵃ10, ᵃ29, ᵇ28; 1220ᵃ7, ᵃ22; 1222ᵃ6; 1223ᵇ30; 1227ᵇ25.

in all the Aristotelian ethics that the occurrence of a medical analogy in a passage cannot provide a decisive piece of evidence for its appurtenance; but a comparison of the *NE* and the *EE* shows that it is in the latter that medicine is most systematically used as a model for ethical method.[1]

1. W. Jaeger collected together the passages in which medicine is used as a model for ethical method in the *NE* and *AE* (Jaeger 1957, 58 ff.). There are a number of passages throughout the *NE* in which medicine appears as an example of a *technē* on an equal footing with other arts such as housebuilding, rhetoric, steersmanship, etc. The important passages where it is singled out (along with the kindred discipline of γυμναστική) are: 1097^a13: medicine is concerned with the individual, not the universal; medicine is practical $1105^b12–18$; the mean is introduced via medical examples 1106^b1 ff.; the importance of a combination of general knowledge of the art and detailed provision for the individual in medicine and education (1180^b7 ff.). Jaeger does not consider the use of the analogy in the *EE* but says 'References to medical discipline and its methods are frequent in it, often occurring in passages that correspond to those in the *Nicomachean Ethics*, but they also occur in places where there is no mention of it in the latter work.' The following list of *EE* and *AE* references documents this:

EE I:	$1214^b14–25$	Constituents of happiness to be distinguished from conditions of happiness, as constituents of health from conditions of health.
	1214^b34	Comparison between medical and ethical chastisement.
	$1216^b17–25$	Ethics like medicine a practical science.
	1218^b16 ff.	Medicine defines end and proves goodness of means; does not prove goodness of end (health).
EE II:	$1220^a2–3$	Virtue like εὐεξία is a whole consisting of parts.
	$122025–38$	Comparison between genesis of εὐεξία and of virtue.
	$1222^a30–40$	Analogy between medicine and ethics with regard to the mean.
	$1226^a9–15$	Neither in medicine nor in ethics do we choose ends.
	1226^a35	Doctors deliberate but not spellers; two types of error in medicine.
	$1227^a27–30$	Health and disease both objects of medicine in different ways.
	$1227^b27–33$	In medicine and other τέχναι the end is the principle and hypothesis.
EE III:	1228^b35 ff., 1229^b20 ff.	Comparison between courage and health.
AE A:	1229^a12 ff.	Points about opposites illustrated by health and εὐεξία.
	$1137^a14–27$	The doctor's knowledge compared with knowledge of justice.
	1138^a30	Comparison between the mean in justice and in medicine.
AE B:	$1138^b30–2$	'What right reasoning prescribes' no more helpful than 'what medicine prescribes'.
	$1141^a22–33$	Ethics, like medicine, is species-oriented.
	1141^b14 ff.	Value of knowledge of particular in medicine.
	$1143^b21–32$	Apparent uselessness of medicine and wisdom compared: medicine neither sufficient nor necessary for being healthy.
	1144^a4	Wisdom comparable not with medicine but with health.
	1145^a7	Relation of wisdom to philosophy is like that of medicine to health.

Aristotle's final methodological remark before proceeding to the examination of justice is that if one of two opposites has a plurality of senses, so does the other. This is applied in the case of justice: there is more than one kind of injustice, therefore there is more than one kind of justice. The practice of distinguishing between the senses of words, and asking in how many different senses words are used, is, along with the technical vocabulary which goes with the practice, more characteristic of the *EE* than of the *NE*; the former, it has long been observed, is more interested in the technicalities of logic (1129ª23–6).[1]

Having distinguished between 'just' as 'equal' and 'just' as 'according to the law', Aristotle defines the subject matter of the first sort of justice and injustice as 'goods subject to good and bad fortune, goods which taken without qualification (*haplōs*) are always good, but for a given individual are not always good' (1129ᵇ1–6). He at once abbreviates this description to the expression '*ta haplōs agatha*', literally 'the without-qualification goods'. This does not mean that they are goods, no matter what may happen, or goods, come what may; just the opposite in fact: it means goods which are good in the absence of special circumstances to upset their goodness. From the contexts in which Aristotle uses the expression it is clear that 'prima-facie goods' or 'things good in the abstract'

AE C:	1147ª5–8	Example of medical syllogism.
	1150ᵇ32–5	Comparison between evil ethical states and types of disease.
EE VII:	1235ᵇ32–ª7	Distinction between goods *simpliciter* and others illustrated from medicine.
	1236ª18–24	Health taken as prime analogate for analogy.
	1237ᵇ22	Wish not enough for health nor for friendship.
EE VIII:	1248ᵇ14	Virtue and health wholes consisting of parts.
	1248ᵇ34	Wealth no more benefits vicious than full diet an invalid.
	1238ᵇ22–5	The standard by which the doctor judges what is healthy

1. The following lexical facts give an indication of this. The expression πλεοναχῶς λέγεσθαι occurs only once in the *NE* (1125ᵇ14). In the much briefer *AE* it occurs twice (1129ª24; 1142ᵇ17) and in the *EE* five times (1230ᵇ9; 1234ᵇ19 and 20; 1236ª7; 1247ᵇ28). Its opposite μοναχῶς λέγεσθαι occurs only in the *EE* (1234ᵇ19).

A synonymous expression, πολλαχῶς λέγεσθαι occurs in the *AE* (1136ᵇ29) and in the *EE* (1217ᵇ27) but not in the *NE*.

A particular instance of plurality of senses, διχῶς λέγεσθαι, occurs twice in the *AE* (1146ᵇ31; 1152ᵇ27) and twice in the *EE* (1217ª36; 1228ᵇ18) but never in the *NE*. ἰσαχῶς λέγεσθαι occurs once in each of the *NE* (1096ª24) and the *EE* (1217ᵇ27). The question ποσαχῶς λέγεται is raised only in the *AE* (1129ª31).

Again, ὁμωνύμως and its cognates, which occur three times in *AE* A alone, and from time to time in the *EE* (e.g. 1236ª17, ᵇ25) appear only once in the whole *NE* (1096ᵇ27). συνώνυμος occurs only in the *AE* (1130ª33). See below, p. 140.

would be a more accurate translation than 'absolute goods' 'unqualified goods' 'intrinsic goods' 'things absolutely good'.[1]

The prima-facie goods are mentioned often in the *EE* and in the *AE* but never in the *NE*.[2] For instance, we are told that 'Some goods are good in the abstract and others good for individuals without being good in the abstract; and the same things are good in the abstract as are pleasant in the abstract' (1235^b32 ff.), and a comparison is developed between those things which are good and pleasant to a healthy body and those things which are advantageous and pleasant to an invalid. The final book of the *EE* contains a long discussion of the prima-facie goods; it uses the expression 'natural goods' (*physei agatha*) as synonymous with 'goods in the abstract' (*haplōs agatha*). (The synonymy is most obvious from the passage 1249^a8-17, where also 'exterior goods' is used as third synonymous expression.) There we are told that if a man is good then the things which are good in the abstract are good for him as an individual also (1248^b27); and we are given a list of these prima-facie goods: honour, wealth, the good qualities of body, good fortune, and power.[3] These, we are told, are good by nature but can be injurious to those of bad character.[4] These goods are contrasted with virtuous character and virtuous activity (1248^b37) which are the finest class of goods and cannot be misused. A man of common goodness may pursue the virtues for the sake of the natural goods; the man of supreme virtue (the *kalos kagathos*) chooses natural goods for the sake of virtue (1249^a6-15).[5]

The prima-facie goods, then, play an important part in the systematic development of the theory of virtue and goodness in the

1. Rackham (Loeb *EE*) and Ross (Oxford *NE*) translate 'things absolutely good'. Grant's 'What are abstractedly goods' is more correct, but seems a little clumsy.

2. The nearest to the concept is at 1157^b27 δοκεῖ γὰρ φιλητὸν μὲν καὶ αἱρετὸν τὸ ἁπλῶς ἀγαθὸν ἢ ἡδύ. The *NE* does not talk of a class of ἁπλῶς ἀγαθά nor does the notion of ἁπλῶς ἀγαθὸν here mentioned play any part in the systematic development of the *NE* theory of goodness.

3. The list which the Scholiast gives in commentary on the passage of *AE* A—health, strength, beauty, good bodily condition, wealth, reputation, and political power—corresponds very accurately to the list in the *EE*, if we take the first four as instances of 'good qualities of body' (*CAG* xx.208).

4. This is a different point from that made in the *NE* that goods can be damaging: for one of the examples given there (1094^b19) that men have died because of their courage is an example of a good which is not just prima facie good but καλὸν according to the *EE* classification.

5. Other places where the *EE* uses the terminology are 1228^b18; 1236^b34; 1238^a3 ff., $^b5$; 1249^b25.

EE. But, as Grant showed long ago, the notion is widespread throughout the disputed books also: at 1134ª10 we hear of 'what is useful in the abstract'; at 1143ᵇ3 we are told that the just ruler does not take more than his share of prima-facie goods for himself, and at 1137ª26 we are told that justice exists among people who share in prima-facie goods. The distinction between goods in the abstract and goods for individuals is made the basis of the rebuttal of Speusippus' attack on pleasure in Book *AE* C (1152ᵇ25).[1] We hear also of things which are bad in the abstract (1129ᵇ8; 1153ᵇ2).[2] This terminology seems still to be one of the strongest indications of a link between the disputed books and the *Eudemian Ethics*.

Having used the notion of prima-facie goods to distinguish the subject matter of justice in the sense of equality or fairness, the justice which contrasts with greediness (*pleonexia*), the taking of overlarge shares, Aristotle turns to the wider sense of justice in which it is obedience to law. In this sense, he says, 'we call "just" those things that produce and preserve happiness and its components for the political society' (1129ᵇ18). Once again a tiny point of terminology gives an indication of the rightful place of the treatise on justice. In speaking of 'happiness and its *components*' Aristotle is here aligning himself with the Eudemian view, according to which happiness is activity in accordance with all the virtues, moral and intellectual, so that each type of virtuous activity is a component of total happiness, and against the Nicomachean view of happiness as the activity of one supreme virtue.[3]

1. See Festugière, 1946, LXX.
2. Grant notes 'It is added that "men pray for these and seek after them, but they should not; they should pray that the absolute goods may be goods to them individually, and that they should choose what is good for themselves." This is in the same style with Eth. Eud. VII.xii.17: τὸ ζητεῖν καὶ εὔχεσθαι πολλοὺς φίλους. But to say what men "ought to pray for" is not after the manner of Aristotle.' Prayer is mentioned in the *NE*, once, in the not very serious context of the man who prayed to have a crane's gullet (1118ª32); but the idea that the desirable situation is to have the prima-facie goods be good for oneself individually parallels *EE* 1249ª13 even more strikingly than the Eudemian passage quoted by Grant.
3. Of the twenty uses of μέρος, μόριον in the *NE* six are for parts of physical objects, four of parts of the soul, four of parts of motion, two of parts of a community, three in expressions like κατὰ μέρος. The *NE* nowhere speaks of parts or components of virtue, vice, or happiness. The nearest it comes to doing so is at 1140ª14 (parts of the common good) and 1180ᵇ30 (science of law-giving part of science of politics). The *AE* on the other hand constantly speaks of parts of virtues and vices (1130ª8, ª14, ª23, ª34, ᵇ11; 1131ª1; 1144ª5) as well as of sciences (1141ª13; 1143ª3). In the *EE* we often hear that happiness is a whole of parts (1214ᵇ5; ᵇ28; 1216ª40; 1219ᵇ14) and parts of virtue(s) are mentioned at 1216ᵇ6; 1219ª38, ª23; 1220ª3, ª14; parts of vices at 1231ª22; 1232ª13. The *EE* and the *AE* are altogether happier than the *NE* about applying mereology to abstract objects. See below, p. 126.

To show that the law covers the whole field of conduct covered by the virtues already considered, Aristotle says:

> The law commands the doing of the acts of a brave man (e.g. not leaving one's post, not running away, and not throwing away one's arms) and those of a temperate man (e.g. not committing adultery, not being wanton) and those of a meek man (e.g. not committing assault or defamation) and similarly with regard to other virtues. (1229^b19-23)

For our present purposes the interest of this list lies in the selection of these three particular virtues as paradigms. It is in the *EE* that these three virtues have pride of place (*EE* III, chapters 1, 2, 3; also 1121^a15-23 in book II). In the *NE* both the preliminary list ($1107^a28-1108^b10$) and in the full-fledged treatment of the virtues in books 3 and 4 meekness appears well down the list; and so far from being a paradigm it is twice described as a virtue that is strictly nameless (1108^a5, 1125^b26).[1]

Of the justice that is law-abidingness Aristotle goes on to say that it is (1) perfect virtue, (2) the use of perfect virtue, (3) using one's virtue in regard to others, (4) not a part of virtue, but total virtue. Every one of these expressions is a Eudemian turn of phrase, as I shall now proceed to show.

At *EE* 1219^a38, when Aristotle has reached his definition of happiness, we read:

> Since happiness, we saw, is something perfect, and life can be either perfect or imperfect, and virtue likewise (for there is total virtue and partial virtue) and since the activity of imperfect things is imperfect, it follows that happiness is the activity of perfect life in accordance with perfect virtue.

Perfect virtue, then, is the totality composed of the individual virtues as parts: it is what is called later in the *EE* *kalokagathia* (1249^a18). Legal justice, he here says, is identical with this perfect virtue: or, to be more accurate, it is a particular aspect of perfect virtue, its utilization in regard to others (1129^a26, 31). The ability to make use of virtue in regard to others is itself added perfection; it gives another sense in which justice is 'perfect' virtue (1129^b31).[2]

---

1. See above p. 23 and below p. 232.
2. Assuming that the ὅτι in line 1129^b31 is correct (despite the disagreement of Kb) the reason there given for the perfection of justice is not the same as the one presupposed by lines 25–31; cf. the Scholiast, *CAG* xx.209.31–210.8 which makes much more sense than the heavy weather made of this passage by most commentators, cf. Gauthier–Jolif (1959, 342).

The notion of the use or utilization of virtue is a Eudemian one. The Greek word for 'use' is employed in the *NE* overwhelmingly for the use of physical objects (eighteen uses out of a total of twenty-five). We hear of one science using another ($1094^{b}4$) and there are references to our making use of our senses ($1103^{a}30$; $1118^{a}28$) of pleasures ($1105^{a}12$) of irony ($1127^{b}30$). Only once in the whole work do we hear of the use of virtue ($1179^{b}3$). In the *Eudemian Ethics*, on the other hand, the notion of the use of a *hexis* is ubiquitous ($1219^{a}1$, $^{a}16$, 18, 25; $1219^{b}2$, $^{b}4$; $1220^{a}33$; $1225^{b}12$; $1227^{a}23$) and there are whole sections devoted to the topic of the use and abuse of sciences and virtues ($127^{a}1$ ff.; $1246^{a}26-^{b}36$).[1]

It has already been shown that the use of the part–whole terminology in connection with virtue is another Eudemian characteristic. Thus the chapter ends, as it began, with Eudemian echoes.[2]

The close examination, then, of this first chapter of the disputed books, has revealed that almost every sentence contains tell-tale indications that the original environment of the books is the Eudemian and not the Nicomachean ethics. To go through every

---

1. In the preliminary *NE* discussion of happiness we read: 'It makes no little difference whether we place the supreme good in possession or in use, in state or in activity' ($1098^{b}32$ f.). If these two pairs of alternatives are meant to mark a single contrast we have here the terminologies of the *EE* and of the remainder of the *NE* brought together. An act of a particular virtue in the *EE* will be described as an activity of that virtue (τῆς ἀρετῆς ἐνέργεια) or as a use of that virtue (passages listed in text). The *NE*'s preferred expression is 'activity in accordance with virtue' (ἐνέργεια κατ᾽ ἀρετήν). This expression is of very frequent occurrence in the *NE* (e.g. $1098^{a}7$, $^{a}17$; $1099^{b}26$; $1174^{a}18$; $1176^{b}26$; $1177^{a}9$-12, 18, 24) and does not occur once in the *EE*. (We do however hear of activity in accordance with passion, $1220^{b}17$, $1223^{a}39$.) Whereas in the *NE* normally a *person* is said to act in accordance with his *hexis*, in the *EE* his life, or his *hexis* acts ($1218^{a}31$-3, 38, $^{b}2$; $1220^{a}8$; cf. *NE* $1177^{b}6$). But altogether the *NE* is much fonder of the terminology of activity (ἐνέργεια ἐνεργεῖν) than the *EE*: see below, p. 142.

Here as usual the *AE* follows the *EE* usage. The activity words occur only seventeen times, thirteen of these in the section on pleasure in *AE* C. In the majority of cases the subject of the ἐνέργεια is a ἕξις, not a person ($1144^{a}6$; $1147^{a}7$; $1152^{b}35$; $1153^{a}14$, $^{b}10$; ἐνέργεια of life, $1154^{a}7$). The expression ἐνέργεια κατ᾽ ἀρετήν is not used. Only in one place is there an echo of the Nicomachean terminology: $1130^{a}17$: κατὰ μὲν γὰρ τὰς ἄλλας μοχθηρίας ὁ ἐνεργῶν ἀδικεῖ.

2. The sentence ἔστι μὲν γὰρ ἡ αυτή, τὸ δ᾽ εἶναι οὐ τὸ αὐτό ($1130^{a}12$) does not give much help for our investigation. The only other sentence of this form in the ethical writings is also in the disputed books $1141^{b}24$. Though the precise way in which the sentence should be read is not clear, its general sense is clear from the many other passages in Aristotelian writings where it occurs (listed by Gauthier–Jolif, 1959, 343). Justice and virtue are the same *hexis*, considered in two different relationships; justice and virtue are the same thing, though what it is to be just is not what it is to be virtuous; in a more modern terminology, 'justice' and 'virtue' have the same reference but not the same sense.

chapter of the *AE* in the same detail would be tedious and unrewarding: each chapter, however, can be made to yield the same minute indications of the original home of the disputed books. Rather than proceed with a line-by-line examination of the style of the *AE*, I shall present the evidence in a cruder but briefer manner in the form of tables exhibiting the results of vocabulary counting. The presentation will be cruder in this way in that it will not permit account to be taken of differences between senses of the same lexical item; but it will have the advantage of providing data sufficiently copious and sufficiently well defined to enable statistical methods of argumentation to be applied. The crudity of the classification will do no harm: it may prevent the detection of stylistic differences between texts where a finer analysis might enable us to discriminate; but it cannot have the effect of producing imaginary distinctions where there are none in reality. If, then, by vocabulary counting and statistical analysis of a simple kind there appear clear differences between the *AE* and one of its competing environments, it is unlikely that later more refined analysis will overturn any conclusions thus reached.

CHAPTER 4

Particles and Connectives in the *Aristotelian Ethics*

THE problem presented by the books common to the *Nicomachean Ethics* and the *Eudemian Ethics* is one which particularly invites investigation by stylistic methods. It is natural to inquire whether the three books which make a double appearance in the manuscript tradition, as books 5, 6, and 7 of the *Nicomachean Ethics* and as books IV, V, and VI of the *Eudemian Ethics*, were originally written for one context rather than another; and one obvious way of undertaking such an inquiry would be to ascertain whether in style the common books show a greater similarity to one or other of the contexts in which they appear. Surprisingly, although scores of Aristotelian scholars have written about the problem of the common books and have pronounced confidently on their provenance, no systematic study of their style or comparison with their Nicomachean and Eudemian contexts has ever been made.[1] The present chapter contains the beginning of such a study: it confines itself to a single aspect of style, vocabulary choice; and within vocabulary choice it concentrates upon a small fragment of vocabulary, namely the use of particles and connectives. Even in such a small area, it will be found, it is possible to detect very striking differences between the degrees to which the common books resemble the competing environments offered by tradition.

Particles and connectives offer a number of advantages as a subject of stylistic study. Students of Greek style have a considerable advantage over students of English style in that Greek is rich in brief words which express nuances of thought-connection and mood which in English are more likely to be expressed by the tone of voice or the tilt of the eyebrow. The frequency of such particles is not affected by variations in subject matter as the

1. The history of scholarly discussion of the disputed books can be conveniently studied in Schächer, 1940, and in Rowe, 1971, chapter III.

frequency of most nouns, verbs, and adjectives is; moreover they occur with sufficient frequency and regularity to enable standard statistical techniques to be used to describe and draw inferences from their distribution. Indeed, as we shall see, about one-quarter of any Aristotelian text consists of uses of these comparatively insignificant and topic-neutral words. Moreover, such studies as have been carried out suggests that the use of particles and connectives in Greek prose may vary in characteristic ways from author to author.

How far authors are consistent in speech habits such as vocabulary choice is a matter of keen debate: fortunately the scope of the present inquiry does not necessitate any participation in the debate. Neither here nor elsewhere am I questioning the consensus of scholars that both the *Eudemian* and the *Nicomachean Ethics* are genuine works of Aristotle; nor am I putting forward any hypothesis about the fixity or fluidity of his stylistic habits. I am merely attempting to discover and compare the regularities to be observed within the undisputed Nicomachean books, within the undisputed Eudemian books, and within the books which are disputed between the two. By seeing how far the regularities in the disputed books resemble the regularities in each of the treatises, we may hope to obtain an indication of the context to which they originally belonged without, for present purposes, making any assumptions about the chronological order of the *NE* and *EE*, or the temporal distance which separates them, or the process by which books belonging in one context became included also in another context. Speculation on all these matters should follow, and not precede, an unpartisan study of the texts of the disputed books and their rival contexts.

Though it is surprising that scholars have so frequently attempted to settle the provenance of the *AE* without a serious study of their style,[1] it is not surprising that the particular features of style studied in the present chapter should not have been investigated. The counting of particles and connectives by hand is a tedious and inaccurate business: the availability of machine-readable texts of Aristotle, of computer programs for word-counts

1. An honourable exception here should be made for Sir Alexander Grant's edition of the *Nicomachean Ethics* (London, 1885), which contains an excellent and almost comprehensive *index verborum*—the work of John Keble—and many judicious observations on particular features of the style of the common books (which he believed to belong to the *Eudemian Ethics*, then regarded as Eudemus' work).

and concordances, and the development of statistical theory and techniques during recent decades make stylometric studies incomparably easier to perform, and potentially more fruitful in outcome, than they were in the 1860s when Rudolf Eucken wrote his dissertation *De Aristotelis dicendi ratione* (Göttingen, 1866) which, to the best of my knowledge, is the only previous study of the Aristotelian vocabulary which is the subject matter of the present chapter.

Eucken studied Aristotle's use of particles in the *Metaphysics*, *Physics*, *de Anima*, *NE*, *Politics*, *Rhetoric*, and *Poetics*. He wrote at a time when the almost universal opinion of scholars held the *EE* to be the work of Aristotle's disciple Eudemus; but he studied the usage of that work, along with Theophrastus' *Characters* and a number of other pseudo-Aristotelian works, in order to investigate how far Aristotle's style differed from that of other members of his school. His work was divided into eight chapters, each devoted to a single particle or group of particles; his conclusion was that there was an astonishing variety of usages and constructions to be found in the Aristotelian treatises, which he hoped might be someday of use in settling the order of their composition. Of most interest in our present context is an appendix: 'Excursus de discrimine dicendi rationis, quod in libris Ethicis invenitur.'

The individual books of the *Ethics*, he maintained, differed so much from each other in particle use that they could hardly have been written in a single stint by Aristotle. They fell into four groups: books 8, 9, and 10 resemble each other closely; furthest from them in style are books 5, 6, and 7, which again form a unified group. The early books stand between, with the first two resembling 5, 6, and 7 more than they resemble 9 and 10, and the third and fourth most resembling the final books. The final books are written in a fluent and elegant style, less argumentative than Aristotle's usual manner: thus *epei*, which is very common in all Aristotle's other works, is rarely found (once in 8, twice in 9, once in 10); in book 7 it occurs twenty-five times and nearly as commonly in books 5 and 6. In the early books, it ranges between six occurrences in book 2 and one in book 4. Similarly *hōste*: four times in book 8, four in book 9, five in book 10, contrasts with twenty-two times in book 7, twenty-three times in book 5, and seventeen in book 6. Books 1 and 2, he said, to some extent resembled the middle books (though *hōste* was much less frequent in them) and books 3 and 4 resembled the final books. In the books in which it rarely appears, Eucken said, it could be said to be replaced by *dē*: indeed, in books 8, 9, and 10 *dē* is used with a frequency which marks these off from every other work of Aristotle's. *Kai de* and *kai dē* are used as conjunctions in the final books with an unparalleled frequency: in book 9 the former expression occurs eleven times and the latter nine times; whereas in the three books of the *AE* they occur only five and two times respectively. The use of *te* also, particularly when used without any other conjunction, is a characteristic of the final books; a mark, Eucken says, of their quasi-poetical character. *Te . . . te* is to be found in the first and final books, not in the *AE; kaitoi, mentoi,* and *alla mēn* are more frequent in the *AE* than elsewhere; whereas *ou mēn,* occurring once only in the *AE,* occurs in the third, fourth and tenth more frequently than in any other work of Aristotle.

The conclusions which Eucken drew from these striking observations were modest. Unusual though the stylistic features of the later books of the *NE* were, there was no reason to regard them as alien to the philosopher's style: it was simply a matter of particles frequent elsewhere being rare here, and usages elsewhere rare being here frequent. The most that should be said was that the ten books of the *Ethics* were written at different times and only later brought together. No conclusion could be drawn about the disputed books, because the style of the *Eudemian Ethics* differed hardly at all from that of genuine works of Aristotle; there was certainly no reason to deny the disputed books to Aristotle once one accepted that the *NE* did not come from Aristotle in the order in which we now have it.[1]

It was a pity that Eucken, having noticed striking differences between the *AE* and other books in the *Ethics*, did not compare the *AE* features with the *EE* to see whether they were not actually closer to the *EE* in those points in which they stood out. He was deterred from doing so by the prevailing scholarly dogma of the time, that to attribute the *AE* to the *Eudemian Ethics* would be to deny that they were genuinely Aristotelian. The success of W. Jaeger in the present century in convincing scholars that the *Eudemian Ethics* are genuine—though not based on any close study of the evidence comparable to Eucken's—has enabled us to look at

1. 'Quod si statuimus quam facile fieri potuerit, ut libri V, VI, VII et Ethicis Nicomacheis et Eudemeis insererentur apparet, utri autem scripto magis apti sunt (de qua re homines docti valde dissentiunt) ex dicendi ratione vix dijudicari potest, quia Ethicorum Eudemeorum sermo fere non distare videtur ab Aristotelis ipsius scriptis' (op. cit. 77).

The Aristotelian Ethics

TABLE 4.1. *Occurrences of thirty-six Particles and Connectives in the* NE, EE, *and* AE

	NE	AE	EE
ἀλλά (inc. ἀλλ')	254	214	311
ἄν (inc. κἄν)	363	97	181
ἄρα (inc. ἀρ')	36	31	31
γάρ	1011	368	577
γε (inc. γ')	76	20	38
δέ (inc. δ')	1851	723	1034
δή	223	46	75
διό	69	44	71
ἐάν	31	17	15
εἰ	181	112	168
εἴπερ	25	15	4
ἐπεί	20	42	60
ἔτι	57	48	45
ἤ	446	182	319
καθάπερ	70	14	10
καί	2633	994	1633
μέν	591	325	451
μέντοι	2	7	17
μή	247	144	230
μήν	25	11	19
ὅθεν	34	1	7
οἷον	136	70	107
ὅταν	34	47	49
ὅτε (inc. ὅτ')	34	5	28
ὅτι	163	133	192
οὐ (inc. οὐκ, οὐχ)	534	288	380
οὐδέ (inc. οὐδ')	232	79	113
οὖν	235	92	97
οὔτε	73	74	82
πότερον	22	11	21
πῶς	47	17	28
τε (inc. τ')	162	56	91
τοίνυν	1	4	17
ὡς inc. ὥς)	203	67	141
ὥσπερ	98	80	123
ὥστε	38	61	96
Total words in text	39525	17041	26330

the question with a more open mind. We shall see that even in the narrow field of particle choice there is a great deal of evidence which confirms Eucken's observation that the *AE* stands out from the rest of the *Nicomachean Ethics*. We shall find also that the *Eudemian Ethics* are not as internally inconsistent as Eucken observed the *NE* to be.

The first step in our inquiry is to discover the number of occurrences of the most frequent particles in the *NE*, *EE*, and *AE*. Table 4.1 sets out the results of such a count. The counts were made on the Oxford ICL 1960A computer by the COCOA concordance and word-count program, from machine-readable texts of the *Ethics* prepared by the Thesaurus Linguae Graecae of Irvine, California; the editions used were Bywater's Oxford Classical Text for the *NE* and *AE*, and Susemihl's Teubner edition for the *EE*.

Each entry in Table 4.1 records the number of tokens of a given word-type to be found in the text of the *NE* (undisputed Nicomachean books), *AE* (disputed books), and *EE* (undisputed Eudemian books) respectively. (The distinction between word-tokens and word-types is familiar to philosophers: tokens are counted as a typographer would count, and types as a lexicographer would count, so that 'Break! Break! Break!' contains three tokens but only one type.) The final line of the table gives the total number of tokens occurring in the respective texts. A glance at the table confirms Eucken's observations, as that *dē* is very much more frequent in the *NE* than the *AE*, and that *hōste* occurs more often in the *AE* than in the *NE*; and it shows that in these two respects, and others, the *AE* feature is reproduced in the *EE*. Some of the expressions which were discussed by Eucken, however, do not figure in the table: a case in point is the conjunction *prin*. These absent expressions are ones which are too infrequent to enable a statistical argument to be based on them. Even if we assume that an author is totally regular in his speech habits, so that any difference in the number of occurrences of a given word between two equal-sized samples of his prose is totally explicable by chance, we still need a sample large enough to contain at least ten occurrences of the word before we can use the sample to form a reliable estimate of the frequency with which the author uses the word.[1]

---

1. The reason is well explained by Ellegård: 'If we postulate that the relative frequency of a word in an author's usage is 0·0001, or one in ten thousand, an actual sample (using this

In the present instance, our over-all strategy will be to endeavour to predict, on the basis of the undisputed Nicomachean books, how many times a given word would occur in the disputed books if its frequency there was the same as that in the Nicomachean; and to predict on the basis of the Eudemian books, how many times a word would occur in the disputed books if its frequency there was the same as the Eudemian one; and then to compare these expected frequencies with the actual ones and to inquire whether the differences between the expected and actual frequencies are such as are explicable by chance alone. For this comparison not to be misleading, we must restrict ourselves to words occurring with sufficient frequency to enable us to say—either on the basis of the Nicomachean evidence or on the basis of the Eudemian evidence— that they would be expected to occur ten times in the *AE*. Since the *NE* contains 39525 words and the *AE* contains 17041 words, a word occurring at the same rate in the *NE* as in the *AE* would occur $(39525/17041) \times 10$ times, or 23·19 times in the *NE* if it occurred ten times in the *AE*; and since the *EE* contains 26330 words, a word occurring with equal frequency in the *AE* and *EE* would occur $(26330/17041) \times 10$ times, or 15·45 times in the *EE* if it occurred ten times in the *AE*. Since words can occur only a whole number of times, we must restrict our consideration to words occurring either twenty-four times or more in the *NE*, or sixteen times or more in the *EE*.

On this basis a word such as *prin* (occurring twice in the *NE* and thrice in the *EE*) must be left out of consideration. But even with this restriction, we can find thirty-six particles and connectives to compare. From one point of view, this may seem an insignificant part of Aristotle's vocabulary: the *EE*, for instance, has a vocabulary of 4750 word-types,[1] so that the particles might be said to make up only three-quarters of 1 per cent of its vocabulary. But

word to refer to consecutive pieces of text also) of 10000 words by this author may well contain no instance of the word at all, or even as many as three or four. (This can be calculated by means of the Poisson formula.) But this also means that a sample of 10000 words is far too small to yield a reliable estimate of the actual frequency of such a word. If, on the other hand we take samples of 100000 words, the observed frequencies will range between at least 4 and at most 16 in 95 per cent of the samples . . . . Generally speaking, to arrive at a realistic estimate of the relative frequency of a word we need a text sample which is about ten times as big as the inversion of the word's relative frequency' (1962, 14).

1. This figure is based on an unlemmatized word-count in which, e.g. διώκω and διώξω count as two types.

in fact a very large proportion of the text is made up of particles: of the 26330 tokens in the *EE* 6861, or 26·05 per cent, consist of occurrences of one or other of these thirty-six words.

Looking at the raw scores recorded in Table 4.1 is not by itself very informative. Apart from the striking discrepancies of the kind already noticed by Eucken, the over-all impression is one of great similarity of usage: a word like *kai* which is frequent in one of the three treatises is frequent also in the other two, and words like *ge* and *ara* which are comparatively rare in one are comparatively rare also in the others. This is, of course, what one would expect in three works of the same author—and indeed some of the features, such as the extreme frequency of *kai*, would be expected to be common to all writers of Greek. Is there any way in which one can discover whether the over-all pattern of the *AE* use of particles revealed by this table resembles more closely the *NE* or the *EE*?

A very simple way to calculate a measure of relative resemblance, which can be carried out by anyone with a pencil and paper, and a minimum of mathematical skill, is to calculate a coefficient of rank correlation. This statistic, which is designated by the Greek letter ρ and called 'Spearman's rho' after its inventor, is familiar to many people involved in education since it is frequently used in order to measure the degree of correlation between gradings and assessments of the same candidates by different examiners. It is a measure of how closely two rank orderings resemble each other. To apply it in the present instance the first step is to rank the particles in order of preference for each treatise—the most frequent particle being given the rank 1, the second the rank 2, and the last the rank 36. The results of doing this are shown in Table 4.2. (Where two particles occur the same number of times—as *poteron* and *men* in the *AE*—both are given the same rank—in this case 31, and the next most frequent is given the next-but-one rank, in this case 33.) In this table it is already more obvious that certain particles are more popular in one treatise than another: *an*, *ge*, *dē*, *kathaper*, *hothen*, *oun*, for instance, are much higher up in the *NE*'s preference ranking than in that of the *EE*, while *epei*, *hotan*, *hoti*, *hōsper*, and *hōste* are higher up in the *EE* list; and in almost all these cases the *AE* ranking mirrors the *EE* ranking rather than the *NE* ranking. But to get a precise figure for the over-all resemblances, we need to apply the formula for calculating the Spearman rho, which will

The Aristotelian Ethics

TABLE 4.2 *Ranking of thirty-six Particles and Connectives in the* NE, EE, *and* AE

	NE	*AE*	*EE*
ἀλλά	8	6	7
ἄν	7	11	10
ἄρα	26	25	26
γάρ	3	3	3
γε	19	26	25
δέ	2	2	2
δή	12	22	20
διό	22	23	21
ἐάν	30	27	29
εἰ	14	10	11
εἴπερ	31	29	36
ἐπεί	34	24	22
ἔτι	23	20	24
ἤ	6	7	6
καθάπερ	21	30	34
καί	1	1	1
μέν	4	4	4
μέντοι	35	33	32
μή	9	8	8
μήν	30	31	31
ὅθεν	28	36	35
οἷον	17	16	15
ὅταν	28	21	23
ὅτε	28	34	27
ὅτι	15	9	9
οὐ	5	5	5
οὐδέ	11	14	14
οὖν	10	12	16
οὔτε	20	15	19
πότερον	33	31	29
πῶς	24	27	27
τε	16	19	18
τοίνυν	36	35	32
ὡς	13	17	12
ὥσπερ	18	13	13
ὥστε	25	18	17

enable us to compare the rankings pairwise. The formula is

$$\rho = 1 - \frac{6 \sum (D^2)}{N(N^2 - 1)}$$

where D is the difference between the rank numbers of any given particle and N the total number of individual particles in the ranking (in this case 36).[1] If we compare the *NE* ranking and the *AE* ranking and go through it line by line, calculating the difference in each line (2 in line 1, for *alla*, 4 in line 2 for *an* and so on) and squaring the difference each time, and then add up all the squares and multiply the total by 6 we get the numerator of the fraction, $6 \sum (D^2)$, which is $6 \times 734 = 4404$. The denominator is $36 \times (1296 - 1) = 46620$. Rho is therefore $1 - (4404/46620) = 0.906$. If we calculate rho for the *AE* and the *EE* in the same manner, we get the result 0.970. Since rho can vary between 1, for perfect correlation, and 0, for complete absence of correlation, the calculation confirms the impression that the three treatises correlate well together (as would be expected on the assumption they are all by Aristotle) but that the *AE* resembles the *EE* more than it resembles the *NE*. But the difference between the two statistics is not sufficiently large for us to be sure that the greater resemblance between the *AE* and the *EE* is not the coincidental result of chance. To investigate this we need to look more closely at the behaviour of the individual particles.

Spearman's rho takes into account only the differences in ranking between the two lists. A more accurate measure of correlation is given by Pearson's product-moment coefficient (r) which, applied to the present material, takes into account not only the difference in the order of preference of particles, but also the size of the preference: it is based not on the simplified data presented in Table 4.2, but on the full data presented in Table 4.1, which gives not just the rank order of Aristotle's particles in each treatise, but the actual number of times they are used. If we calculate Pearson's r for each pair of ethical treatises, for the thirty-six particles, we find that the correlation is very good in each case,[2] though closer between the *AE* and the *EE* than between the *AE* and the *NE*. r for *AE* and *NE* is

1. The procedure for calculating Spearman's rho can be found in any statistics textbook, e.g. Ary and Jacobs, 1976, 227 ff. An alternative method of dealing with ties is to give the value $n + 0.5$ to two items tying for rank n. With this procedure, and a formula available for tie-correction, the value of ρ for *NE* and *AE* is 0.9047.

2. The formula for Pearson's r is not given: it is complicated, and in practice nowadays the statistic is seldom worked out with pencil and paper. See Ary and Jacobs, 1976, 162–81.

o·9848, *r* for *AE* and *EE* is o·9954. This very high correlation is in part due to the effect of the five particles which are commonest in each of the three treatises (*kai, de, gar, men, ou*). If we remove these particles from our list, and study the remaining thirty-one particles, we find that that the figures for *r* are now: for *AE* and *NE* o·8015; for *AE* and *EE*, o·9753.

TABLE 4.3 *Scattergram of Occurrences of Particles and Connectives in the NE and AE*

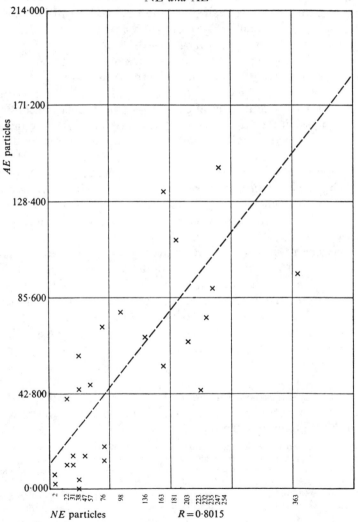

NE particles   *R* = 0·8015

Standard deviation of *Y* data against regression line is 31·46

The relationships between the treatises can be represented graphically. A scattergram is a graph in which a single dot or cross is used to represent the position of an individual in two dimensions: the pattern formed by the dots illustrates the correlation. Each cross in our scattergrams will represent a single word-type (e.g. *alla*). Each axis of the graph will be a scale to measure the frequency of

TABLE 4.4 *Scattergram of Occurrences of Particles and Connectives in the EE. and AE*

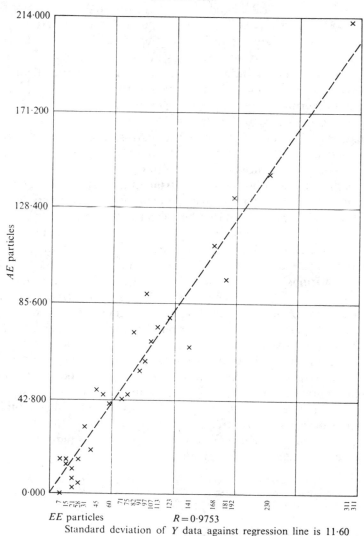

EE particles   R = 0·9753
Standard deviation of Y data against regression line is 11·60

that word in a given ethical treatise: if we wish to correlate the *NE* and the *AE*, for instance, we can plot the *NE* frequencies along one axis, and the *AE* frequencies along another. If Aristotle's use of particles in the two treatises was totally consistent, there would be perfect positive correlation between the frequencies in each treatise, and the crosses in the scattergram could be connected with a single straight line. In fact, of course, the crosses scatter to a greater or less extent, spreading in either direction from a regression line—i.e. a line which can be calculated on the basis of the data as giving the best possible estimate of a word's frequency in one treatise given information about its frequency in the other. Table 4.3 gives a scattergram for thirty-one particles in the *NE* and the *AE*: each cross represents an individual particle (they are not identified individually so as not to clutter the graph): the position of each cross is determined by the particle's frequency in the *AE*, as given by the vertical axis, and its frequency in the *NE*, as given by the horizontal axis. The dashes give the regression line around which the actual values cluster: the standard deviation against the regression line is a measure of the degree of their spread. Table 4.4 gives the same graphical representation of the data for the *AE* and the *EE*. It will be seen that just as the correlation between the *AE* and the *EE* is higher than that between the *AE* and the *NE*, so the crosses in the *AE* graph are much less scattered and more compactly clustered around the regression line, with a much smaller standard deviation.[1] This brings out in a visible manner the closer relationship between the *AE* and the *EE* which the study of particle usage suggests. If one wished to predict the frequency of a word in the *AE*, information about its frequency in the *EE* would be much more useful than information about its frequency in *NE*.

More informative than the raw scores for each particle are the scores expressed as a relative frequency, as in Table 4.5. Here the frequency scores are the ratio of the number of occurrences of the word-type in question to the total number of word-tokens in the text. Thus, since *kai* occurs 994 times in the *AE*, which contains 17041 words, its relative frequency is 0·0583. To avoid a superfluity of zeros, the frequencies are expressed in the text as percentages, so that the frequency of *kai* is given as 5·83 per cent, and the figure of

---

1. The graphs, and other similar graphs later in this book, were produced by the BIVAR package for bivariate analysis, written by Mr. F. Pettit of the Oxford computer teaching staff as a statistical demonstration program.

TABLE 4.5 *Frequencies of Particles and Connectives in the* NE, EE, *and* AE

		NE	*AE*	*EE*
ἀλλά	frequency (%)	0·64	1·26	1·18
	standard error	0·04	0·09	0.07
ἄν	f.	0·92	0·57	0·69
	s.e.	0·05	0·06	0·05
ἄρα	f.	0·09	0·18	0·12
	s.e.	0·02	0·03	0·02
γάρ	f.	2·56	2·16	2·19
	s.e.	0·08	0·11	0·09
γε	f.	0·19	0·12	0·14
	s.e.	0·02	0·03	0·02
δέ	f.	4·68	4·24	3·93
	s.e.	0·11	0·15	0·12
δή	f.	0·56	0·27	0·28
	s.e.	0·04	0·04	0·03
διό	f.	0·17	0·26	0·27
	s.e.	0·02	0·04	0·03
ἐάν	f.	0·08	0·10	0·06
	s.e.	0·01	0·02	0·01
εἰ	f.	0·46	0·66	0·64
	s.e.	0·03	0·06	0·05
εἴπερ	f.	0·06	0·09	0·02
	s.e.	0·01	0·02	0·01
ἐπεί	f.	0·05	0·25	0·23
	s.e.	0·01	0·04	0·03
ἔτι	f.	0·14	0·28	0·17
	s.e.	0·02	0·04	0·03
ἤ	f.	1·13	1·07	1·21
	s.e.	0·05	0·08	0·07
καθάπερ	f.	0·18	0·08	0·04
	s.e.	0·02	0·02	0·01
καί	f.	6·66	5·83	6·20
	s.e.	0·13	0·18	0·15
μέν	f.	1·50	1·91	1·71
	s.e.	0·06	0·10	0·08
μέντοι	f.	0·01	0·04	0·06
	s.e.	0·00	0·02	0·02
μή	f.	0·62	0·85	0·87
	s.e.	0·04	0·07	0·06
μήν	f.	0·06	0·06	0·07
	s.e.	0·01	0·02	0·02

TABLE 4.5 (*contd.*)

		NE	AE	EE
ὅθεν	f.	0·09	0·01	0·03
	s.e.	0·01	0·01	0·01
οἷον	f.	0·34	0·41	0·41
	s.e.	0·03	0·05	0·04
ὅταν	f.	0·09	0·28	0·19
	s.e.	0·01	0·04	0·03
ὅτε	f.	0·09	0·03	0·11
	s.e.	0·01	0·01	0·02
ὅτι	f.	0·41	0·78	0·73
	s.e.	0·03	0·07	0·05
οὐ	f.	1·35	1·69	1·44
	s.e.	0·06	0·10	0·07
οὐδέ	f.	0·59	0·46	0·43
	s.e.	0·04	0·05	0·04
οὖν	f.	0·59	0·54	0·37
	s.e.	0·04	0·06	0·04
οὔτε	f.	0·18	0·43	0·31
	s.e.	0·02	0·05	0·03
πότερον	f.	0·06	0·06	0·08
	s.e.	0·01	0·02	0·02
πῶς	f.	0·12	0·10	0·11
	s.e.	0·02	0·02	0·02
τε	f.	0·41	0·33	0·35
	s.e.	0·03	0·04	0·04
τοίνυν	f.	0·00	0·02	0·06
	s.e.	0·00	0·01	0·02
ὡς	f.	0·51	0·39	0·54
	s.e.	0·04	0·05	0·04
ὥσπερ	f.	0·25	0·47	0·47
	s.e.	0·03	0·05	0·04
ὥστε	f.	0·10	0·36	0·36
	s.e.	0·02	0·05	0·04

0·12 against *ge* does not mean that 0·12 of the text consists of *ge*, but that 0·12 *of a per cent* of the text consists of *ge*.

Associated with each frequency given in Table 4.5 will be found a *standard error*. This is a measure of how much reliance can be placed on the frequency in question as an indicator of the author's general usage, on the assumption of a certain regularity in his vocabulary habits. When we are counting the occurrences of a certain word-type in an author's text we are looking on each word-token as a binomial event, that is as an event which may have one of two possible outcomes: either the token is an instance of the type in question or it is not; just as each toss of a coin must be either heads or tails. The frequency given in the table records the proportion of such binomial events which had the first of the two possible outcomes. The standard error is calculated in accordance with the statisticians' formula for the standard error of a proportion, σ per cent $=\sqrt{pq/n}$ where sigma is the standard error, p is the proportion, $q = 1 - p$, and n is the number of events (in this case, word-tokens in the whole text).

We are treating each of our texts as providing data about the vocabulary usage of its author at the time of writing: each text is taken as a sample drawn from the indefinitely large universe or population of Greek prose which Aristotle wrote, or could have written, consistently with his stylistic habits at the time of writing. What these habits were is something that we can now only discover by a study of the texts themselves; and we have to call in aid the statistical theory of sampling in order to discover what inferences to features of the larger population we are entitled to draw from features of the sample text, and what degree of error our generalizations are subject to. When we compare the *AE* with the *NE* and the *EE* in turn, one thing which we wish to discover is whether the *AE* and the *NE*, or on the other hand the *AE* and the *EE*, can be regarded as two samples from a single population. Clearly, as Table 4.5 shows, there are differences between the frequencies in the *AE* and the frequencies in the *NE*, and also differences between the frequencies in the *AE* and the frequencies in the *EE*: but we wish to know whether these differences, in one or other or both cases, can be regarded as due solely to chance or whether they mark a genuine stylistic difference. For if any two samples of any data are drawn from a given population, there will be some differences between the statistics of the samples which call for no other explanation than chance variation in selection, as hands dealt at bridge from the same pack by fair dealers differ from deal to deal.

The use of the standard-error formula enables us to separate out chance differences from ones which call for some other explanation. It is possible to calculate the probability of two samples from the same population having statistics which differ from each other by multiples of the standard error. As a rule of thumb, where the statistics of two works differ by more than twice the sum of the relevant standard errors, it is improbable that the differences between them can be accounted for as chance variations among two samples from the same population. This rule of thumb, with the calculations on which it is based, rest on certain assumptions about the nature of the population, which in the case of literary texts may be questioned, and will be questioned later in the present study. But for the moment, let us return to Table 4.5 to see whether a provisional judgement can be made as to how far the *AE*, the *NE*, and the *EE* can be regarded as samples from a single population exhibiting only chance differences, and whether the differences between the *AE* and the *NE* are more or less significant than those between the *AE* and the *EE*.

If we look first at the frequencies alone, we can already see that

TABLE 4.6 *Agreements and Disagreements between* AE, NE, *and* EE *in respect of Particle Use*

Particle	Does *AE* agree with *NE*?	Does *AE* agree with *EE*?	Particle	Does *AE* agree with *NE*?	Does *AE* agree with *EE*?
ἀλλά	No	Yes	μή	No	Yes
ἄν	No	Yes	μήν	Yes	Yes
ἄρα	Yes	Yes	ὅθεν	No	Yes
γάρ	No	Yes	οἷον	Yes	Yes
γε	Yes	Yes	ὅταν	No	Yes
δέ	Yes	Yes	ὅτε	No	No
δή	No	Yes	ὅτι	No	Yes
διό	Yes	Yes	οὐ	No	Yes
ἐάν	Yes	Yes	οὐδέ	Yes	Yes
εἰ	No	Yes	οὖν	Yes	Yes
εἴπερ	Yes	No	οὔτε	No	Yes
ἐπεί	No	Yes	πότερον	Yes	Yes
ἔτι	No	Yes	πῶς	Yes	Yes
ἤ	Yes	Yes	τε	Yes	Yes
καθάπερ	No	Yes	τοίνυν	Yes	Yes
καί	No	Yes	ὡς	Yes	Yes
μέν	No	Yes	ὥσπερ	No	Yes
μέντοι	No	Yes	ὥστε	No	Yes

the *AE* resembles the *EE* considerably more than it resembles the *NE*. Of the thirty-six particles studied, the *AE* frequency is closer to the *EE* frequency than to the *NE* frequency in twenty-seven cases, and closer to the *NE* frequency than to the *EE* frequency only in nine cases. If we apply our rule of thumb, and ask whether the differences between the respective features are more than twice the sum of the standard errors of the proportions, the situation becomes even more striking, as can be seen in Table 4.6. This sets out in the case of each particle in turn whether the *AE* frequency 'agrees with'—i.e. differs by less than twice the sum of the standard errors from—the *NE* frequency and the *AE* frequency. It will be seen from the table that the differences between the *NE* and the *AE* are in a majority of cases—twenty out of thirty-six—too great to be attributable to chance in the form of sampling error. Whereas the differences between the *AE* and the *EE* in every case but two (*eiper* and *hote*) are such as to require no explanation other than chance. This result is very striking: can we achieve a more precise evaluation of the significance of the result and of the probabilities involved?

To calculate the significance between two sampling proportions statisticians proceed as follows. First, the value of a statistic z is calculated by dividing the observed difference between the proportions by the appropriate standard error of the difference.[1] The theoretical probability of the difference between two proportions of samples reaching a particular z value is known in advance and can be ascertained from tables to be found in any statistical textbook: the probability of a z value greater than $1\cdot96$, for instance, is $0\cdot05$, or one in twenty; the probability of a z value greater than $2\cdot58$ is $0\cdot01$ or one in a hundred. If the probability that the difference arises from sampling error falls below an acceptable level, then the null hypothesis, i.e. the hypothesis that the two samples have been drawn from the same population, is rejected, and

---

1. The value of z is calculated from the data by means of the formula

$$z = \frac{(p_1 - p_2)}{\sqrt{\{p(1-p)(1/n_1 + 1/n_2)\}}} \quad \text{where} \quad p = \frac{n_1 p_1 + n_2 p_2}{n_1 + n_2}$$

In testing the difference between the *NE* proportion and the *AE* proportion p_1 is the *NE* proportion, p_2 the *AE* proportion, n_1 is the number of words in the *NE* (39525), n_2 the number in the *AE* (17041). This formula, and the explanation of the method of testing the significance between sample proportions, is derived from Caulcott, 1973, 85.

the differences between them are described as statistically significant. It has to be decided in advance what level of probability is regarded as acceptable: the decision is to a certain extent arbitrary and to a certain extent guided by the purpose of the test (e.g. we must ask whether it would have more serious consequences to reject the null hypothesis when it should not be rejected, or to accept it when it should be rejected). The two levels most commonly used are the 0·05 and 0·01 level: for our purposes the appropriate procedure is to test for significance at the 0·01 level (it is more important not to discover imaginary stylistic differences than it is to be sure of discovering all genuine ones).

Table 4.7 gives the z values of the differences between the *AE* and *NE* and of the differences between the *AE* and *EE* for each particle. It will be seen that twenty-one of the differences between the *AE* and *NE* are statistically significant at the 1-per-cent level. Some of the values are extremely significant: at $z = 4·00$ the

TABLE 4.7 *Significance of the Difference between Frequencies of Particles in the* AE, NE, *and* EE

Particle	NE and AE value of z	EE and AE value of z	Particle	NE and AE value of z	EE and AE value of z
ἀλλά	7·39	0·69	μή	2·90	0·31
ἄν	4·24	1·51	μήν	0·06	0·29
ἄρα	2·88	1·73	ὅθεν	3·52	1·55
γάρ	2·82	0·22	οἶον	1·21	0·07
γε	1·99	0·75	ὅταν	5·48	1·94
δέ	2·31	1·63	ὅτε	2·36	2·84
δή	4·67	0·29	ὅτι	5·57	0·60
διό	2·04	0·23	οὐ	3·09	2·04
ἐάν	0·80	1·60	οὐδέ	1·82	0·53
εἰ	3·03	0·24	οὖν	0·79	2·65
εἴπερ	1·02	3·54	οὔτε	5·35	2·09
ἐπεί	6·46	0·39	πότερον	0·40	0·57
ἔτι	3·48	2·44	πῶς	0·62	0·21
ἤ	0·63	1·37	τε	1·43	0·30
καθάπερ	2·69	1·91	τοίνυν	2·43	1·90
καί	3·69	1·57	ὡς	1·91	2·10
μέν	3·56	1·49	ὥσπερ	4·32	0·03
μέντοι	3·12	1·02	ὥστε	6·83	0·11

probability of two samples coming from the same population is only 0·00005, or one in 20000: the values for *an*, *dē*, and *hōsper* are all between four and five. For $z = 5$, the probability is only 0·0000006, less than one in a million and a half; the z values for *alla*, *epei*, *hotan*, *hoti*, *oute* are all above this. On the other hand, all but three of the differences between the *AE* and the *EE* are statistically insignificant at our chosen level. *Eiper* and *hote* had already been revealed as mavericks by the application of our rule of thumb: *oun*, where the difference previously appeared to be just within the limits of sampling error, is now shown to be just outside them.

When we say that it is enormously unlikely that the differences between the *AE* and the *NE* should have come about by chance, that does not of course mean that we can say without further ado that it is enormously unlikely that the *AE* and the *NE* were originally part of the same work. For the differences, though not due to chance, may be due to a number of other things: a conscious wish by Aristotle to vary his usage in one part of his work; the influence of subject matter; varied degrees of revision and polishing, and the like. What our study has shown so far is that it is a much more economical hypothesis to regard the *AE* as belonging originally to the *EE*; for almost all the differences between the *AE* and the *EE* in respect of the vocabulary so far studied call for no other explanation than chance.

We cannot yet be said, however, to have satisfactorily quantified the likelihood of chance accounting for the observed differences between the *NE* and *AE* in respect of particle usage. For the statistical procedures which have been adopted are ones which are strictly applicable only in situations where the outcome of each of the binomial events to be counted is independent of the outcome of each other event. In the case of the occurrences of a word in a text this assumption is clearly unrealistic: the choice of a word at one point in a text affects the likelihood of its being chosen at other points in the text. The matter has been vividly illustrated by A. Q. Morton (1966, 70):

> *Kai* occurs at a rate of about 0·05, so that two successive occurrences of *kai* would be found, if the occurrence was a matter of pure chance, at a rate of 0·05 × 0·05 = 0·0025, i.e. in four hundred words of text you could expect to find two successive *kai*s. In Greek prose two successive *kai*s are found about once in a million words of text.

But though the choice of a word has an effect on the choice of other words in its immediate context, it seems reasonable to expect that this effect can be discounted if we make our samples sufficiently large: there seems no reason to expect that the fact that Aristotle used *kai* on a particular line of the first page of book 1 of the *NE* should affect his decision to use it on a particular line of the last page of book 10. One might well hope that samples as large as the *AE*, *NE*, and *EE* would be big enough to allow the local interdependence of word-choices to be discounted. But this hope must be put to the test. What size a sample has to be for the occurrence of a given word in a text to conform to the conditions of simple sampling is an empirical matter which must be discovered by counting and calculation. To discover whether the *AE*, *NE*, and *EE* display the degree of internal homogeneity which would justify making statistical inferences about their relationship, we must break up the text of each of them into smaller units, and count the occurrences of words in each of these new samples. A significance test known as the chi-squared test enables one to assess whether the occurrence of the word complies with the conditions of simple sampling or whether there are statistically significant differences between the rates of occurrence in different samples.

The obvious smaller units into which to break the treatises are the individual books that compose them. Considered as samples these books have the disadvantage that they are of different sizes, which complicates some of the calculations; but taking them as separate wholes has the advantage of keeping open the possibility, suggested by many scholars, that they may have existed once as separate units which were perhaps only later combined into the more lengthy treatises that we know. Obtaining statistics for them separately will not only help us to assess the degree of reliance which can be placed on our conclusions concerning the treatises as a whole: it may also enable us to detect any anomalies which may make individual books stand out from the other books to which they are traditionally united.

Some of the particles we have so far studied occur too infrequently to make it profitable to study their occurrences in particular books. As before, we cannot make reliable estimates of frequencies from samples unless the expression in question can be expected to occur a minimum of ten times within them. Since the *NE* consists of seven books, this means very roughly that only particles with an over-all occurrence of seventy or more will repay study in individual books; and similarly, only those with an occurrence in the *EE* of fifty or more will repay study in the individual five books of the *EE*. If we exclude from our list of particles those which do not occur either seventy or more times in the *NE* or fifty or more times in the *EE*, we reduce our list from thirty-six to twenty-four, with the omission of *ara, ean, eiper, eti, mentoi, mēn, hothen, hotan, hote, poteron, pōs, toinun*. It will be noted that the new shorter list consists entirely of particles whose frequencies in the *AE* and *EE* differ by only insignificant degrees. Of the new list, fifteen show significant disagreements between *NE* and *AE*, while nine agree in *NE* and *AE* usage.

Table 4.10 sets out the occurrences of the twenty-four particles in each of the seven books of the *NE*, and Table 4.11 in the five books of the *EE*. The chi-squared value for each particle is calculated in a way which may be illustrated from the case of *ei* in the *EE*, whose occurrences are given in Table 4.8. We first set out its occurrences in the form of a table known as a contingency table.

TABLE 4.8 *Occurrences of* εἰ *in the* EE

EE book	Occurrences of εἰ	Occurrences of other words	Total words in book
I	18	3366	3384
II	27	4645	4672
III	52	7043	7095
VII	52	8566	8618
VIII	19	2542	2561
Total	168	26162	26330

We wish to know whether the differences in the figures from book to book can be explained simply as the result of sampling error. If so, we would expect the proportion of *ei*s in each book to be the same as the proportion in the whole of the *EE*. Accordingly, we work out, for each book, the expected occurrences of *ei* and the expected occurences of other words, on the assumption that the proportion remains thus constant. The results of the calculation are inserted in brackets in Table 4.9.

TABLE 4.9 *The Calculation of Chi-squared*

EE book	Occurrences of $\epsilon\hat{\iota}$ actual (expected)		Occurrences of other actual (expected)		Total
I	18	(21·6)	3366	(3362·4)	3384
II	52	(45·3)	7043	(7049·7)	7095
III	27	(29·8)	4645	(4642·2)	4672
VII	52	(55·0)	8566	(8563·0)	8618
VIII	19	(16·3)	2542	(2544·7)	2561
Total	168		26162		26330

For each cell we now square the difference between the actual and expected values and divide the result by the expected value: thus for the first cell (*ei*s in book I) we square (21·6–18) and divide the square by 21·6, obtaining the result 0·60. When we have performed this operation for each cell in the table, we add all the results together, and that gives the value of chi-squared for the table as a whole. In this case chi-squared $= 2·46$.

The significance of a chi-squared has to be discovered by consulting a table; but first one must ascertain the number of degrees of freedom associated with it. The number of degrees of freedom is the number of ways in which the data represented in the table are free to vary independently of each other within the constraints set by the characteristics of the total. In each book, given the number of occurrences of *ei*, the number of occurrences of words other than *ei* is not free to vary independently but is fixed: therefore in each line of the table we have only one degree of freedom. Given the number of *ei*s in each of the first four lines of the table, the number in the fifth is not free to vary but can be deduced by subtraction from the total: therefore the degrees of freedom from line to line are four. The number of degrees of freedom of the table as a whole is four by one, i.e. four. If we enter a table of chi-squared in a statistical textbook at the entry for four degrees of freedom we find that the probability of a chi-squared of 2·46 is above 0·50: a distribution of *ei* parallel to that in the *EE* would be found by chance in one case out of two. Clearly, the differences between the rates of occurrence in one book and the next are statistically non-significant and the occurrence of *ei* in the *EE* conforms to the conditions for simple sampling.[1] A study of Tables 4.10 and 4.11 reveals how far, within the *NE* and within the *EE*, Aristotle was regular in his habits of use of particular connectives. The tables contain a number of surprises. *Kai*, which because of its extreme commonness and apparent topic-

TABLE 4.10 *Particles and Connectives in Individual Books of the* NE

	1	2	3	4	8	9	10	χ^2 for 6 degrees of freedom
ἀλλά	37	30	60	38	37	22	30	16·27
ἄν	60	18	53	50	40	55	87	33·50
γάρ	128	76	151	170	195	135	156	29·41
γε	18	3	17	15	3	5	15	20·41
δέ	267	216	302	295	298	234	239	15·94
δή	28	10	42	28	31	38	46	16·37
διό	5	10	14	11	10	10	9	4·51
εἰ	44	13	37	15	9	21	42	41·28
ἐπεί	4	6	4	2	1	2	1	N.A.
ἤ	63	35	93	67	58	71	59	14·96
καθάπερ	19	3	3	3	10	21	11	36·75
καί	419	298	398	440	362	320	396	17·97
μέν	75	108	104	85	84	67	68	42·85
μή	28	9	61	59	30	34	26	43·11
οἷον	16	13	33	21	20	18	15	8·50
ὅτι	21	22	39	16	10	34	21	26·65
οὐ	41	48	91	115	80	65	94	35·24
οὐδέ	18	22	43	43	31	27	48	14·50
οὖν	25	32	35	32	30	39	42	7·66
οὔτε	16	16	12	15	5	4	5	23·18
τε	17	14	11	22	24	26	48	30·85
ὡς	19	19	42	43	25	23	32	13.89
ὥσπερ	12	14	15	18	6	13	20	8·48
ὥστε	11	4	5	4	5	4	5	N.A.
Totals	5644	4242	6338	5953	5827	5291	6230	

For 6 degrees of freedom, a value of 16·81 or more is significant at the 1-per-cent level.

1. The procedure for calculating chi-square can be found in any statistics textbook; e.g. Caulcott, 1973, 114 ff.

TABLE 4.11 *Particles and Connectives in Individual Books of the* EE

	I	II	III	VII	VIII	χ^2 for 4 degrees of freedom
ἀλλά	32	78	43	112	46	14·07
ἄν	26	34	34	56	31	15·38
γάρ	68	131	104	225	49	12·49
γε	5	13	3	10	7	6·26
δέ	103	287	198	362	84	13·01
δή	5	25	8	22	15	13·93
διό	0	17	14	35	5	13·93
εἰ	18	52	27	52	19	2·46
ἐπεί	1	18	11	22	8	7·16
ἤ	38	115	60	67	39	26·00
καθάπερ	4	3	2	1	1	N.A.
καί	165	469	312	526	161	14·26
μέν	58	121	84	148	40	0·55
μή	26	74	40	80	10	10·00
οἷον	15	32	21	29	10	1·73
ὅτι	24	56	20	67	25	8·66
οὐ	45	100	46	133	56	17·83
οὐδέ	27	28	17	29	12	13·25
οὖν	15	19	17	29	17	8·80
οὔτε	13	20	25	22	2	13·67
τε	17	25	18	24	7	4·15
ὡς	14	25	18	67	17	17·65
ὥσπερ	9	23	23	52	16	10·94
ὥστε	11	35	12	29	9	5·07
Totals	3384	7095	4672	8618	2561	

For 4 degrees of freedom, a value of 13·28 or more is significant at the 1-per-cent level.

neutrality might have been expected to occur with constant frequency, is irregular in appearance in both the *NE* and the *EE*: there are differences between the rate of occurrences in individual books which, in each treatise, are just significant at the 1-per-cent level. Similarly the negation signs *ou* and *oute* occur at significantly different rates in different books within each treatise, and so does the particle *an*. It is not, then, the commonest or most apparently topic-neutral particles that occur with the greatest regularity. The other particles all occur in at least one of the treatises in accordance with the conditions of simple sampling, and therefore enable inferences to be drawn from the frequency of their use in either the *NE* or in the *EE* to an expected frequency in the *AE*.

Before proceeding to the comparison with the analogous data for the *AE*, we may notice that our tables reveal that the *EE*, despite the greater variation in the length of the individual books that compose it, displays a considerably greater degree of uniformity in respect of particle usage. Disregarding the four particles irregular in both, we find that fourteen out of the other twenty in the *EE* occur at rates showing only insignificant differences between books. In the *NE* only ten are similarly regular; twelve display significant fluctuations in rate of occurrences, and in two cases the chi-squared test is not applicable.[1]

If the *AE* was originally part of the *EE*, we would expect that those regularities which are displayed in the particle use in the *EE* would continue to be regular, and regular at approximately the same rate, in the *AE*; similarly, if the *AE* was originally all of one piece with the *NE* one would expect it to reflect the regularities to be observed there. We can therefore use the fourteen observed regularities from the *EE*, and the ten observed regularities from the *NE*, to make predictions as to the regularities in particle usage to be expected in the *AE*. Table 4.12, which sets out the figures for the individual books of the *AE*, enables us to begin to compare these expectations with the observed data to see whether the Nicomachean hypothesis or the Eudemian hypothesis best fits the facts.

The most striking feature of Table 4.12 is that it shows the *AE* as much more uniform than either the *EE* or the *NE*. In twenty-two out of twenty-four cases the differences between the individual books are statistically insignificant. Only in the cases of $\bar{e}$ and *hōsper* are the between-books differences significant at the 1-per-cent level. This fact is not negligible in view of the fact that some scholars have wished to solve the problem of the disputed books by

---

1. For a chi-squared test to be applicable, at least 80 per cent of the cells in the frequency table must have an expected value of no less than five. Because ἐπεί and ὥστε each occur less than forty times in the *NE* this is not so. The inapplicability of the chi-squared test in this case is of course not because the difference between the *NE* and *EE* in this respect is too small, but because it is too enormous. The test is inapplicable for analogous reasons to καθάπερ in the *EE*.

TABLE 4.12 *Particles and Connectives in Individual Books of the* AE

	A	B	C	χ^2 for 2 degrees of freedom
ἀλλά	88	43	83	2·55
ἄν	34	32	31	3·78
γάρ	133	102	133	9·93
γε	5	5	10	1·68
δέ	280	161	282	2·29
δή	12	20	14	8·94
διό	15	15	14	2·15
εἰ	53	20	39	5·09
ἐπεί	10	7	25	8·61
ἤ	90	30	62	12·28
καθάπερ	1	3	10	7·79
καί	362	240	392	1·50
μέν	114	71	140	4·27
μή	54	31	59	1·00
οἷον	34	10	26	5·25
ὅτι	45	39	49	1·76
οὐ	114	62	112	1·54
οὐδέ	20	28	31	7·06
οὖν	32	21	39	0·89
οὔτε	20	24	30	4·26
τε	27	10	19	2·89
ὡς	30	14	23	1·46
ὥσπερ	23	13	44	10·45
ὥστε	23	17	21	0·43
Totals	6430	4198	6413	

For 2 degrees of freedom, a value of 9·21 or more is significant at the 1-per-cent level.

splitting them up, assigning one or more of them to the *NE* and the remainder of the *EE*.[1]

The irregular occurrence of *hōsper* contrasts with the regularities to be found in both *NE* and *EE*; the irregularity of *ē* parallels its irregularity in the *EE*, and conflicts with the prediction of regularity from the *NE*. Otherwise, all predictions of regularity from either *EE* or *NE* are fulfilled by the *AE*. We now have eight cases (*alla, de,*

1. Thus Rowe, op. cit. 90–114 sees *AE* B as being wholly Nicomachean, whereas A and C, he thinks, have a Eudemian base.

dē, dio, hoion, oude, oun, hōs) where we can compare the regularity found in the *NE* with that found in the *AE*; and thirteen cases (*gar, ge, de, ei, epei, men, mē, hoion, hoti, oude, oun, te, hōste*) where we can compare regularities in the *AE* and the *EE*. We already know, from Table 4.6, that in six out of the eight *NE* cases, and in every one of the thirteen *EE* cases, the differences between the frequencies in the

TABLE 4.13 *Comparison of two contexts for the* AE *in respect of Particle Use*

Particle	AE and NE χ^2 for 9 degrees of freedom	AE and EE χ^2 for 7 degrees of freedom
ἀλλά	*71·08*	*16·86*
ἄν	*58·44*	*22·12*
γάρ	*40·48*	*14·51*
γε	*28·22*	8·79
δέ	*23·84*	*17·67*
δή	*46·27*	*22·95*
διό	10·90	*16·41*
εἰ	*52·14*	7·68
ἐπεί	*66·07*	*16·12*
ἤ	*27·41*	*40·49*
καθάπερ	*55·37*	N.A.
καί	*34·10*	*18·50*
μέν	*57·31*	7·30
μή	*48·63*	11·21
οἷον	*15·41*	7·01
ὅτι	*54·63*	10·62
οὐ	*44·14*	*22·56*
οὐδέ	*24·74*	*20·52*
οὖν	9·33	15·56
οὔτε	*52·20*	*21·33*
τε	*38·31*	7·12
ὡς	20·49	*25·29*
ὥσπερ	*40·89*	*21·40*
ὥστε	*51·39*	5·55

For 9 degrees of freedom, a value of 21·66 or more is significant at the 1-per-cent level.

For 7 degrees of freedom, a value of 18·48 or more is significant at the 1-per-cent level.

Values of χ^2 significant at the 1-per-cent level are italicized.

treatises as a whole are not significant; but we are now in a position to make a comparison which takes account not only of the frequency of the particles in each treatise considered as a whole, but also of the distribution of the particles in the particular books of the treatises. We can place the three books of the *AE* in their rival contexts in turn, and see which experiment produces the more homogeneous resulting whole. We do so by putting the seven books of the *NE* together with the three books of the *AE*, and applying a chi-squared test to the ten-book whole thus produced (the traditional *Nicomachean Ethics*); and similarly, lumping together the *EE* and the *AE* and applying a chi-squared test to the resulting eight-book *Eudemian Ethics*. The results of this experiment are shown in Table 4.13.

It leaps to the eye that in respect of particle usage the traditional *Eudemian Ethics* is a much more homogeneous work than the traditional *Nicomachean Ethics*. In the former, there are only nine cases where the differences between books are significant; in the latter the differences are statistically significant in twenty out of twenty-four cases. If we restrict ourselves to a consideration of the cases recently isolated, we find that only in four of the eight cases where an *NE* regularity corresponded to an *AE* regularity can the two homogeneous treatises be combined to form a third homogeneous whole; whereas in the thirteen cases where *EE* and *AE* agreed in displaying regularities, the regularities are preserved if we combine the two treatises together. Every irregularity to be found in the *Eudemian Ethics* containing the disputed books is already to

TABLE 4.14 *Bar Charts of the Use of* ἐπεί *and* ὥστε *in the traditional* NE *and* EE

TABLE 4.14a ὥστε *in the traditional* NE. *Proportions in per cent*

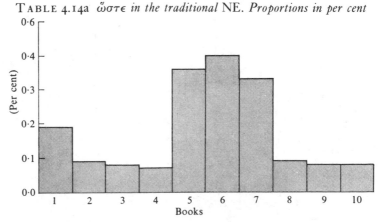

TABLE 4.14b ὥστε *in the traditional EE. Proportions in per cent*

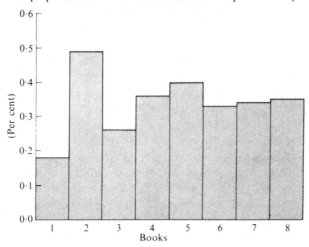

TABLE 4.14c ἐπεί *in the traditional NE. Proportions in per cent*

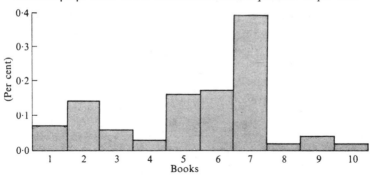

TABLE 4.14d ἐπεί *in the traditional EE. Proportions in per cent*

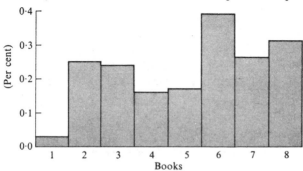

be found in the *EE* alone; and even those particles (such as *alla*) which display irregularity in the narrower context of the *EE* no longer do so if placed in the wider context of the traditional *Eudemian Ethics*.

The way in which the disputed books look much more at home in a Eudemian than in a Nicomachean context can be illustrated graphically in the cases of the particles *hōste* and *epei*. Table 4.14 gives bar charts of the occurrences of these particles, first in the *Nicomachean Ethics* taken as including the disputed books as its fifth, sixth, and seventh books; and then in the *Eudemian Ethics* taken as including the disputed books as its fourth, fifth, and sixth books. The sore thumb which is conspicuous in the first chart of each pair is noticeably lacking in the second one of each pair.

We must now take a further look at the irregularities discovered between books within the undisputed *NE* and the undisputed *EE*. Is it possible to discover whether these irregularities in the use of particular particles are concentrated in particular books of these treatises which render anomalous an otherwise homogeneous whole? The raw scores given in Tables 4.10, 11, and 12 do not render this perspicuous: the matter is more easily studied in Tables 4.15 and 16 which give the proportions and standard errors of the particles in individual books.

TABLE 4.15 *Frequencies of Particles and Connectives in Individual Books of the* NE

		1	2	3	4	8	9	10
ἀλλά	frequency (%)	0·66	0·71	**0·95**	0·64	0·63	0·42	0·48
	standard error	0·11	0·12	0·10	0·10	0·10	0·11	0·10
ἄν	f.	1·06	0·42	0·84	0·84	0·69	1·04	1·40
	s.e.	0·13	0·15	0·12	0·12	0·13	0·13	0·12
γάρ	f.	2·27	1·79	2·38	2·86	3·35	2·55	2·50
	s.e.	0·21	0·24	0·20	0·20	0·21	0·22	0·20
γε	f.	0·32	0·07	0·27	0·25	0·05	0·09	0·26
	s.e.	0·06	0·07	0·05	0·06	0·06	0·06	0·06
δέ	f.	4·73	5·09	4·76	4·96	5·11	4·42	3·84
	s.e.	0·28	0·32	0·27	0·27	0·28	0·29	0·27

		1	2	3	4	8	9	10
δή	f.	0·50	0·24	0·66	0·47	0·53	0·72	0·74
	s.e.	0·10	0·11	0·09	0·10	0·10	0·10	0·09
διό	f.	0·09	0·24	0·22	0·18	0·17	0·19	0·14
	s.e.	0·05	0·06	0·05	0·05	0·05	0·06	0·05
εἰ	f.	0·78	0·31	0·58	0·25	0·15	0·40	0·67
	s.e.	0·09	0·10	0·08	0·09	0·09	0·09	0·09
ἐπεί	f.	0·07	0·14	0·06	0·03	0·02	0·04	0·02
	s.e.	0·03	0·03	0·03	0·03	0·03	0·03	0·03
ἤ	f.	1·12	0·83	1·47	1·13	1·00	1·34	0·95
	s.e.	0·14	0·16	0·13	0·14	0·14	0·15	0·13
καθάπερ	f.	0·34	0·07	0·05	0·05	0·17	0·40	0·18
	s.e.	0·06	0·06	0·05	0·05	0·06	0·06	0·05
καί	f.	7·42	7·02	6·28	7·39	6·21	6·05	6·36
	s.e.	0·33	0·38	0·31	0·32	0·33	0·34	0·32
μέν	f.	1·33	2·55	1·64	1·43	1·44	1·27	1·09
	s.e.	0·16	0·18	0·15	0·16	0·16	0·17	0·15
μή	f.	0·50	0·21	0·96	0·99	0·51	0·64	0·42
	s.e.	0·10	0·11	0·10	0·10	0·10	0·11	0·10
οἷον	f.	0·28	0·31	0·52	0·35	0·34	0·34	0·24
	s.e.	0·08	0·08	0·07	0·08	0·08	0·08	0·07
ὄη	f.	0·37	0·52	0·62	0·27	0·17	0·64	0·34
	s.e.	0·09	0·09	0·08	0·08	0·08	0·09	0·08
οὐ	f.	0·73	1·13	1·44	1·93	1·37	1·23	1·51
	s.e.	0·15	0·18	0·14	0·15	0·15	0·16	0·15
οὐδέ	f.	0·32	0·52	0·68	0·72	0·53	0·51	0·77
	s.e.	0·10	0·11	0·10	0·10	0·10	0·11	0·10
οὖν	f.	0·44	0·75	0·55	0·54	0·51	0·74	0·67
	s.e.	0·10	0·11	0·10	0·10	0·10	0·11	0·10
οὔτε	f.	0·28	0·38	0·19	0·25	0·09	0·08	0·08
	s.e.	0·06	0·06	0·05	0·05	0·06	0·06	0·05
τε	f.	0·30	0·33	0·17	0·37	0·41	0·49	0·77
	s.e.	0·09	0·09	0·08	0·08	0·08	0·09	0·08
ὡς	f.	0·34	0·45	0·66	0·72	0·43	0·43	0·51
	s.e.	0·09	0·10	0·09	0·09	0·09	0·10	0·09
ὥσπερ	f.	0·21	0·33	0·24	0·30	0·10	0·25	0·32
	s.e.	0·07	0·07	0·06	0·06	0·07	0·07	0·06
ὥστε	f.	0·19	0·09	0·08	0·07	0·09	0·08	0·08
	s.e.	0·04	0·04	0·04	0·04	0·04	0·04	0·04

TABLE 4.16 *Frequencies of Particles and Connectives in Individual Books of the* EE

		I	II	III	VII	VIII
ἀλλά	frequency (%)	0·95	1·10	0·92	1·30	**1·80**
	standard error	0·19	0·13	0·16	0·12	0·21
ἄν	f.	0·77	0·48	0·73	0·65	**1·21**
	s.e.	0·14	0·10	0·12	0·09	0·16
γάρ	f.	2·01	1·85	2·23	**2·61**	1·91
	s.e.	0·25	0·17	0·21	0·16	0·29
γε	f.	0·15	0·18	0·06	0·12	0·27
	s.e.	0·06	0·04	0·05	0·04	0·07
δέ	f.	3·04	4·05	4·24	4·20	3·28
	s.e.	0·33	0·23	0·28	0·21	0·38
δή	f.	0·15	0·35	0·17	0·26	0·59
	s.e.	0·09	0·06	0·08	0·06	0·10
διό	f.	**0·00**	0·24	0·30	0·41	0·20
	s.e.	0·09	0·06	0·08	0·06	0·10
εἰ	f.	0·53	0·73	0·58	0·60	0·74
	s.e.	0·14	0·09	0·12	0·09	0·16
ἐπεί	f.	0·03	0·25	0·24	0·26	0·31
	s.e.	0·08	0·06	0·07	0·05	0·09
ἤ	f.	1·12	1·62	1·28	0·78	1·52
	s.e.	0·19	0·13	0·16	0·12	0·22
καθάπερ	f.	0·12	0·04	0·04	0·01	0·04
	s.e.	0·03	0·02	0·03	0·02	0·04
καί	f.	4·88	6·61	6·68	6·10	6·29
	s.e.	0·41	0·29	0·35	0·26	0·48
μέν	f.	1·71	1·71	1·80	1·72	1·56
	s.e.	0·22	0·15	0·19	0·14	0·26
μή	f.	0·77	1·04	0·86	0·93	**0·39**
	s.e.	0·16	0·11	0·14	0·10	0·18
οἷον	f.	0·44	0·45	0·45	0·34	0·39
	s.e.	0·11	0·08	0·09	0·07	0·13
ὅτι	f.	0·71	0·79	0·43	0·78	0·98
	s.e.	0·15	0·10	0·13	0·09	0·17
οὐ	f.	1·33	1·41	1·41	1·54	2·19
	s.e.	0·20	0·14	0·17	0·13	0·22
οὐδέ	f.	**0·80**	0·39	0·36	0·34	0·47
	s.e.	0·11	0·08	0·10	0·07	0·13

TABLE 4.16 (*contd.*)

		I	II	III	VII	VIII
οὖν	f.	0·44	0·27	0·36	0·34	0·66
	s.e.	0·10	0·07	0·09	0·07	0·12
οὔτε	f.	0·38	0·28	0·54	0·34	0·08
	s.e.	0·10	0·07	0·08	0·07	0·11
τε	f.	0·50	0·35	0·39	0·28	0·27
	s.e.	0·10	0·07	0·09	0·08	0·12
ὡς	f.	0·50	0·35	0·39	0·78	0·66
	s.e.	0·13	0·09	0·11	0·08	0·14
ὥσπερ	f.	0·27	0·32	0·49	0·60	0·62
	s.e.	0·12	0·08	0·10	0·07	0·14
ὥστε	f.	0·18	0·49	0·26	0·34	0·35
	s.e.	0·10	0·07	0·09	0·06	0·12

The formula for calculating the standard error of the proportions given differs from that used for the ethical treatises as wholes and explained on pp. 84–5 above. Earlier, we were treating the ethical treatises as being each a sample from the indefinitely large population of Aristotelian prose: now, we are regarding each book as a sample from a population of known size and known characteristics, namely the whole treatise from which the book is taken. We are asking, of each book, whether its characteristics are those which would be expected of a sample drawn randomly from the population constituted by the whole treatise. In such a case, in calculating the standard error of the sample proportion we make use of the known proportion, for each word, of the population as a whole. The formula used to work out the standard error of the sample proportion is

$$(\text{se } p) = \sqrt{\{\theta(1-\theta)/n\}}$$

where p is the observed proportion in the sample, θ is the population proportion and n is the sample size.[1] We can use the standard error thus calculated as a standard unit to express the observed difference between the sample and population proportions as a z-score thus:

$$z = \frac{p-\theta}{\text{se } p}$$

1. Caulcott, 1973, 83.

Where a z score is 2·58 or more (or −2·58 or less) there is less than one chance in a hundred of the word-frequency in question having occurred simply as the result of random sampling, and we say that the difference between the frequency in the particular book and the frequency in the treatise as a whole is statistically significant at the 1-per-cent level. In Table 4.15 the proportions and standard errors for each particle in each book of the *NE* is given, the standard errors being calculated on the basis of the known frequencies for the *NE* as a whole, as already given in Table 4.5. The z-value for the

TABLE 4.17 *Frequencies of Particles and Connectives in Individual Books of the* AE

	A		B		C	
	Frequency (%)	Standard error	Frequency (%)	Standard error	Frequency (%)	Standard error
ἀλλά	1·37	0·14	1·02	0·17	1·29	0·14
ἄν	0·53	0·09	0·76	0·12	0·48	0·09
γάρ	2·07	0·18	2·43	0·22	2·07	0·18
γε	0·11	0·04	0·12	0·05	0·16	0·04
δέ	4·35	0·25	3·88	0·31	4·40	0·25
δή	0·19	0·06	0·48	0·08	0·22	0·06
διό	0·23	0·06	0·36	0·08	0·22	0·06
εἰ	0·82	0·10	0·48	0·12	0·69	0·10
ἐπεί	0·16	0·06	0·17	0·08	0·39	0·06
ἤ	1·40	0·13	0·71	0·16	0·97	0·13
καθάπερ	0·02	0·04	0·07	0·04	0·16	0·04
καί	5·63	0·29	5·72	0·36	6·11	0·29
μέν	1·77	0·17	1·69	0·21	2·18	0·17
μή	0·84	0·11	0·74	0·14	0·92	0·11
οἷον	0·53	0·08	0·24	0·10	0·41	0·08
ὅτι	0·70	0·11	0·93	0·14	0·76	0·11
οὐ	1·77	0·16	1·48	0·20	1·75	0·16
οὐδέ	0·31	0·08	0·67	0·10	0·48	0·08
οὖν	0·50	0·09	0·50	0·11	0·61	0·09
οὔτε	0·31	0·08	0·57	0·10	0·47	0·08
τε	0·42	0·07	0·24	0·09	0·30	0·07
ὡς	0·47	0·08	0·33	0·10	0·36	0·08
ὥσπερ	0·36	0·09	0·31	0·11	0·69	0·09
ὥστε	0·36	0·07	0·40	0·09	0·33	0·07

difference between the sample frequency and the population frequency was calculated in each case; these values are not given in the table, but wherever a z-score had an absolute value of more than 2·58 the proportion figure in the table is printed in bold type: the bold-type values, therefore, are those which differ from the over-all frequency in the *NE* by a statistically significant amount. Table 4.16 sets out analogous data for the *EE*, and Table 4.17 for the *AE*: in each case the standard errors are calculated on the basis of the frequencies for the whole treatises given in Table 4.5, and in each case values differing from the treatise value by an amount significant at the 1-per-cent level are in bold type.

The first fact which meets the eye on studying these tables is the great general regularity of particle use to be found in the ethical treatises. Of the 360 values recorded of frequencies in these tables, only thirty-three, roughly 9 per cent, are anomalous in the sense of being different by a significant amount from the over-all frequency of the treatise to which they belong. In all other cases chance is an adequate account of the differences observed. It should be stressed again that in the anomalous cases no inference, about authorship, chronology, interpolation, context, etc. can be drawn from the anomaly alone: all the anomaly means is that some explanation other than chance is needed. But such explanations are often very easy to find. For instance, it will be noticed in Table 4.16 that the frequency of *kai* in the first book of the *Eudemian Ethics* is significantly less than the frequency of *kai* in the other books of the *EE* (it is indeed much the lowest to be found in any of the books in the three tables). Scholars have long noticed in book I of the *EE* evidence of careful stylistic revision—hiatus is avoided, for instance—and it may well be that when polishing up his style Aristotle, like many other writers, removed paratactic constructions in favour of more elegant periods; this would account for the anomalous value. There may be similar particular explanations for the other particular anomalies: what is important in the tables are the regularities revealed by the *absence* of anomalies in the great majority of the cases.

If we look at Table 4.15, we notice that book 2 stands out to some extent from the other books: seven out of the twenty-five anomalous values to be found in the *NE* books occur in this book alone. What is most striking is that in each of these cases the book 2 value is nearer to the *EE* mean proportion than it is to the *NE* mean proportion. This affinity between *NE* 2 and the *EE* may deserve further investigation.

Table 4.16 shows that the *EE* is more homogeneous in respect of particle use than the *NE*: there are eight anomalies in 120 cases (6.7 per cent) as against twenty-five anomalies in 168 cases (14·9 per cent). Books I and VIII, with two anomalies each, stand slightly apart from books II, III, and VII, which are highly regular with the unusually high *gar* score for book VII as the only anomaly. Most regular of all the ethical books are the common books of the *AE*: no anomaly at all is to be found in any of the three books. This is surely a striking result in view of the fact that many scholars have claimed that the common books form a patchwork of writings from different periods, some from Eudemian original material, some from Nicomachean. If this is patchwork it is highly remarkable patchwork, with the pieces so well matched as to make a more regular pattern than the originals from which the pieces have been cut.

We may use the same data to test the fit of the *AE* into its two rival contexts in the following manner. If we compute the mean proportion for the ten books made up of the *NE* plus the *AE*, we can again compute standard errors and z-scores for each of the frequencies of each of the ten books, and record anomalies as we did for the seven-book *NE*, and similarly we can compute mean proportions for the eight books of the traditional *Eudemian Ethics* (*EE* plus *AE*) and with their aid reckon standard errors and z-scores for each particle in each book. The scores so computed cannot be set out without an inordinate degree of reduplication of data: but Tables 4.18 and 19 show the anomalies which are produced by this procedure. It will be seen that the effect is to make the *NE* considerably less homogeneous than it was (there are now fifty-one anomalies out of 240 cases, or 21·3 per cent) while the *EE* is made very slightly more homogeneous (with twelve anomalies in 192 cases, 6·25 per cent); the *EE* remains very much more homogeneous than the *NE*. If we look in particular at the disputed books, we find that in their Nicomachean context they display eighteen anomalies (25 per cent), in their Eudemian context only two (2·8 per cent). *NE* book 2, which stood out in a purely Nicomachean context, is now more at home with the disputed books to keep it company; in the new arrangement the most anomalous of the undisputed Nicomachean books is book 10. The only crumb of comfort for those who defend a Nicomachean origin for some of the common books is that B (*NE* 6) is as comfortable in the ten-book Nicomachean context as are any of the undisputed books. But that does not alter the fact that it is more at home in the Eudemian context (where it displays only one anomaly, in the use of *ē*) than in the Nicomachean context (where it displays three).

We have noticed that the common books, taken by themselves, form one of the most homogeneous blocks in the Aristotelian ethical corpus. Can we proceed further and see whether this uniformity is

TABLE 4.18 *Particles: Books as Samples from the Traditional* NE *as a Single Population*

	1	2	3	4	5	6	7	8	9	10
ἀλλά	0	0	0	0	1	0	1	0	1	1
ἄν	0	1	0	0	0	0	1	0	0	1
γάρ	0	1	0	0	0	0	0	1	0	0
γε	1	0	0	0	0	0	0	0	0	0
δέ	0	0	0	0	0	0	0	0	0	1
δή	0	0	0	0	1	0	1	0	0	1
διό	0	0	0	0	0	0	0	0	0	0
εἰ	0	0	0	1	1	0	0	1	0	0
ἐπεί	0	0	0	0	0	0	1	0	0	0
ἤ	0	0	1	0	0	0	0	0	0	0
καθάπερ	1	0	0	0	1	0	0	0	1	0
καί	1	0	0	1	0	0	0	0	0	0
μέν	0	1	0	0	0	0	1	0	0	1
μή	0	0	1	1	0	0	0	0	0	1
οἷον	0	0	0	0	0	0	0	0	0	0
ὅτι	0	0	0	1	0	1	1	1	0	0
οὐ	1	0	0	1	0	0	0	0	0	0
οὐδέ	0	0	0	0	1	0	0	0	0	0
οὖν	0	0	0	0	0	0	0	0	0	0
οὔτε	0	1	0	0	0	1	1	1	1	1
τε	0	0	1	0	0	0	0	0	0	1
ὡς	0	0	0	1	0	0	0	0	0	0
ὥσπερ	0	0	0	0	0	0	1	1	0	0
ὥστε	0	0	0	0	1	1	1	0	0	0

0 denotes an absolute *z*-score less than 2·58; 1 denotes a *z*-score greater than 2·58 and therefore significant at the 1-per-cent level.

displayed within each of the books in question? This is of interest given the prevalence of theories which divide the disputed books into pieces of varying dates. Altogether the common books total 17041 words. It is therefore possible to divide them into seventeen samples, each of approximately 1000 words, and repeat the tests which we have carried out on the books as a whole.[1] The limits and

TABLE 4.19 *Particles: Books as Samples from the Traditional* EE *as a Single Population*

	I	II	III	IV	V	VI	VII	VIII
ἀλλά	o	o	o	o	o	o	o	1
ἄν	o	o	o	o	o	o	o	1
γάρ	o	o	o	o	o	o	o	o
γε	o	o	o	o	o	o	o	o
δέ	1	o	o	o	o	o	o	o
δή	o	o	o	o	o	o	o	1
διό	1	o	o	o	o	o	o	o
εἰ	o	o	o	o	o	o	o	o
ἐπεί	o	o	o	o	o	o	o	o
ἤ	o	1	o	o	1	o	1	o
καθάπερ	o	o	o	o	o	1	o	o
καί	1	o	o	o	o	o	o	o
μέν	o	o	o	o	o	o	o	o
μή	o	o	o	o	o	o	o	o
οἷον	o	o	o	o	o	o	o	o
ὅτι	o	o	o	o	o	o	o	o
οὐ	o	o	1	o	o	o	o	o
οὐδέ	1	o	o	o	o	o	o	o
οὖν	o	o	o	o	o	o	o	o
οὔτε	o	o	o	o	o	o	o	o
τε	o	o	o	o	o	o	o	o
ὡς	o	o	o	o	o	o	o	o
ὥσπερ	o	o	o	o	o	o	o	o
ὥστε	o	o	o	o	o	o	o	o

o denotes a z-score less than 2·58; 1 denotes a z-score greater than 2·58 and therefore significant at the 1-per-cent level.

1. The samples are not exactly equal in word-length. For technical reasons it was easier to deal with samples measured by number of lines than with samples measured by number of words.

the contents of the samples which result may be indicated as follows:

1. $1129^a1{-}30^b8$; bk. A chs. 1–2; general and particular justice.
2. $1130^b8{-}32^a15$; bk. A chs. 2–4; distributive justice.
3. $1132^a15{-}33^a22$; bk. A chs. 4–5; corrective justice and reciprocity.
4. $1133^a22{-}34^a26$; bk. A chs. 5–8; justice as mean; political justice, nature, and law.
5. $1134^a26{-}36^b32$; bk. A chs. 8–9; justice, voluntariness, and involuntariness.
6. $1136^h32{-}38^b1$; bk. A chs. 9–11; equity, *aporiai* about justice.
7. $1138^b1{-}40^a1$; end of bk. A, bk. B chs. 1–3; intellectual virtues, man as agent.
8. $1140^a1{-}41^b2$; bk. B chs. 4–7; art, wisdom, and learning.
9. $1141^b2{-}43^a5$; bk. B chs. 7–10; wisdom and its parts and satellites.
10. $1143^a5{-}44^b5$; bk. B chs. 10–13; wisdom in relation to learning and intellect.
11. $1144^b5{-}46^a6$; bk. B ch. 13, bk. C, chs. 1–2; wisdom and virtue; opinions on *akrasia*.
12. $1146^a6{-}47^b8$; bk. C chs. 2–3; *akrasia* and knowledge.
13. $1147^b8{-}49^a12$; bk. C chs. 3–5; the sphere of *akrasia*.
14. $1149^a12{-}50^b12$; bk. C chs. 5–7; different kinds of *akrasia*.
15. $1150^b12{-}52^a13$; bk. C chs. 7–10; continence, incontinence, intemperance.
16. $1152^a13{-}53^b13$; bk. C chs. 10–13; is pleasure a good?
17. $1153^b13{-}54^b35$; bk. C chs. 13–14; conclusion of discussion of pleasure.

Table 4.20 gives the raw scores for each particle in each sample. Proportions, standard errors, and z-scores were computed as before; these statistics are not reproduced, but where the z-score revealed an anomaly the raw score has been printed in bold type. The final column for each particle gives the value of chi-squared for 16 degrees of freedom, calculated in the manner explained above on p. 92.

Inspection of Table 4.20 suggests that the general regularity we have observed in Aristotle's use of particles continues to be observable even at a comparatively microscopic level. Twenty-one

TABLE 4.20 *Particles and Connectives in Seventeen Samples of the AE*

Sample	1	2	3	4	5	6	7	8	9	10	11	12	13	14	15	16	17	χ^2 for 16 degrees of freedom
ἀλλά	13	11	7	15	17	18	10	8	15	8	14	16	15	7	11	13	13	15·60
ἄν	2	3	7	4	9	6	4	**12**	6	6	9	6	5	5	2	5	4	20·93
γάρ	17	25	22	18	24	23	19	18	24	31	22	27	12	19	21	23	19	13·84
γε	2	5	3	3	1	0	0	1	0	2	3	3	0	0	3	1	1	—
δέ	42	49	35	68	44	38	35	33	49	34	39	38	45	49	55	39	28	28·70
δή	3	1	4	0	2	1	6	4	7	3	2	2	0	2	2	3	4	—
διό	1	0	5	5	1	3	4	2	5	4	0	0	3	3	2	3	3	—
εἰ	8	6	**17**	3	11	6	5	7	2	0	5	14	3	12	1	3	3	**51·45**
ἐπεί	2	3	0	3	1	1	1	3	3	8	1	2	4	2	5	7	4	—
ἤ	13	8	11	16	**25**	14	6	6	12	8	13	11	16	14	11	9	9	26·82
καθάπερ	0	0	0	1	0	0	1	1	0	0	4	1	4	2	0	0	0	—
καί	61	59	53	63	47	73	49	55	57	68	51	47	76	62	50	69	49	**32·87**
μέν	21	23	8	24	19	17	18	11	20	16	21	20	25	20	**32**	19	7	28·61
μή	3	4	**17**	8	13	8	10	9	1	9	5	15	5	11	11	4	9	**37·49**
οἷον	8	5	8	5	4	4	2	4	1	2	2	5	8	2	4	4	2	—
ὅτι	14	3	6	8	5	8	4	11	12	4	**15**	7	5	10	2	12	7	—
οὐ	11	10	7	15	35	23	8	16	19	11	5	14	17	10	**29**	19	16	—
οὐδέ	3	1	2	4	5	5	2	9	9	3	**10**	3	4	3	3	8	5	27·27
οὖν	5	7	5	4	3	6	10	3	2	5	6	7	6	7	4	6	6	11·85
οὔτε	2	0	3	2	5	3	4	**12**	5	2	1	4	0	2	7	4	7	—
τε	7	7	3	1	4	3	2	2	3	2	6	1	3	2	1	3	2	—
ὡς	5	**11**	1	2	4	7	3	1	4	6	3	3	4	2	3	4	3	21·27
ὥσπερ	1	0	6	3	7	5	2	4	2	4	6	0	9	10	**11**	5	5	**32·90**
ὥστε	3	5	5	2	4	3	2	6	3	4	3	6	0	4	4	3	3	—

χ^2 of more than 32 significant at the 1-per-cent level for 16 degrees of freedom.

anomalies occur out of 408 cases, a mere 5 per cent. None of the sample sections displays a remarkably large number of anomalies; sample 11 has the largest number, namely four; this section, interestingly enough, is one where Aristotle is recording, perhaps to some extent in their own words, the opinions of other philosophers on the nature of *akrasia*. Once again, there is no real support for the view that the common books of the *AE* are patchwork of disparate material.

A word of warning is necessary, however, about the significance of the statistical results at this point. The tests described on pp. 84, 87 and 103, are all based on the assumpton that the sampling distribution of the values to be studied is a normal one. In fact, where we are dealing with the proportion of a number of discrete events falling into one of two classes (as we are with the occurrences of words) we know that the appropriate theoretical sampling distribution is not the normal distribution but the binomial distribution. Moreover, when the proportion of events falling into one of the two classes is very small (as it is in the case of rarely occurring words) the appropriate discrete distribution is not the binomial, but some other such as the Poisson distribution.[1] None the less, it is regular statistical practice to use the binomial distribution instead of the Poisson, and the normal distribution in turn instead of the binomial, provided that we are dealing with a reasonably large number of trials; for in such cases the distributions approximate very closely to each other, and the use of the normal distribution greatly facilitates computation. In the case of the statistics for the *NE*, *AE*, *EE* as wholes, and for the individual books as wholes, the length of the books (and therefore the number of trials in question, each word-choice counting as a trial) was sufficiently great for this approximation to be reliable. But now that we have reached the consideration of samples of no more than 1000 words, the effect of treating the distribution as a normal one may become misleading in the case of the less frequently occurring particles. The approximation of the Poisson distribution to the normal one is sufficiently close provided that the number of trials multiplied by the proportion of successes is at least five. In the case of the 1000-word samples, therefore, the approximation is reliable in the case of particles occurring with a frequency of at least 0·50 per

1. See Caulcott, 1973, 28–33.

cent. We have already encountered in connection with the chi-squared test the fact that where individual cells of the table of values have an expected value of less than five in more than 80 per cent of cases, the test is unreliable. For analogous reasons, in Table 4.20 where the chi-squared test is inapplicable, the z-values on which the specification of values is based cannot be regarded as any precise measure of statistical probability.

In a later chapter we shall see a method of circumventing some of the difficulty of accurately measuring the statistical significance of stylistic features even in small samples. In the present one, enough has been done to show that in respect of the use of particles, the common books of the *AE*, whether considered as a single unit, or as individual books, or in 1000-word samples, resemble the *Eudemian Ethics* far more than they resemble the *Nicomachean Ethics*.

CHAPTER 5

Prepositions, Adverbs, and Pronouns in the Ethical Treatises

PREPOSITIONS

PREPOSITIONS, like particles, furnish abundant material for the statistical study of style. They occur with considerable frequency and are comparatively, though not totally, free from fluctuations due to change of subject matter. Table 5.1 sets out the occurrences and frequencies of the nineteen prepositions commonest in the *NE*, *AE*, and *EE*. It will be seen that tokens of these prepositions constitute roughly 6 per cent of the total text to be considered. Prepositions occur slightly less frequently in the *AE* than in the *EE*, and considerably less frequently in the *AE* than in the *NE*; but neither of the differences is statistically significant.

In the majority of cases the frequency in the *AE* is not significantly different either from that in the *NE* or from that in the *EE*. But once again the differences which do exist show that the *AE* resembles the *EE* more than it does the *AE*. If we plot the occurrences of each of the prepositions in the *AE* against those in the *NE* we find that the correlation between frequency in the *AE* and frequency in the *NE* is 0·87 for the nineteen prepositions: the corresponding correlation between the frequency in the *AE* and the frequency in the *EE* is higher, 0·97. The favourite preposition in the *NE* is *en*; in the *AE* and *EE* it is *kata* with the accusative.

When we apply the test described above in chapter 4 to see whether the treatises can be regarded as samples from a single population, we find that only in three cases are the differences between preposition usage in the *EE* and the *AE* statistically significant at the 1-per-cent level. This is in the case of the prepositions *dia* with the genitive, *eis* with the accusative, and *epi* with the dative. In every one of these cases there is also a significant, and in fact larger, difference between the usage in the *NE* and the

TABLE 5.1 *Nineteen Common Prepositions in the* NE, AE, *and* EE

Preposition	NE		AE		EE	
	Occur-rences	Propor-tion %	Occur-rences	Propor-tion %	Occur-rences	Propor-tion %
ἄνευ	18	0·05	23	0·13	31	0·12
ἀπό	64	0·16	22	0·13	58	0·22
διά + acc.	245	0·62	138	0·81	199	0·76
διά + gen.	62	0·16	8	0·04	34	0·13
εἰς	83	0·21	13	0·08	48	0·18
ἐκ (ἐξ)	130	0·33	50	0·29	63	0·24
ἐν	482	1·22	117	0·69	223	0·85
ἕνεκα (−εν)	49	0·12	22	0·13	56	0·21
ἐπί + acc.	85	0·22	19	0·11	38	0·14
ἐπί + gen.	75	0·19	37	0·22	48	0·18
ἐπί + dat.	82	0·21	17	0·10	55	0·21
κατά + acc.	363	0·92	152	0·89	249	0·95
μετά	42	0·11	24	0·14	31	0·12
παρά + acc.	25	0·06	36	0·21	40	0·15
παρά + g./d.	23	0·06	3	0·18	6	0·22
περί + acc.	233	0·59	90	0·53	116	0·44
περί + gen.	111	0·28	88	0·52	105	0·40
πρός + acc.	255	0·65	107	0·63	171	0·24
ὑπό	61	0·15	20	0·12	34	0·13
Total of 19	2488	6·29	986	5·79	1605	6·10

The figures for each preposition were obtained from a word-count made by the COCOA program. As the program did not discriminate between cases where the preposition occurred with different cases, the figures for such expressions as *epi* are the result of an apportionment of the computer total between the different cases on the basis of an independent hand-count of the complete text.

usage in the *AE*. The differences probably show simply that prepositions are not quite as topic-neutral as might at first appear: the higher frequency of *epi* with the dative in both *NE* and *EE* by comparison with *AE* is due largely to the occurrences of *eph' hēmin* in the discussions of voluntariness in the second book of the *NE* and the second book of the *EE*.

Thus, in sixteen out of nineteen cases the differences between the *EE* and the *AE* are only such as might be expected by chance; and there is no non-chance difference between the *EE* and the *AE* not matched by a greater difference between the *NE* and the *AE*. There are five cases, on the other hand, where the *NE* differs significantly from the *AE* without a correspondingly significant difference between *AE* and *EE*. This is in the case of *aneu* (twice as frequent in *AE* and *EE* as in *NE*), *en* (much more popular in the *NE* than in the others), *epi* with the accusative (another Nicomachean favourite), *para* with the accusative (very much less frequent in the *NE*), and *peri* with the genitive (similarly infrequent in the *NE*). It is again possible that some of these differences may be due to the effect of subject matter: but it is unlikely, since the subject matter of the *NE* and that of the *EE* so closely resemble each other. Once again, the most economical hypothesis to explain the data is that the common books, as they stand, belong to the *EE* rather than to the *NE*.

ADVERBS

After particles, connectives, and prepositions, adverbs present a promising field for the statistician. They occur frequently and in a variety of contexts, and being indeclinable they are easy to collect from an unlemmatized print-out of a word-count. Many adverbs in Greek as in English are formed by terminal modification of a descriptive adjective: in general such adverbs will not be the subject of a special study here, but will be treated as forms of the adjective. There are many other adverbs and adverbial expressions whose study reveals striking differences between the *Nicomachean* and *Eudemian Ethics* which can then be used for comparison with the *AE*.

One such group of expressions is a set of adverbial modifiers of degree: *hēkista* (least), *hētton* (less), *hikanōs* (enough), *lian* (too much), *māllon* (more), *malista* (most), *panu* (altogether). The *Nicomachean Ethics* is uncommonly fond of expressions of this group: as will be seen from Table 5.2 they make up over 1 per cent of its entire text (as against 0·32 per cent for the *AE* and 0·55 per cent for the *EE*). This difference, as the table shows, can be observed throughout the various books of the treatises: the lowest proportion in any book of the *NE* (0·71 per cent in book 1) is approximately the same as the highest proportion in any book of the *EE* (0·73 per cent in book III), and no book in the *AE* contains these words in so high a proportion (highest is 0·45 per cent for book C). When the *AE* is compared with either the *NE* or the *EE* the

TABLE 5.2 *Adverbial Modifiers of Degree in Individual Books of the* NE, AE, *and* EE

Book	ἥκιστα	ἧττον	ἱκανῶς	λίαν	μᾶλλον	μάλιστα	πάνυ	Total	Proportion %
NE									
1	1	3	6	2	14	13	1	40	0·71
2	0	7	1	0	17	8	1	34	0·80
3	1	14	0	1	33	14	5	68	1·07
4	3	6	0	4	51	13	2	79	1·32
8	3	9	0	0	20	26	8	66	1·13
9	1	2	1	1	26	32	2	65	1·22
10	1	10	3	2	33	15	2	66	1·06
Total	10	51	11	10	194	121	21	418	1·06
AE									
A	0	4	2	0	8	1	0	15	0·23
B	0	2	1	0	4	4	0	11	0·26
C	0	6	1	1	16	5	0	29	0·45
Total	0	12	4	1	28	10	0	55	0·32
EE									
I	0	0	0	1	13	8	0	22	0·65
II	0	2	0	1	17	6	0	26	0·37
III	0	5	1	0	18	8	2	34	0·73
VII	1	3	1	2	27	24	0	58	0·67
VIII	1	0	0	0	4	1	0	6	0·23
Total	2	10	2	4	79	47	2	146	0·55

differences, for the group of words as a whole, appear greater than those to be expected as a result of sampling error: when the *AE* is compared with the *EE* there is an absolute z-score of 3·47, when it is compared with the *NE* the z-score is 8·81. But the differences between the *AE* and the *NE* are very much greater than those between the *AE* and the *EE*, and both diverge in the same direction: the occurrence of these Nicomachean favourite expressions is much less in the *AE* than in either the *EE* or the *NE*.

Two adverbs which, by contrast, are Eudemian favourites are *monon* (only) and *haplōs* (without qualification). Table 5.3 sets out

TABLE 5.3 ἁπλῶς *and* μόνον *in Individual Books of the* NE, AE, *and* EE

Book	ἁπλῶς	μόνον	Total	Proportion %
NE				
I	5	4	9	0·15
2	6	3	9	0·21
3	5	I	6	0·09
4	I	2	3	0·05
8	10	4	14	0·24
9	0	2	2	0·03
10	0	5	5	0·08
Total	27	21	48	0·12
AE				
A	23	11	34	0·53
B	7	9	16	0·38
C	28	15	43	0·67
Total	58	35	93	0·55
EE				
I	I	9	10	0·30
II	11	4	15	0·21
III	7	2	9	0·19
VII	40	17	57	0·66
VIII	4	5	9	0·39
Total	63	37	100	0·38

the occurrences of these words in the individual books of the treatises. The lowest scoring books of the *AE* and *EE* (*EE* II, with 0·21 per cent and *EE* III with 0·19 per cent) score just below the highest scoring books of the *NE* (2, with 0·21 per cent and 8, with 0·24 per cent). Just as, in Table 5.2, we saw that the *AE* has a more than Eudemian distaste for the Nicomachean favourite adverbs, so here we see that the *AE* has a more than Eudemian liking for the adverbs most popular in the *EE*. But in this case the differences between the *AE* and *EE* proportions are not significant, while those between the *AE* and *NE* proportions are.

The adverbs *isōs* (perhaps) is a distinct Nicomachean favourite,

TABLE 5.4 Expressions of Doubt and Certainty in Individual Books of the NE, AE, and EE

Book	1 ἴσως	2 δοκεῖ	3 δόξειε(ν)	4 ἔοικε(ν)	5 φαίνεται	6 Total 1–5 (+ proportion) %	7 ἀνάγκη	8 δῆλον	9 φανερόν	10 Total 7–9 (+ proportion) %
NE										
1	16	14	5	10	29	74 (1·31)	0	18	0	18 (0·32)
2	2	2	0	0	4	8 (0·19)	0	2	2	4 (0·09)
3	13	18	6	16	15	68 (1·07)	1	7	1	8 (0·12)
4	1	18	5	11	8	43 (0·72)	0	7	0	7 (0·12)
8	8	24	3	25	10	70 (1·20)	0	5	1	6 (0·10)
9	15	10	13	18	12	68 (1·28)	0	5	0	5 (0·09)
10	15	28	10	11	9	73 (1·17)	0	14	1	15 (0·24)
Total	70	114	42	91	87	404 (1·02)	1	58	5	64 (0·16)
AE										
A	3	14	2	1	2	22 (0·34)	6	15	6	27 (0·42)
B	1	8	1	2	3	15 (0·35)	2	9	4	15 (0·35)
C	4	12	2	5	1	24 (0·37)	5	7	5	17 (0·27)
Total	8	34	5	8	6	61 (0·36)	13	31	15	59 (0·35)
EE										
I	2	2	0	1	2	7 (0·21)	2	5	4	11 (0·32)
II	2	15	5	1	3	26 (0·37)	22	22	9	53 (0·75)
III	2	12	5	1	6	26 (0·56)	6	6	2	14 (0·30)
VII	4	25	4	4	8	45 (0·52)	8	17	10	35 (0·41)
VIII	0	6	0	2	0	8 (0·31)	3	6	4	13 (0·50)
Total	10	60	14	9	19	112 (0·43)	41	56	20	126 (0·48)

occurring in the *NE* with a frequency of 0·18 per cent by comparison with 0·05 per cent in the *AE* and 0·04 per cent in the *EE*. It turns out that this is just one of a number of tentative expressions which are markedly more popular in the *NE* than in the *AE* or the *EE*. The five commonest of these—*isōs* (perhaps), *dokei* (seems), *doxeie* (would seem), *eoike* (seems likely), *phainetai* (appears)—are studied in Table 5.4 which gives the occurrences, book by book, of each. It will be seen that these expressions, between them, add up to over 1 per cent of the whole Nicomachean text. By this crude measure, the *EE* is only half as tentative as the *NE* (these expressions amount to 0·43 per cent of the text) and the *AE* is even less tentative (0·36 per cent). Other, less frequent, expressions of tentativeness, not shown in the table, exhibit the same pattern, such as *tacha* (possibly) and *adēlon* (unclear), which occur between them twenty two times in the *NE*, four times in the *EE*, and twice in the *AE*.

It will be noted that the tentative expressions occur very much less frequently in *NE* 2 than in any other Nicomachean book: the proportion is only 0·19 per cent. Here, as in particle usage, *NE* 2 resembles the *EE* pattern in some respects more than the pattern of its fellow Nicomachean books. If we leave this book aside, we find that the lowest-scoring *NE* book (*NE* 4, with 0·72 per cent) scores considerably higher than the highest-scoring *EE* or *AE* book (*EE* III, with 0·56 per cent). Once again the *AE* is more un-Nicomachean than the *EE* is; but the difference between *AE* and *EE* is again statistically non-significant, for the group considered as a whole.

Table 5.4 shows, in addition to these five expressions of tentativeness, three contrasting expressions of certainty or clarity—*anagkē* (necessarily), *dēlon* (clearly), *phaneron* (obviously). Consistently with the hypothesis that the *EE* is less tentative than the *NE*, these expressions are about three times as popular in the *EE*, where they make up 0·48 of the text, as they are in the *NE*, where they account for no more than 0·16 of the text. The *AE*, with 0·35 per cent, is less prone to use these words than the *EE*, but not by a significant amount; its difference from the *NE*, however, is significantly large.

The data presented in Table 5.4, taken together, amount to quite a striking demonstration of the greater closeness of the *AE* to the *EE* than to the *NE*. The occurrence of each of the expressions in the

TABLE 5.5 *Scattergram of Occurrences of Expressions of Doubt and Certainty in* AE *and* EE

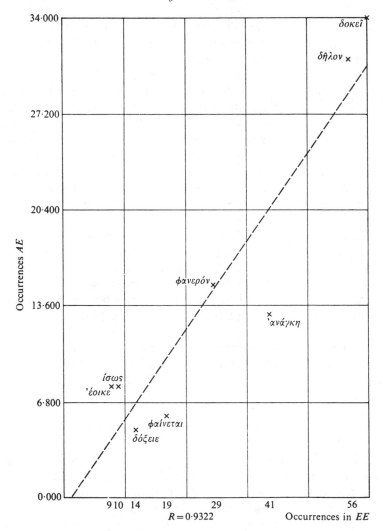

AE is not significantly different, when tested by the usual test,[1] from the occurrence in the EE; by the same test, when we compare the EE and the NE, the null hypothesis is rejected at the 1-per-cent

1. See above, p. 84.

TABLE 5.6 *Scattergram of Occurrences of Expressions of Doubt and Certainty in* NE *and* EE

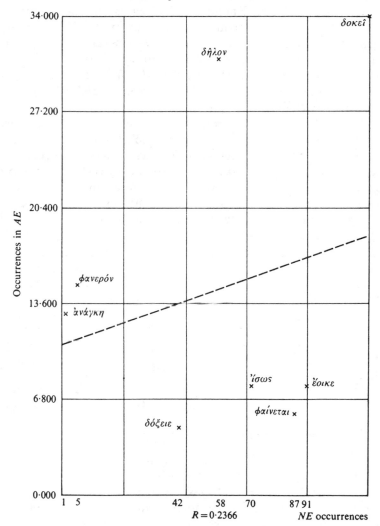

level for six out of the eight expressions (all except *dokei* and *dēlon*). When we take the tentativeness group as a whole, there is no significant difference between the figure for the *EE* and the *AE* ($z = 1.09$), but there is between the *NE* figure and the *AE* figure

($z = 8\cdot03$); similarly with the figures for the certainty group as a whole (z for *NE* and *AE* is $4\cdot32$, for *EE* and *AE* it is $2\cdot07$).

We can present the data graphically in a pair of scattergrams in which the values for individual expressions in the *AE* are plotted against those in the *EE* and those in the *NE* respectively. The result of this for the *AE* and *EE* is shown in Table 5.5, and for the *NE* and *EE* in Table 5.6. It will be seen that *AE* and *EE* correlate well ($r = 0\cdot9322$), whereas the correlation between *AE* and *NE* is so poor that the regression line is valueless.

There seems to be less information for our purpose to be gained from the study of other adverbs in the ethical treatises. Two temporal adverbs are Eudemian favourites, *hama* (at once) and *aei* (always); in the case of *hama* the *AE* frequency is closer to the *NE* one, and in the case of *aei* closer to the *EE* one, but in neither case are the differences between the *AE* frequency and either of the others significant. The values are set out below, along with those of three other frequent adverbs:

	NE		AE		EE	
	Occur-rence	Propor-tion %	Occur-rence	Propor-tion %	Occur-rence	Propor-tion %
ἀεί	24	0·06	20	0·12	24	0·09
ἅμα	18	0·05	9	0·05	35	0·13
ὅλως	35	0·09	15	0·09	24	0·09
ὁμοίως	94	0·24	29	0·17	50	0·19
οὕτως	51	0·13	20	0·12	34	0·13

In the case of *holōs*, *houtōs*, and *homoiōs* the frequencies in each of the three treatises are too close together to be used for any discriminatory purpose. The evidence provided by the use of these words cannot be used unless they can be suitably grouped with other words—e.g. their parent adjectives—to yield statistically significant results. We shall see later how this can be done, as it can with some other adverbs here omitted because they occur, in isolation, less than twenty-four times in the *NE* and less than sixteen times in the *EE*.

PRONOUNS AND DEMONSTRATIVES

When we turn from indeclinable adverbs to pronouns and demonstratives, and later when we come to consider adjectives, nouns, and verbs, we encounter a new difficulty in handling the data. The COCOA program used for word-counting does not lemmatize: that is to say, each separate form of a declining noun or conjugating verb appears listed in alphabetical order, not grouped under the form under which the noun or verb would appear in an ordinary lexicon. Almost all the data considered so far have involved only a single entry in the print-out of the computer word-count (the exceptions being contractions such as *all'* which get counted as forms of the uncontracted word, and forms containing a terminal *n*, such as *eoiken*, which are counted with the unterminated form). When counting Aristotle's usage of a pronoun, a noun, or verb, we have to group together by eye, and total by hand, the occurrences of each of the separate unlemmatized forms which together constitute the score for the single dictionary entry. There is ample scope for human error in omitting a form or incorrectly adding a total. This should be borne in mind henceforth.

Two of the commonest pronouns are *houtos* (this) and *autos* (self, he, same). Between them they make up about 3 per cent of the text of each of the three ethical treatises. Though there are slight differences between the frequencies with which they occur in the different treatises, these differences are not significant. (Approximate frequencies for *houtos*: *NE* 1·51 per cent, *AE* 1·46 per cent, *EE* 1·75 per cent; for *autos*: *NE* 1·44 per cent, *AE* 1·34 per cent, *EE* 1·50 per cent.) Similarly the figures for the two Greek words for 'nobody', *oudeis* and *mēdeis*, show no significant differences between the treatises (provided that *oudeis* and *outheis* are taken together, and likewise *mēdeis* and *mētheis*). The figures and proportions are:

	NE		AE		EE	
	Occur-rence	Propor-tion %	Occur-rence	Propor-tion %	Occur-rence	Propor-tion %
οὐδείς	160	0·40	78	0·46	91	0·35
μηδείς	43	0·11	14	0·08	21	0·08

TABLE 5.7 *Pronouns and Pronominal Adjectives in Individual Books of the NE, AE, and EE*

Book	1 ἕκαστος	2 τοιοῦτος	3 τοσοῦτος	4 Total 1–3 (+proportion %)	5 ἀλλήλων	6 ἄλλος	7 ἐκεῖνος	8 ἔνιοι	9 ἕτερος	10 Total 5–9 (+proportion %)
NE										
1	19	29	5	53 (0·94)	0	44	3	3	13	63 (1·12)
2	6	11	2	19 (0·45)	8	21	4	2	2	37 (0·87)
3	24	63	1	88 (1·39)	0	21	3	9	11	44 (0·69)
4	12	34	4	50 (0·84)	0	20	3	3	3	29 (0·49)
8	16	40	8	64 (1·10)	39	16	17	3	16	91 (1·56)
9	16	32	9	57 (1·08)	9	14	12	1	10	46 (0·87)
10	31	42	3	76 (1·22)	6	27	1	3	33	70 (1·12)
Total	124	251	32	407 (1·03)	62	163	43	24	88	380 (0·96)
AE										
A	12	14	4	30 (0·47)	5	27	11	5	35	83 (1·29)
B	13	16	1	30 (0·71)	2	33	6	4	16	61 (1·45)
C	14	22	1	37 (0·58)	3	18	5	21	22	69 (1·08)
Total	39	52	6	97 (0·57)	10	78	22	30	73	213 (1·25)
EE										
I	15	15	0	30 (0·89)	1	23	7	5	16	52 (1·54)
II	15	26	1	41 (0·58)	9	25	9	6	13	62 (0·87)
III	10	34	2	46 (0·98)	5	23	7	8	10	53 (1·13)
VII	13	21	4	38 (0·44)	38	47	28	4	28	145 (1·68)
VIII	7	10	0	17 (0·66)	0	25	6	0	4	35 (1·37)
Total	60	106	7	173 (0·66)	53	143	57	23	71	347 (1·32)

But there are other pronouns and kindred adjectives which are more popular in the Nicomachean treatise than in the Eudemian, and vice versa. Three Nicomachean favourites are *hekastos* (each), *toioutos* (such), and *tosoutos* (so big). Their distribution, book by book, is shown in Table 5.7. It will be seen that, taken together, these three expressions account for over 1 per cent of the *NE*, but only 0·57 per cent of the *AE* and 0·66 per cent of the *EE*. In the case of none of these words is there significant difference of frequency between the *EE* and the *AE*, but in the case of the group as a whole, and of *toioutos* considered singly, the differences between *NE* and *AE* show up on the test as significant at the 1-per-cent level. Table 5.7 also contains the figures for five words which are relatively more frequent in the *EE* than in the *NE* and which between them constitute 1·32 per cent of the *EE* text but only 0·96 per cent of the *NE* text. The frequency of this group—*allēlōn* (each other), *allos* (other), *ekeinos* (that), *enioi* (some), and *heteros* (the other)—in the *AE* is much closer to its frequency in the *EE* than to its frequency in the *NE*. The differences between the *AE* frequency and the *EE* frequency are non-significant in the case of every word except *allēlōn*: it is clear from a glance at the table that the discussion of the topic of friendship (in books 8 and 9 of the *NE* and book VII of the *EE*) causes a massive increase in the frequency of this pronoun. When we compare the individual expressions between the *NE* and the *AE* we find highly significant differences not only in the case of *allēlōn* but also in the case of *enioi* and *heteros*. It will be seen from the table that in the *NE* the figures for the Nicomachean group and the Eudemian group commonly approximate to each other; in the *EE* and the *AE* the Eudemian group in every book scores more heavily than the Nicomachean group, and in the treatises as a whole occurs at least twice as frequently as it.

Another pronoun which occurs significantly more frequently in the *NE* than in the other two treatises is the reflexive *heautou* (oneself): it is to be found eighty-three times in the *NE*, fourteen in the *AE*, and twenty-four in the *EE*. It has not been included in Table 5.7, however, since its between-books occurrence in the *NE* is even more irregular than that of *allēlōn*: forty-eight of its Nicomachean occurrences occur in the single book 9.

Words concerned with multitude and magnitude, wholes, parts, and shares form a group which repays study in the ethical treatises. Though the commonest word for 'all', which comes in two forms, *pās* and *hapās*, does not tell us anything of interest—there are no significant differences between the frequency of either of these forms, or in the relationship between them, from treatise to treatise—many other words in the group are favourittes of one or other treatise. The *Eudemian Ethics* is more interested in wholes and parts,[1] as is shown by the figures for occurrences of the word for 'whole' (*holos*) and of two words for 'part' (*meros, morion*):

	NE	AE	EE
ὅλος	40	38	35
μέρος	12	28	14
μόριον	8	10	17
Total	60 (=0·15%)	76 (=0·45%)	66 (=0·25%)

This interest, it will be seen, is shared in an exaggerated form by the *AE*, which in respect of these words as a group differs significantly from both the other treatises. The *Nicomachean Ethics* has a liking for two words to do with parts and sharing (*koinos*, 'common', and *loipos*, 'rest', for which the figures are respectively: *NE* 48, *AE* 12, *EE* 21; *NE* 39, *AE* 3, *EE* 2); but has a more general preference for words to do with multitude (such as *oligos*, 'few', and *polys*, 'many') and magnitude (such as *pleiōn* and *pleistos*, the comparative and superlative of *polys*; and *mikros*, 'small', and its comparative *elattōn* and superlative *elachistos*). The figure for occurrences of these words are as follows. *Megas* ('great') with its comparative and

	NE	AE	EE
ὀλίγος	27	3	8
πολύς	145	26	76
πλιωνρπλεῖστος	75	33	39
μικρός	56	3	21
ἐλάττωνρελάχισπος	27	31	17
Total	330 (=0·83%)	96 (=0·56%)	161 (=0·61%)

superlative is also a Nicomachean favourite, but it will be more convenient to consider it later in a different context.

---

1. See above, p. 66.

THE DEFINITE ARTICLE

One might expect in advance that if any word at all displayed regularity within the work of an author, it would be the definite article, so colourless and so topic-neutral. When we compare the use of the different cases of the article in the three ethical treatises, this expectation is not fulfilled. Between the *EE* and the *AE* we find statistically significant differences between the frequencies for two of the cases of the article, the masculine dative singular $t\bar{o}(i)$ and the masculine nominative plural *hoi*. Between the *NE* and the *AE* we find statistically significant differences in seven cases (the frequencies for *ho*, $h\bar{e}$, *to*, *hoi*, *tous*, *tois*, and *tais*). But the most striking feature which differentiates the use of the article in the *NE* from its use in the *EE* is the much greater preference which the latter has for the singular forms. The figures below give the proportion (per cent) of each book constituted by (a) singular forms of the article, (b) plural forms of the article, (c) the sum-total of both singular and plural forms.

Book	*NE* 1	*NE* 2	*NE* 3	*NE* 4	*NE* 8	*NE* 9	*NE* 10
Sing.	7·26	9·31	7·51	8·32	7·86	7·96	8·14
Plur.	5·71	5·00	5·82	4·47	5·46	5·05	5·97
Total	12·97	14·31	13·33	12·79	13·32	13·01	14·11

Book	*EE* I	*EE* II	*EE* III	*EE* VII	*EE* VIII
Sing.	9·25	9·54	8·73	9·98	7·97
Plur.	5·41	3·62	4·92	3·78	3·20
Total	14·66	13·16	13·65	13·76	11·17

It will be seen that four out of five of the Eudemian books have a proportion of singular forms of the article of more than 8·5 per cent. Only one of the Nicomachean books, *NE* 2, whose similarity to the Eudemian books has several times been remarked, has a score in excess of this. If we take the plural forms, only the first of the Eudemian books has a score of more than 5 per cent here; all except book 4 of the Nicomachean treatise score over 5 per cent. Here, as so often, the disputed books display the Eudemian features in an accentuated form. The figures for these books are as follows:

Book	*AE* A	*AE* B	*AE* C
Sing.	10·90	9·31	9·37
Plur.	2·72	4·10	4·04
Total	13·61	13·41	13·41

Altogether, the proportion of all occurrences of the article constituted by singular forms is 59·7 per cent in the *NE*, 69·5 per cent in the *EE*, and 75·7 per cent in the *AE*.

GROUPING INDICATOR WORDS

The words which we have so far studied amount to some 53 per cent of the entire treatises. In each treatise, roughly 25 per cent consists of particles and connectives, 6 per cent of prepositions, 9 per cent of adverbs, pronouns, and similar words, and 13 per cent of the definite article. In respect of every feature so far in which there was a significant difference between Nicomachean and Eudemian usage the common books resembled the Eudemian pattern more than the Nicomachean. Undeniably the results so far presented amount to a substantial argument in favour of assigning these disputed books to an original Eudemian context.

However, there are two ways in which the case so far presented has been incomplete. In the first place, many of the vocabulary habits studied in the present chapter have been too irregular to form the basis of any rigorous statistical argument. From time to time a test has been used to determine which frequency differences were significant and which were not. This procedure in the present context is useful as a rough discriminator: but the result of the test can only be regarded as giving an accurate measure of the probability of a difference in frequency being the result of chance if the data in question conform to the conditions of simple sampling. In chapter 4 a chi-squared test was undertaken to ensure that this condition was met, and it was found that in the case of the majority of particles studied it was indeed satisfied. In the present chapter no such test has been undertaken: but it is obvious to the naked eye when we study the book-by-book occurrences of several of the expressions that more than chance fluctuations occur between one book and another. It would be desirable to find a procedure which would enable us to tighten up the statistical argument from one treatise to another.

In the second place, even the most powerful argument to show that, considered as a single unit, or even book by book, the *Aristotelian Ethics* belong with the *Eudemian* would be insufficient to settle the age-long scholarly dispute about the origin of the common books. For, as has been remarked, many scholars favour a solution which sees the common books as made up of different strata from different periods, forming a patchwork. At the end of chapter 4 we considered the occurrence of particles in each of seventeen 1000-word samples of the *AE*: the results were interesting in that they showed no trace of patchwork composition; but in the case of many particles the frequencies were too small for complete confidence to be placed in the result. It would be desirable to employ a method of studying the small samples which would generalize the inquiry to include words occurring even less frequently than particles, while enabling firmer statistical conclusions to be drawn.

We can achieve both these results if we take words together in groups and count not the occurrence of single words, but the occurrence of a group, the occurrence of any word in the group counting as an occurrence of the group. To serve our purposes, a group must satisfy two conditions. First, the group must be one which is characteristic either of the *Nicomachean* or the *Eudemian Ethics*: it must consist in general of words which are either Nicomachean favourites or Eudemian favourites; and the occurrence of the group as a whole must be substantially more frequent in one of the treatises than in the other. If this is not so, the occurrence of the group within the *AE* will be useless as a discriminator and will yield no information about its likely original context. Secondly, the group must be one which occurs frequently enough in the treatise of which it is characteristic to enable us to make a reliable prediction of its occurrence in any randomly selected 1000-word sample of material homogeneous with that treatise. If this is not so, it will be impossible to tell, when the actual occurrence in the sample differs from the expectation derived from one of the rival contexts, whether this is due to a genuine difference of style or merely to a chance sampling fluctuation.

We can ensure that our groups satisfy the former condition by calculating, for each word and group a *distinctiveness ratio*.[1] In the

---

1. The notion of distinctiveness ratio is adapted from Ellegård, 1962, 20 ff.

present context, the D.R. of an expression is the ratio of its frequency in one treatise to its frequency in the other. Let us express the D.R. of an expression occurring in the ethical treatises as its Nicomachean frequency divided by its Eudemian frequency. Thus, a word which occurs more frequently in the *Nicomachean Ethics* will have a D.R. greater than unity, a Eudemian favourite will have one between one and zero, and a word which is used with the same relative frequency in each will have a D.R. of one.

We may expect the D.R. of many words, in two treatises by the same author, to be very close to one: words with such a D.R. will obviously be useless as discriminators. For our purposes we must look for words, or groups of words, whose D.R. is some distance from unity—say more than 1·4 or less than 0·7; words, in other words, which occur about three times or more in one treatise for every twice they occur in the other. When we group words, it is not necessary that every word in the group should have a marked D.R., but it is important that the group as a whole should have: that is, that the occurrence of a-word-from-the-group should be a considerably more frequent event in one treatise than in the other.

To ensure that our group enables predictions to be made of its occurrence in samples as small as 1000 words it is necessary to insist on a minimum absolute frequency as well as a characteristic relative frequency. In practice, we need groups which will enable us to predict an absolute occurrence of not less than ten in each sample of 1000 words. Since the *Nicomachean Ethics* is 39525 words long, this means that we can make predictions based on Nicomachean frequencies of 400 and above: for if a word or group occurs 400 times in a text of about 40000 words it can be expected to occur ten times in a 1000-word sample homogeneous with it. The *Eudemian Ethics* is 26330 words long, and so for predictions based on Eudemian frequencies we need words or groups occurring at least 260 times in the *EE*.

We shall look, therefore, for groups of words with the following characteristics. A group should be either a Nicomachean favourite group with at least 400 occurrences in the *NE* and a distinctiveness ratio of at least 1·4; or it should be a Eudemian favourite group with at least 260 occurrences in the *EE* and a D.R. of less than 0·7. On the basis of the Nicomachean favourite groups we can calculate a Nicomachean expectation for each of our seventeen samples of the *AE*, and on the basis of the Eudemian favourite groups we can calculate a Eudemian expectation. By comparing the expected number of occurrences of each group in each case with the actual occurrences, we can determine for each sample in turn whether it resembles the *Nicomachean Ethics* more than the *Eudemian*. Any substantial patching, say, of an original Eudemian text with Nicomachean material should display itself in a fluctuation between one sample and another in respect of comparative resemblance.

It turns out that it is possible, from the data that we have already recorded, to assemble six Nicomachean and six Eudemian groups answering to these specifications. The first Nicomachean group is formed by taking together five particles popular in the *NE*: *dē*, *eiper*, *kathaper*, *hothen*, and *oun*. Taken as a whole the group has a D.R. of 2·00 and occurs 587 times in the *NE*, so that words from the group could be expected to occur 14·85, i.e. fifteen times, in a 1000-word sample homogeneous with the *NE*. The second group consists of the single preposition *en*, with a D.R. of 1·44 and a total of 482 occurrences in the *NE*. The third group has already been studied as a group: the qualifying adverbs *hēkista*, *hētton*, *hikanōs*, *līan*, *mallon*, *malista*, *pany* occur altogether 418 times in the *NE*, and the group as a whole has a D.R. of 1·93. Even more distinctive is the group of expressions of tentativeness already studied: *isōs*, *dokei*, *doxeie*, *eoike*, *phainetai*. This group occurs 404 times and has a D.R. of 2·37. Three Nicomachean favourite pronouns and demonstratives—*hekastos*, *toioutos*, and *tosoutos*—form another group with a D.R. of 1·56 and 407 occurrences in the *NE*. The final Nicomachean group is made by putting together the two Nicomachean favourites *koinos* and *loipos* with the 'multitude and magnitude' group of *oligos* with *mikros* and *polys* and their comparatives and superlatives. This group has a total occurrence in the *NE* of 417 and a D.R. of 1·51.

The six Eudemian groups are made up as follows. The conjunction *alla* is popular enough to constitute a group on its own, with 311 occurrences in the *EE* and a D.R. of 0·54. The two connectives *dio* and *hoti* form a group occurring 263 times with a D.R. of 0·58. A third group can be made up from three more Eudemian connectives, *hōsper*, *hōste*, and *epei*: this highly character-istic group has a D.R. of 0·38 and occurs 279 times in the *EE*. We have already seen that *anagkē*, *dēlon*, and *phaneron* form a characteristically Eudemian set of expressions, but as they make up only 0·48 per cent of the Eudemian text they are not by themselves

TABLE 5.8 *Nicomachean Favourites in Seventeen Samples of the AE: Part One*

Group	NE total	D.R.	Expectation in 1000	Actual occurrences in samples																	Mean actual occurrences
				1	2	3	4	5	6	7	8	9	10	11	12	13	14	15	16	17	
N I (*dē, eiper kathaper, hothen oun*)	587	2·00	14·85	8	8	10	7	7	7	19	9	9	10	12	10	10	12	8	10	12	9·9
N II (*en*)	482	1·44	12·19	10	20	5	6	5	9	11	6	4	5	7	6	3	6	6	2	5	6·8
N III (*hēkista, hēton, hikanōs, līan, māllon, malista, pany*)	418	1·93	10·58	3	2	2	2	1	5	2	1	5	3	4	3	3	6	3	6	2	3·2
N IV (*isōs, dokei, doxeie, eoike, phainetai*)	404	2·37	10·22	9	2	2	2	1	4	2	3	5	4	2	2	1	2	4	3	8	3·2
N V (*hekastos, toioutos, tos-outos*)	407	1·56	10·30	4	3	6	8	2	5	2	7	9	8	7	7	11	2	8	5	1	5·5
N VI (*oligos, polys, pleōn, mikros,* etc., *koinos, loipos*)	417	1·51	10·55	8	20	12	12	5	6	5	2	5	2	2	0	2	8	7	7	3	6·2
Total N I–VI	2715		68·69	42	55	37	37	21	36	41	28	37	32	34	27	30	36	36	33	31	34·8

TABLE 5.9 *Eudemian Favourites in Seventeen Samples of the AE: Part One*

Group	EE total	D.R.	Expectation in 1000	Actual occurrences in samples																	Mean actual occurrences
				1	2	3	4	5	6	7	8	9	10	11	12	13	14	15	16	17	
E I (*alla*)	311	0·54	11·81	13	11	7	15	17	18	10	8	15	8	14	16	15	7	11	13	13	13·8
E II (*hoti, dio*)	263	0·58	9·99	15	3	11	13	6	11	8	13	17	8	15	7	8	13	4	15	10	9·8
E III (*hōsper, hōste, epei*)	279	0·38	10·60	6	8	11	8	12	9	5	13	8	8	10	8	13	16	20	15	12	11·4
E IV (*anagkē, dēlon, phaneron, monon, haplōs, mentoi, toinun*)	256	0·30	9·72	14	12	5	13	10	13	6	7	12	4	6	9	13	16	7	11	5	9·6
E V (*aneu, heneka, para+acc. peri+gen. hama*)	267	0·48	10·14	9	6	2	7	16	10	13	14	13	16	17	12	16	6	9	5	6	10·8
E VI (*ekeinos, heteros, allos enioi, allēlōn*)	380	0·73	14·43	17	12	16	17	10	11	12	23	10	9	13	13	12	8	8	13	6	12·4
Total E I–VI	1756		66·69	74	62	52	73	71	72	54	79	75	51	75	65	67	66	59	72	52	65·8

frequent enough to make up one of our test groups. The group remains too small if we add to it the 0·38 per cent of the text made up by the characteristically Eudemian adverbs *haplōs* and *monon*. We may add further two particles, *mentoi* and *toinun*, which we saw in chapter 4 to be Eudemian favourites. This brings our group to a total of 256 occurrences, near enough to 260 occurrences to predict an expectation in 1000 words approximating to ten. The D.R. of the group so formed is 0·30: it is thus an extremely characteristic Eudemian group. For the next group we take four prepositions popular in the *EE*—*aneu*, *heneka*, *para* with the accusative, and *peri* with the genitive—and add to them the popular adverb *hama*. This gives us a group with D.R. 0·48 which occurs 267 times in the *EE*. The pronouns and pronominal adjectives which we noticed earlier as characteristic of the *EE*—*allēlōn*, *allos*, *ekeinos*, *enioi*, *heteros*—will make up a sixth and final group, as they occur in total no less than 380 times. But the group is not as distinctive as the others, with a D.R. as high as 0·73.

Table 5.8 compares the expected frequency per 1000 words of the Nicomachean groups with the actual frequencies in the seventeen approximately 1000-word samples of the *AE*, and Table 5.9 compares the expected frequency of the Eudemian favourites with the actual occurrences in the same samples. The final line of each table gives the mean occurrence per sample. As in the case of the particles studied in the seventeen samples in chapter 4, the results are strikingly uniform in their tendency. In none of the samples does the actual occurrence of the Nicomachean indicator words reach higher than 80 per cent of the Nicomachean expectation; in most of them the actual occurrence is about half the expectation, and the mean is exactly 0·51 of the expectation. If we turn to the Eudemian favourites we find that in nine of the sixteen samples the actual occurrence surpasses the Eudemian expectation; and the mean of the actual occurrences is 0·99 of the expectation. In every single sample the Eudemian expectation is approximated better than the Nicomachean one: once again there is no sign of patchwork. Indeed, even in the case of the Nicomachean favourites the actual occurrences in the seventeen samples are closer to the expectation which would be derived from the Eudemian use of the same expressions than to the Nicomachean expectations. This can be seen in the following list:

Group	I	II	III	IV	V	VI
N-Exp.	14·85	12·19	10·58	10·22	10·30	10·55
E-Exp.	7·42	8·47	5·48	4·30	6·60	6·99
Actual mean	9·9	6·8	3·2	3·2	5·5	6·2

But of course the Eudemian frequency of these words (which *ex hypothesi* are much rarer in the *EE* than in the *NE*) is not as accurate an indicator of the frequency to be expected in the *AE* if that is homogeneous with the *EE* as the Nicomachean frequency is of the frequency to be expected in the *AE* if that is homogeneous with the *NE*. In the case of these groups, therefore, the failure to meet the *NE* expectation is of greater moment than the degree of approximation to the *EE* expectation.

The grouping procedure we have adopted goes some way to remedy the incompleteness of the statistical argument hitherto. Grouping words helps to smooth out the fluctuations of individual words from book to book of a treatise and to approximate the conditions of simple sampling; the greater frequency of group occurrences in comparison with word occurrences also means that the underlying binomial distribution approximates more closely to the normal distribution presupposed by the most easily employable significance tests. The grouping also means that we are able to apply the large amount of information about vocabulary frequency available from the comparatively lengthy texts of the *NE* and *EE* to small portions of the *AE* no larger than 1000 words in length. We shall see in chapter 6 how this procedure can be carried even further.

The particular groupings adopted have been to a considerable extent arbitrary. It is important that the reader should appreciate that this does not affect the validity of the statistical procedure adopted. The application of statistical techniques to vocabulary choice is based on the fact that the choice of a word-token in a text can be considered as a binomial event which can have one of two outcomes: either the word-token in question is an instance of a word-category or it is not. For the statistical techniques to be applicable what is necessary is that it should be unambiguously decidable whether the token falls under the category or not. But it is no more difficult to decide whether a given token, say the seventeenth word in the second of the disputed books, is a token of *either* of the types *hoti* or *dio* than to decide whether it is a token of the type *hoti*; and indeed a decision whether a word-token counts as an occurrence of one of our groups is exactly the same kind of decision as the decision whether it is an instance of the lexicon-word-type *logos* (i.e. is it *logos*, or *logon*, or *logou*, etc.). The argument could have proceeded in the same way if we had made our groups of 400 Nicomachean occurrences, or 260 Eudemian occurrences, out of words sharing a common distinctiveness ratio, or a common initial letter. The grouping has been chosen to reflect incidentally certain features of the *NE* and *EE* other than their statistical relationships—attention has been drawn, for instance, to the fondness of the *NE* for adverbs of degree and expressions of tentativeness. The judgement that the *NE* is more tentative than the *EE* is, of course, one that goes beyond the merely statistical evidence: it involves judgements—as the statistical data do not—on the *meaning* of the words being counted. The reader will be able to evaluate for himself such judgements in the light of the data and of his knowledge of Greek; but the judgements could all be mistaken, and the groupings totally incongruous, while leaving unaffected the statistical argument to the effect that the *AE* resembles the *EE* much more than it does the *NE*.[1]

1. The grouping procedure is an adaptation of that to be found in Ellegård, 1962. My method differs from his principally in that I have adapted the notion of distinctiveness ratio so that it fits a problem of determining between two rival contexts for a text, rather than a problem of assigning a text to one of an indeterminate number of authors, and in that I have grouped my words on the basis of syntactical and semantical criteria rather than on the basis of D.R.

CHAPTER 6

The Use of Technical Terms
in the Ethical Treatises

Most of the words studied so far have been ones which are comparatively little affected by changes in subject matter: function words which are likely to occur with comparative frequency whatever the topic of discussion. Few words are completely unaffected by changes of topic: at the end of chapter 5, for instance, it could be seen from Table 5.8 that words such as 'more' and 'less' occur with more than their usual frequency when justice is the subject being considered. And in philosophy above all, no word is completely topic-neutral; for even the most colourless words such as 'if' and 'therefore' may themselves provide the topic of discussion. But in comparison with most nouns, verbs, and adjectives the words we have studied suffer little fluctuation due to subject matter.

In the present chapter we shall turn to the remainder of the vocabulary of the ethical treatises to see what information it can yield about the original context of the disputed books. We can no longer hope to be able to trace regularities which continue from book to book with only sampling variations: the best we can aim to do is to detect the influence of stylistic preferences in fluctuations which are the resultant not only of style but principally of topic. We cannot aim to locate the origin of the *AE* by asking whether there is one of its rival contexts which it differs from only in statistically insignificant ways: we must expect it to differ significantly from each of the *NE* and *EE* and it will be only from the comparative magnitude of the differences that we may hope to draw any conclusions. Given that the topics treated in the *AE* differ from those treated in the *NE* and *EE* more than these do from each other, we may well expect that the *NE* and *EE* will resemble each other more than either of them resembles the *AE*. But, as before, we shall be on the look-out for words in which the *NE* and *EE* do not closely resemble each other, words with a high distinctiveness ratio. For any such comparison to be meaningful we shall need words which, though not topic-neutral, are not connected exclusively with topics which are treated *only* in the *AE*, or *only* in the *NE* and *EE*. We shall therefore not consider names of particular virtues and vices, as such, nor words for the cluster of concepts surrounding friendship (discussed only in *NE* and *EE*), nor the names of the intellectual characteristics listed in *AE* B, nor the like. We shall discuss words connected with the topics which to a greater or lesser extent run through all three of the treatises: verbs of saying and thinking; logical, metaphysical, and psychological technical terms of Aristotle's philosophy; general evaluative expressions and words linked with pervasive ethical concepts rather than particular ethical topics. The borderline between usable and unusable material will not be a sharp one, and arbitrary decisions of exclusion or inclusion will have to be taken from time to time. Fortunately, as will be seen, such arbitrary decisions are unlikely to have affected the over-all outcome.

VERBS OF SAYING

The commonest verbs of saying in the ethical treatises are *lego*, *phēmi*, and the available tenses of *erō* and *eipon*. The figures for these verbs are:

	NE		*AE*		*EE*	
	Occur-rences	Propor-tion %	Occur-rences	Propor-tion %	Occur-rences	Propor-tion %
λέγω	189	0·48	97	0·57	149	0·57
φημί	44	0·11	46	0·27	54	0·21
ἐρῶ	103	0·26	32	0·19	43	0·16
εἶπον	36	0·09	17	0·10	22	0·08
Total	372	0·94	192	1·13	268	1·02

It will be seen that verbs of saying, as a whole, are more popular in the *EE* than in the *NE*, and more popular again in the *EE*: but these differences do not appear to be significant. What is significant is the greater frequency of *phēmi* in the *AE* and *EE* than in the *NE*: this comes out both absolutely (where the difference between the *AE* and the *NE* is highly significant by our test) and relatively to the other verbs of saying (*phēmi* makes up only 12 per cent of the verbs of saying in the *NE* as against 20 per cent in the *EE* and 24 per cent in the *AE*). Like *phēmi*, *lego* is both absolutely and relatively more popular in the *EE* than in the *NE* (56 per cent in the *EE* vs. 51 per cent in the *NE*); while both *erō* and *eipon* are both absolutely and relatively more popular in the *NE* than in the *EE* (making up between them 38 per cent as against 24 per cent). In the case of *erō* the *AE* approximates more closely to the *EE* frequency, and in the case of *eipon* to the *NE* frequency; but in neither of these cases are the differences, considered in isolation, significant. If we turn to particular forms of the verbs, we find that *legetai* is an *EE* favourite (frequency 0·13 vs. 0·08 per cent in the *NE*) whereas *eirētai* is an *NE* favourite (0·15 vs. 0·09 per cent). The *AE* goes with the *NE* in respect of *legetai* (0·08 per cent), with the *EE* in respect of *eirētai* (0·08 per cent). In neither case are the differences significant.

LOGICAL TERMINOLOGY

Scholars have often remarked that the *EE* is 'more logical' than the *NE*. To verify this one may construct a list of logical terms, Aristotelian technicalities, and investigate whether their occurrence is more frequent in the *EE* than in the *NE*. Table 6.1 sets out the results of such an inquiry. It will be seen that the twenty-two logical terms and their cognates which are listed in the table occur more than twice as frequently in the *EE* as in the *NE*, amounting in the *EE* to about an eightieth of the entire text. The frequency of these logical technical terms is even higher in the *AE*, where about one word in every sixty-five is a term of logic from the list. Part of the high frequency in the *AE* is no doubt due to the fact that the second of the three books of the *AE* deals with the intellectual virtues; but the results shown in the table cannot be explained simply as the result of variations in subject matter. If that were so, the frequencies in the *NE* and the *EE* should resemble each other in contrast to the *EE*. In fact, in spite of the difference in subject matter between the *AE* and the *EE*, we have once again a situation in which the difference in over-all frequency between the *AE* and *EE* is not significant by our test, whereas the differences between either of them and the *NE* are highly significant.

Five other words which are too homespun to be called logical technicalities, but which occur frequently in logical contexts,

TABLE 6.1 *Logical Terms in the* NE, AE, *and* EE

	NE	AE	EE
ἀκριβής, ἀκρίβεια	10	3	5
ἀμφισβητέω, ἀμφισβήτησις	11	5	11
ἀναλογία, ἀνάλογος	9	27	16
ἀναλυτικά	0	2	3
ἀντίκειμαι, ἀντιτίθημι, ἀντίθεσις	17	8	7
ἀποδείκνυμι, ἀπόδειξις, δείκνυμι	6	16	15
ἀπορέω, ἀπορία, διαπορέω	24	13	23
ἀποφάναι, ἀπόφασις, κατάφασις, φάσις	6	11	4
ἀφορίζω, διορίζω, ὁρίζω, προσδιορίζω	41	20	37
διαιρέω, διαίρεσις	9	8	20
ἐλέγχω, ἔλεγχος	1	1	2
ἐπαγωγή	1	3	3
ἐναντίος, ἐναντιόω, ὑπεναντίος, ὑπεναντιόω	37	29	74
καθόλου	12	22	9
λογίζεσθαι, λογισμός	6	10	25
λύω, λύσις	0	6	3
μεταφέρω, μεταφορά	2	4	5
ὁμώνυμος, συνώνυμος	1	3	2
πολλαχῶς etc. λέγεσθαι	3	5	7
συλλογισμός, πρότασις, συμπεραίνειν, ὅρος	2	40	37
τίθημι, ὑποτίθημι, ὑπόθεσις	28	10	25
ὑπολαμβάνειν, ὑπόληψις	10	15	5
Totals	236 (=0·60%)	261 (=1·53%)	338 (=1·28%)

display the same pattern. They are *alēthēs* (with *alētheia*), *orthos* (with *orthotēs*), *logos*, and *pseudēs* (with *pseudos* and *diapseudesthai*), and *onoma*. Here again we have a substantially greater frequency in the *EE* than in the *NE* for the group as a whole, and a frequency in the *AE* greater than either; but here for the group as a whole, and for *orthos* in particular, the *AE* frequencies are significantly different from either of the other treatises.

	NE		AE		EE	
	Occur-rence	Propor-tion %	Occur-rence	Propor-tion %	Occur-rence	Propor-tion %
ἀληθής	41	0·10	31	0·18	33	0·13
λόγος	106	0·29	84	0·49	107	0·41
ὄνομα	7	0·02	18	0·11	8	0·03
ὀρθός	33	0·08	49	0·29	30	0·11
ψευδής	7	0·02	10	0·06	5	0·02
Total	194	0·49	192	1·13	183	0·70

METAPHYSICAL TERMS

We may turn from logical technicalities to the technical expressions of Aristotelian metaphysics. Table 6.2 sets out the figures, book by book, for words expressive of eight fundamental concepts which contribute to the construction of the metaphysical framework of the ethical treatises. It will be seen that four of the expressions, or groups of expressions, are Nicomachcan favourites, and four are Eudemian favourites. The notion of *becoming*, expressed in the noun *genesis* and the verb *ginomai*, is twice as prevalent in the *NE*, where these expressions form 0·70 per cent of the text, as in the *EE* where they form only 0·28 per cent. (In the *AE* these expressions form 0·40 per cent.) The Aristotelian technical terms for *operation* or *actuality*, the noun *energeia* and the cognate verb *energein*, are likewise favourites of the *NE*, with a frequency there of 0·33 per cent against 0·10 per cent in the *AE* and 0·13 per cent in the *EE*. Two other notions which occur much more frequently in the *NE* are those of *perfection* (expressed by the adjective *teleios* and the verb *teleioō*) and that of something's being *naturally proper* (*oikeios*) to something else. It will be seen that there is a considerable fluctuation from one book to another of the *NE*, and two books of the *NE* (3 and 4) score less highly in respect of this group than the highest-scoring book of the *EE* (II). The fluctuation cannot be due entirely to subject matter, since the highest-scoring *EE* book has very much the same subject matter as the two lowest-scoring *NE* books. If we take the figures for the treatises as a whole, we find that in every case a test shows the differences between the

TABLE 6.2 *Metaphysical Technical Terms in Individual Books of the NE, AE, and EE*

Book	1 γένεσις γίνομαι	2 ἐνέργεια ἐνεργέω	3 οἰκεῖος	4 τέλειος τελειόω	5 Total 1–4 (+ proportion %)	6 ἀρχή ἄρχω	7 ἐνδέχομαι	8 συμβαίνω	9 φύσις φυσικός	10 Total 6–9 (+ proportion %)
NE										
I	26	28	8	21	81 (1·44)	12	5	9	8	34 (0·60)
2	42	6	0	1	48 (1·13)	2	1	2	11	16 (0·28)
3	31	7	1	1	40 (0·63)	20	0	4	15	39 (0·62)
4	17	1	5	0	23 (0·39)	2	0	3	0	5 (0·08)
8	58	4	8	3	73 (1·25)	24	5	7	8	42 (0·72)
9	52	16	14	0	82 (1·55)	8	7	10	12	37 (0·70)
10	50	70	21	32	173 (2·78)	5	6	8	11	30 (0·48)
Total	276	132	57	58	523 (1·32)	73	24	43	65	205 (0·52)
AE										
A	23	1	2	5	31 (0·48)	19	9	16	18	62 (0·96)
B	18	1	2	0	21 (0·50)	27	23	2	12	64 (1·53)
C	26	15	0	4	45 (0·70)	10	5	19	43	77 (1·20)
Total	67	17	4	9	97 (0·57)	56	37	37	73	203 (1·19)
EE										
I	12	0	5	0	17 (0·50)	5	4	5	11	25 (0·74)
II	27	17	1	5	50 (0·70)	29	11	11	27	78 (1·10)
III	7	0	0	0	7 (0·15)	4	0	7	9	22 (0·47)
VII	26	14	6	2	48 (0·55)	28	18	17	29	92 (1·07)
VIII	2	2	0	1	5 (0·15)	17	3	4	28	52 (2·03)
Total	71	33	12	8	127 (0·42)	83	26	44	104	267 (1·01)

EE and the *AE* to be non-significant, and those between the *NE* and
the *AE* significant. But any conclusions to be drawn from this must
be drawn in the light of the marked between-books fluctuation.

The first Eudemian favourite is the notion of *principle*, expressed
by the noun *archē* and its cognate verb *archō*. These expressions

TABLE 6.3 *Scattergram of Occurrences of Metaphysical Technical Terms in*
NE *and* AE

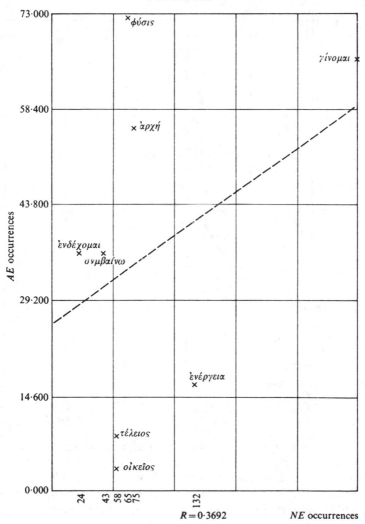

$R = 0.3692$ NE occurrences

TABLE 6.4 *Scattergram of Occurrences of Metaphysical Technical Terms in*
EE *and* AE

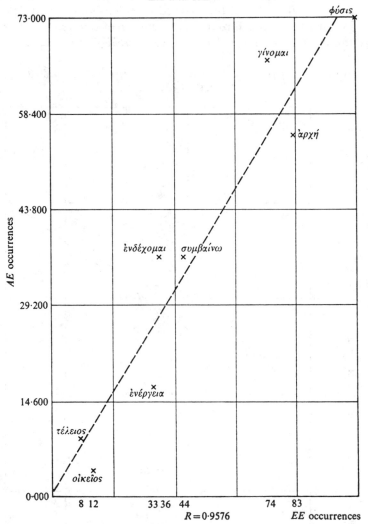

occur with a frequency between them of 0·32 per cent in the *EE*,
and approximately the same frequency (0·33 per cent) in the *AE*;
they are just over half as frequent (0·18 per cent) in the *NE*. The *EE*
is fond of two words to express contingency, *endechesthai* (which
often occurs in the context of, or as an abbreviation for, the

expression *endechesthai allōs echein,* to be capable of being otherwise) and *sumbainein* (which occurs frequently in the form *kata sumbebēkos,* meaning *per accidens*). Finally the *EE* is much more interested than in the *NE* in the notion of *nature*: the words *physis* and *physikon* occur in the *EE* with a frequency of 0·39 per cent, in the *NE* with only 0·16 per cent. In the *AE* they occur at a rate of 0·43 per cent, a frequency higher, but not significantly so, than in the *EE*. Once again there is a considerable variation from book to book, one book of the *EE* scoring less than 0·50 per cent for this group while four books of the *NE* score above that figure.[1]

Table 6.3 shows the result of plotting the *AE* scores for each of these words against the *NE* scores: the correlation, it will be seen, is very low, 0·3692. Table 6.4 shows the result of plotting the *AE* scores against the *EE* scores: the correlation this time is high, *r* being 0·9576.

Other metaphysical technical terms, such as 'potentiality', *dynamis,* plus *dynamai,* and *dynaton* (*NE* 76 = 0·19 per cent, *AE* 41 = 0·24 per cent, *EE* 59 = 0·22 per cent) and 'function', *ergon* (*NE* 63 = 0·15 per cent, *AE* 16 = 0·09 per cent, *EE* 45 = 0·17 per cent) are not sufficiently distinctive of one or other treatise to serve as discriminators.

PSYCHOLOGICAL TERMS

In the realm of psychology as in metaphysics we can identify Nicomachean and Eudemian favourite expressions. There are two verbs for 'think'—*axioō* and *oiomai*—that are more frequent in the *Eudemian Ethics*: the figures are *NE* 20, *AE* 0, *EE* 29 and *NE* 18, *AE* 24, *EE* 32 respectively. But it is with affective, rather than cognitive terms, that we see a distinct pattern of preferences emerging. Table 6.5 sets out the occurrences in each book of three Nicomachean and five Eudemian sets of expressions relating to affective states and attitudes. *Haireomai,* 'choose' and its verbal adjective *hairetos* are more popular in the *NE*; whereas the more technical word for 'choice', *prohaireomai,* with the adjective

---

1. The one constant feature of Table 6.3 is that for every book of the *NE*, the frequency for the *NE* favourites is higher than that for the *EE* favourites; while for every book of the *EE* and for every book of the *AE* the frequency for the *EE* favourites is higher than that of the *NE* favourites. This constancy is all the more striking given the violent fluctuations which the table displays otherwise.

TABLE 6.5 Expressions for Volitional States in Individual Books of the NE, AE, and EE

Book	1 αἱρέομαι αἱρετός	2 ἐφίεμαι	3 ἥδομαι	4 χαίρω	5 Total 1–4 (+ proportion %)	6 βουλεύω βούλευσις	7 ἐπιθυμέω ἐπιθυμία	8 θυμός	9 ὀρέγομαι ὄρεξις	10 προαιρέομαι προαίρεσις	11 Total 6–10 (+ proportion %)
NE											
1	15	5	1	2	23 (0·41)	0	0	1	3	6	10 (0·18)
2	2	0	1	5	8 (0·19)	0	3	1	2	4	10 (0·24)
3	15	1	4	18	38 (0·60)	22	29	18	9	37	115 (1·82)
4	3	4	3	2	12 (0·20)	0	1	1	3	3	8 (0·13)
8	4	11	1	16	32 (0·55)	0	0	0	6	5	11 (0·19)
9	24	6	7	5	42 (0·79)	0	3	0	6	3	12 (0·23)
10	31	8	12	9	60 (0·96)	0	2	0	5	5	12 (0·19)
Total	94	35	29	57	215 (0·54)	22	38	21	34	63	178 (0·45)
AE											
A	5	0	0	0	5 (0·08)	0	1	3	1	11	16 (0·25)
B	4	0	0	0	4 (0·09)	22	0	0	8	10	40 (0·95)
C	13	0	2	11	26 (0·41)	5	33	16	2	19	75 (1·12)
Total	22	0	2	11	35 (0·21)	27	34	19	11	40	131 (0·77)
EE											
I	4	3	0	1	8 (0·24)	0	1	0	1	2	4 (0·12)
II	3	0	0	5	8 (0·11)	27	30	15	19	62	153 (2·16)
III	2	0	1	7	10 (0·21)	0	4	12	0	2	18 (0·39)
VII	28	0	0	9	31 (0·36)	0	13	0	14	13	40 (0·46)
VIII	2	0	0	0	2 (0·08)	5	8	0	4	2	19 (0·74)
Total	39	3	1	22	58 (0·22)	32	56	27	38	81	215 (0·82)

prohairetos and the noun *prohairesis*, is preferred in the *EE*. The verb *bouleuō* with its cognates, closely connected in sense with *prohaireomai*, is also commoner in the *EE* than in the *NE*. For 'want', as a general verb of appetition, *ephiesthai* is common in the *NE*, *oregomai* in the *EE*. (The commonest verb for 'want', *boulomai*, is slightly more frequent in the *EE*—the proportions are *NE* 0·24, *AE* 0·08, *EE* 0·27 per cent for the word and its cognates—but the *NE* and *EE* frequencies are too close to make it worth including in the table.) The words *thymos* and *epithymia*, with the verb *epithymein*, words for the two lower parts of the Platonic tripartite soul and their functions of anger and sensual desire, are considerably commoner in the *EE* than in the *NE*. Two verbs for taking pleasure, *hēdesthai* and *chairein*, are popular in the *NE*. Once again there is considerable fluctuation due to subject matter: in both the *NE* and the *EE* the majority of the occurrences of the Eudemian favourites occur in the books in which *prohairesis* is being explicitly discussed; but again differences due to subject matter are combined with differences due to vocabulary preference: both within the *prohairesis* book itself, and in the other books taken separately, the Eudemian frequency of the Eudemian favourites is much higher. Taking the groups as a whole and the works as a whole, it will be seen that as usual the *AE* frequencies are close to the *EE* ones and distant from the *NE* ones. For the Nicomachean group the *EE* frequency is 0·22 per cent and the *AE* frequency is 0·21 per cent: in each case less than half the *NE* frequency of 0·54 per cent. For the Eudemian group the *EE* frequency is 0·82 per cent and the *AE* frequency is 0·77 per cent: in each case much higher than the *NE* frequency of 0·45 per cent.

One psychological term which is much more frequent in the *EE* than in the *NE* is the word 'soul' itself: *psychē*. The figures here are *NE* thirty-one (0·08 per cent), *EE* fifty-five (0·21 per cent). In respect of this word the *AE* resembles the *NE* rather than the *EE*, with fourteen occurrences (0·08 per cent).

TECHNICAL TERMS OF ETHICS

Several of the technical terms of Aristotle's ethics, such as the names of particular virtues and vices, are useless for our inquiry since their occurrences are virtually confined to single locations in the treatises. There are, however, a number of terms which occur in a variety of contexts in whose use we can detect Eudemian and

Nicomachean preferences. Seven such Eudemian favourites are
listed as follows:

	NE		AE		EE	
	Occur-rences	Propor-tion %	Occur-rences	Propor-tion %	Occur-rences	Propor-tion %
αἴτιος (inc. αἰτία)	35	0·09	8	0·05	63	0·24
βία, βίαιον	12	0·03	3	0·02	47	0·18
ἕξις	59	0·15	57	0·33	64	0·24
ἑκών	11	0·03	30	0·18	25	0·10
ἑκούσιον	42	0·11	24	0·14	45	0·17
ἀκών	11	0·03	8	0·05	11	0·04
ἀκούσιον	21	0·05	11	0·06	23	0·09
Total	191	0·48	141	0·83	278	1·06

It will be seen that taken together the words of this group occur
twice in the *EE* for every once in the *NE*. The rate in the *AE*, for the
words as a group, is between the two and closer to the *EE*; but for
certain words taken individually, such as *aitios* and *bia*, there are for
once striking differences between the *AE* and the *EE*.

Besides these Eudemian favourites, there are some ethical
concepts whose expressions are more frequent in the *Nicomachean
Ethics*. The notion of a life, or way of life, expressed by the noun *bios*
and the verb *bioō*, is much more Nicomachean than Eudemian; and
the notion of happiness, though obviously pervasive in both ethics,
finds expression in the adjectives *eudaimōn* and *makarios* with its
cognates, and in the noun *eudaimonia*, more than twice as often in
the *NE* than in the *EE*. For the three treatises we have:

	NE		AE		EE	
	Occur-rences	Propor-tion %	Occur-rences	Propor-tion %	Occur-rences	Propor-tion %
βίος etc.	75	0·19	5	0·03	10	0·04
εὐδαίμων etc.	100	0·25	14	0·08	38	0·14
μακάριος etc.	37	0·09	1	0·01	4	0·02
Total	212	0·54	20	0·12	52	0·20

Here again we see a combination of the effects of subject matter and of vocabulary preference: but even so, by our test the differences between *AE* and *EE* are insignificant, those between *AE* and *NE* significant.

Another group of Nicomachean-favoured ethical terms are terms for excess and defect, prominent in discussions of the theory of the mean:

	NE		AE		EE	
	Occur-rences	Propor-tion %	Occur-rences	Propor-tion %	Occur-rences	Propor-tion %
ἐλλείπω,—ψις	74	0·19	12	0·07	28	0·11
ὑπερβάλλω,—βολή	97	0·25	34	0·20	38	0·14
ὑπερέχω,—οχή	29	0·07	8	0·05	21	0·08
Total	200	0·51	54	0·31	87	0·33

Though terms for excess in general are more frequent in the *NE*, the *EE* is fonder than the *NE* is of expressing excess by *hyperochē* rather than *hyperbolē*. The differences between the *NE* and the *AE* for *elleipō* and *elleipsis* and for the group as a whole are significant; none of the other differences is. Two verbs of obligation, *deō* and *opheilō*, make a final group of Nicomachean ethical favourites: *deō* (*NE* 274, *AE* 75, *EE* 128) has a D.R. of 1·43 and *opheilō* (*NE* 21, *AE* 0, *EE* 4) has a D.R. of 3·5.

EVALUATIVE EXPRESSIONS

Besides words which have a more or less technical role in ethics, the ethical treatises are naturally rich also in common evaluative expressions, words which with varying nuances are more or less equivalent to the word 'good' with its adverb, comparatives, and superlatives. It is interesting to study the use of the common word for 'good', *agathos*, and its adverb 'well', *eu*, and its various comparative and superlative forms, *kreittōn* and *kratistos*, *ameinōn* and *aristos*, *beltiōn* and *beltistos*; with it one can study the words '*epieikēs*', '*kalos*', '*spoudaios*', which have technical meanings in particular contexts but can also be used as general pro-words. The results of studying in each book the use of these words—along with

TABLE 6.6 *Evaluative Expressions in Individual Books of the NE, AE, and EE*

Book	1 ἐπιεικής	2 εὖ	3 καλός κάλλος	4 κρείττων κράτιστος	5 σπουδαῖος	6 σύμφερος ὠφέλιμος	7 Total 1-6 (+ proportion %)	8 ἀγαθός	9 ἀμείνων ἄριστος	10 βελτίων βέλτιστος	11 χρήσιμος	12 Total 8-11 (+ proportion %)
NE												
I	1	13	31	2	8	1	56 (0·99)	69	12	12	4	97 (1·72)
2	0	26	4	0	5	3	38 (0·90)	15	3	3	0	21 (0·50)
3	2	2	35	4	4	1	48 (0·76)	18	5	1	1	25 (0·39)
4	10	13	29	0	1	4	57 (0·96)	13	4	4	1	22 (0·34)
8	9	11	10	1	2	18	51 (0·86)	81	6	3	31	121 (2·08)
9	21	16	34	2	18	6	97 (1·83)	43	3	6	6	61 (1·15)
10	13	3	30	13	11	1	71 (1·14)	30	13	9	9	53 (0·85)
Total	56	84	173	22	49	34	418 (1·05)	269	46	38	47	400 (1·01)
AE												
A	22	2	2	4	5	6	43 (0·67)	22	3	5	0	30 (0·46)
B	5	12	7	0	5	5	34 (0·81)	15	3	3	2	23 (0·55)
C	2	0	5	2	12	0	21 (0·33)	31	5	10	0	46 (0·74)
Total	29	14	16	6	22	11	98 (0·58)	68	11	18	2	110 (0·65)
EE												
I	1	7	22	4	0	1	35	63	14	2	4	83
II	0	7	5	1	7	1	21	16	15	28	0	59
III	3	3	13	2	1	1	23	10	2	10	2	24
VII	5	24	9	0	14	7	39	94	2	7	50	143
VIII	0	6	24	3	1	1	35	34	3	1	0	38
Total	9	47	73	10	23	11	153 (0·50)	217	36	48	56	357 (1·35)

three words for instrumental goodbess, or utility, *sympheron,
ōphelimon, chrēsimon*—are shown in Table 6.6. Once again clear
Nicomachean and Eudemian preferences emerge; but for once the
AE does not completely share the preferences of the *EE*. It
continues to resemble the *EE* more than the *NE*, the coefficient of
correlation between the *EE* and *AE* usage being 0·8185 as against

TABLE 6.7 *Scattergram of Occurrences of Evaluative Expressions in the* EE
and AE

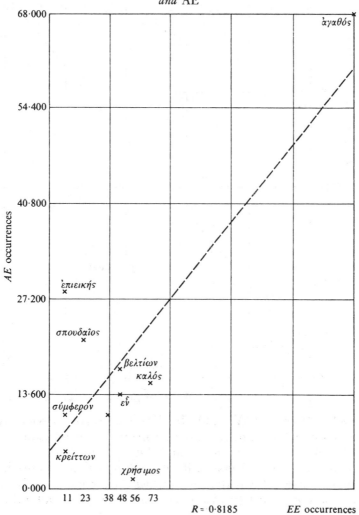

R = 0·8185   EE occurrences

TABLE 6.8 *Scattergram of Occurrences of Evaluative Expressions in the NE and AE*

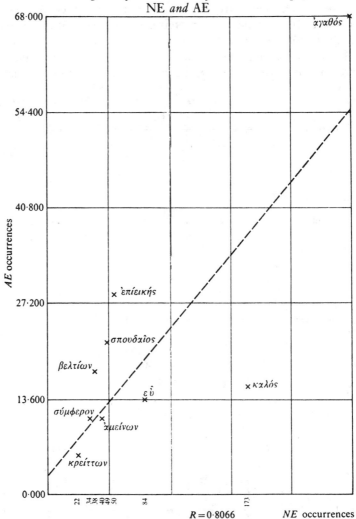

$R = 0.8066$ *NE* occurrences

0·8066 between the *NE* and *AE*, but it does not correlate very highly with either. The result of plotting the *AE* uses against each of the other treatises is shown in Tables 6.7 and 6.8.

In this group of expressions it will be seen that the Nicomachean favourites follow the pattern with which we are now familiar: the *NE* stands on its own (with a proportion of 1·05 per cent for the six groups of expressions) while the *AE* and the *EE* are very close together (0·58 per cent each)—and this despite the fluctuation in the frequency of *epieikēs* due to the fact that while normally it is something of a synonym for *agathos* it is used in the first common book, and there alone, in a special technical sense. But with the Eudemian favourites the pattern is unusual: the words are much more frequent in both the *NE* and *EE* than in the *AE*, and the *AE* is closer to the *NE* than to the *EE*.

GLORY AND THE FAMILY

If we search through word lists of the *NE* and *EE*, looking for words with a high distinctiveness ratio, two rather surprising and interesting groups of Nicomachean favourites emerge. We discover that the *Nicomachean Ethics* has a consistently higher score first in words which concern glory, honour, praise, and their converses humiliation, shame, and blame, and secondly in words for family relationships and for youth and age. *Aischros*, 'shameful', with the compounds formed from it, is a Nicomachean favourite, as is *geloion*, 'ridiculous', and the verb *psegō*, 'blame', with its adjective *psektos*. So, on the other hand is the verb *epainein*, 'to praise', with its adjective *epainetos*, and the noun *timē*, 'honour', with its cognate verb *timān* and adjective *timios*. The *NE* is also fond of the adjective *megas*, 'great', with its comparatives *meizōn* and *megistos* and of compounds formed from the root *megal* such as *megalopsychos* and *megaloprepēs*. The figures for the treatises are:

	NE		AE		EE	
	Occur-rences	Propor-tion %	Occur-rences	Propor-tion %	Occur-rences	Propor-tion %
αἰσχρός etc.	53	0·13	7	0·04	9	0·03
γέλοιος	17	0·04	0	0·00	5	0·02
ἐπαινέω etc.	64	0·16	7	0·04	31	0·12
μέγας, μεγαλ-	156	0·39	6	0·04	80	0·30
τιμή etc.	92	0·23	11	0·06	19	0·07
ψέγω etc.	24	0·06	8	0·05	12	0·05
Total	406	1·03	39	0·23	165	0·63

Here the *EE* frequency for the group is just under two-thirds that for the *NE*; the *AE* is significantly less than either the *NE* or the *EE*.

If we take a group of words referring to youth vs. age and family relationships—*adelphos*, 'brother', *goneis* 'parents', *neos* 'youth', *pais* and its cognates, 'child' and 'childish', and *patēr and patrikos*, 'father' and 'paternal', *uios*, 'son', *teknon*, 'child', and *mētēr*, 'mother', we again find that the group as a whole is substantially more frequent in the *NE* than in either of the other two treatises. The group occurs 129 times in the *NE* (0·33 per cent), 28 times in the *AE* (0·16 per cent), and 53 times in the *EE* (0·20 per cent).

TESTING GROUPS OF INDICATOR WORDS AGAINST SMALL SAMPLES

In respect of the words studied in the present chapter, as in the earlier ones, the *AE* as a whole resembles the *EE* much more than the *NE*; though the considerable book-to-book fluctuation within the *EE* and the *NE* makes the results more difficult to interpret than in chapters 4 and 5 above. We may now try to apply the findings of the present chapter, as we applied the findings of chapters 4 and 5, to small samples of the *AE* to see whether the material we have been studying allows us to detect any sign of piecemeal construction or stratification within the *AE*.

The first step, as before, is to attempt to construct groups of words with a sufficiently high frequency and a sufficiently marked distinctiveness ratio. If we consider first Nicomachean groups, we find that the Nicomachean favourite metaphysical terms provide a group of 523 words with a D.R. of 2·74, and the Nicomachean favourite ethical terms (happiness-words plus excess-and-defect words) a group of 412 words with a D.R. of 2·13. The Nicomachean evaluative words occur 418 times in the *NE* and have a distinctiveness ratio of 1·82: they will form a third suitable group. A fourth group can be made up of the 'glory' words (406 occurrences, with a D.R. of 1·64); to make a fifth group we can take the 'family' words (145) and the 'obligation' words *deo* and *opheilo* (295 occurrences) to make a group of 440 with a D.R. of 1·53. The Nicomachean psychological words (215 occurrences) are not sufficiently numerous to make a group: we can, however, add them to some other assorted Nicomachean favourites to make a final,

Group	NE total	D.R.	Expecta-tion in 1000	1	2	3	4	5	6	7	8	9	10	11	12	13	14	15	16	17	Mean actual occur-rences
										Actual occurrences in samples											
N VII (*genesis* etc., *en-ergein* etc., *oikeios*, *te-leios* etc.)	523	2·74	13·23	8	5	9	3	3	1	8	3	4	4	6	6	2	1	0	20	10	5·47
N VIII (*bios* etc., *euda-imōn* etc., *elleipō* etc., *uperballō* etc., *uperecō* etc.)	412	2·13	10·42	1	0	9	9	0	4	4	2	0	3	2	0	8	7	2	60	20	4·53
N IX (*eu* etc., *epieikēs* etc., *kalon* etc., *kreitton* etc., *spoudaios* etc., *sympheron*, *ōphelimon*)	418	1·82	10·58	5	3	2	4	4	22	2	8	13	13	3	2	3	1	5	3	5	5·76
N X (*aischros*, *geloios*, *epainos*, etc., *megas* etc., *timē* etc., *psego* etc.)	406	1·64	10·27	2	1	3	4	0	4	2	1	3	1	5	2	8	6	1	1	1	2·65
N XI (*adelphos*, *goneus*, *neos*, *pais*, *patēr*, *huios*, *mētēr*, *teknon*, *deō*, *opheilō*)	440	1·53	11·13	1	1	20	3	5	2	6	2	14	6	5	8	9	6	7	3	5	6·06
N XII (*erō*, *eipon*, *dia-phero*, *homoiōs*, *chronos*, *rhadios*, *haireomai*, etc., *ephiesthai* etc., *hēdes-thai*, *chairein*)	611	1·67	15·46	8	10	3	18	10	11	6	6	7	4	3	10	12	10	7	12	10	9·12
Total *N* VII–XII	2810		71·09	25	20	46	41	22	44	28	22	41	31	24	28	42	31	22	45	51	33·12

TABLE 6.10 *Eudemian Favourites in Seventeen Samples of the AE: Part Two*

Group	EE total	D.R.	Expectation in 1000	1	2	3	4	5	6	7	8	9	10	11	12	13	14	15	16	17	Mean actual occurrences
E VII (legō, phēmi, oio-mai, axioō)	271	0·68	10·29	10	4	8	4	9	4	10	10	7	14	16	14	17	10	5	10	11	9·53
E VIII (logos etc., enantion, aporeō etc., diaireō etc., orthos)	279	0·51	10·59	8	7	2	1	4	10	22	14	17	10	21	17	6	7	26	5	6	10·94
E IX (archē etc., endechesthai, symbainein, physis etc.)	267	0·51	10·14	3	3	6	22	18	6	23	25	3	11	10	6	12	8	10	20	19	12·06
E X (psychē, bouleuō, etc., thymos, epithymia, oregesthai, prohai-reomai, etc.)	270	0·64	10·25	1	0	0	3	10	1	22	4	17	6	4	10	13	30	12	7	1	8·29
E XI (aitios etc., bia etc., hexis, hekōn etc., akōn etc.)	278	0·45	10·55	6	9	5	6	28	10	8	12	2	6	7	4	2	4	2	10	5	7·4
E XII (agathos, ameinōn, etc., beltiōn etc., chrēsimon)	357	0·75	13·55	10	5	1	4	1	7	2	4	4	9	7	3	3	1	3	20	15	5·82
Total E VII–XII	1722		65·40	38	28	22	40	70	38	87	69	50	56	65	54	53	60	58	72	57	53·94

rag-bag group. Into this bag we can throw the two Nicomachean verbs of saying, *ero* and *eipon* (139 occurrences), and four other words which the *NE* specially favours: (a) *diaphero* and *diaphora*, *NE* 92, *AE* 20, *EE* 30; (b) *homoios*, *NE* 94, *AE* 29, *EE* 50; (c) *chronos*, *NE* 40, *AE* 5, *EE* 12; (d) *radios*, *NE* 31, *AE* 5, *EE* 8. This will give us a total group with 611 occurrences and a D.R. of 1·67.

Six Eudemian groups can be constructed to match these six Nicomachean groups. The first is provided by the Eudemian verbs of saying, *lego* and *phemi*, plus the Eudemian verbs of thinking, *oiomai* and *axioo*: these give a group with 271 occurrences and a D.R. of 0·68. From the logical and quasi-logical words we can select the occurrences of *logos*, *logismos*, and its verb, *enantion*, *aporeo* and its cognates, *diaireo*, and *orthos*: this will make up a group with a total of 279 occurrences in the *EE*, and a D.R. of 0·51. The Eudemian metaphysical terms give a group with an occurrence of 267 and a D.R. of 0·51; if we add *psyche* to the volitional terms we get a group of psychological terms occurring 270 times with a D.R. of 0·64. The Eudemian ethical terms occur 278 times, and make a group with a D.R. of 0·45; the evaluative ones 357 times with a D.R. of 0·75.

Armed with these twelve groups, we can set out to record their occurrences in each of the seventeen samples of the *AE* with which we are familiar from chapters 4 and 5. The outcome of this exercise can be seen in Tables 6.9 and 6.10. It will be seen that once again the overwhelming impression is of a greater similarity with the *EE* than with the *NE*. In none of the samples does the actual occurrence of the Nicomachean indicator words reach more than 72 per cent of the Nicomachean expectation; in most of them the actual occurrence is less than half the expectation, and the mean is only 0·47 of the expectation. In all but two of the samples, on the other hand, the actual occurrence of the Eudemian favourites is above 58 per cent of the Eudemian expectation and in four cases the Eudemian expectation is exceeded. The mean of the actual occurrences is 0·83 of the expectation. However, in the case of these groups VII–XII, unlike the groups studied earlier, the influence of subject matter occasionally triumphs over stylistic preference. While in fifteen out of the seventeen cases the Eudemian expectation is approximated by the sample better than the Nicomachean expectation, in two cases the Nicomachean expectation is better approximated. In each case, the reason is not far to seek: in the case of sample 3 (which reaches 56 per cent of the *N*-expectation, but only 34 per cent of the Eudemian) the high Nicomachean score is due to the twenty occurrences of the verb *deō* in the discussion of corrective justice and reciprocity. In the case of sample 6, where the actual occurrences reach 62 per cent of the *N*-expectation but only 58 per cent of the *E*-expectation, the explanation is to be found in the technical use of *epieikēs* in the discussion of equity, which boosts the score for *N*-group-IX to twenty-two. This latter anomaly in fact is the result of the greater similarity of the *AE* to the *EE*: in the *AE* and the *EE* the use of *epieikēs* as a synonym for 'good' is rare, because of the reservation of the term for the technical use in *AE* A. That is why *epieikēs* appears as an *N*-favourite and yet is common in sample 6, where the technical sense is discussed. Thus, the two anomalies reveal the limits of the comparatively crude vocabulary tests applied rather than any genuine Nicomachean element in the samples of the disputed books. Allowing for discrepancies due to particular subject matters (the high score of *NE*-group-XII in samples 16 and 17, for instance, is due to pleasure being there the topic of discussion) the over-all picture remains as before, of general similarity between the *AE* and the *EE*. There is no support for the patchwork theory: the two sections which approximate the *NE* expectation better than the *EE* expectation are not places which scholars on other grounds have regarded as particularly Nicomachean, and in each case if the scores of the groups I–VI (see above, pp. 132–3) are added to the scores of groups VII–XII the sections emerge as over all closer to the *EE* expectation.

We may conclude our stylometric examination, therefore, with the verdict that the overwhelming weight of the evidence suggests that the common books are more at home in the context of the *Eudemian Ethics* than in the context of the *Nicomachean Ethics*. Our twelve groups of Nicomachean favourites and our twelve groups of Eudemian favourites have provided twenty-four independent tests to apply to the disputed books. Twenty-three out of these twenty-four independent tests give an unambiguous answer that the common books, considered as a whole, resemble the *EE* more than the *NE*.[1] When we take the twenty-four tests together and apply

---

1. Only the twelfth of the Eudemian groups suggests otherwise. Here the actual occurrence in the *AE* reaches only 43 per cent of the Eudemian expectation. This failure can only partly be explained through considerations of subject matter.

them as a group to each of the seventeen 1000-word samples of the *AE*, they indicate in the case of each individual sample that it is closer to the *EE* than to the *NE*. None of our tests gives any support to the theory that the *AE* is a patchwork of mixed Eudemian and Nicomachean material. The conclusions of these test-groups are confirmed by those of other vocabulary tests (such as the study of the singular and plural forms of the definite article) which are independent of the vocabulary elements which contributed to the groups constituting the twenty-four tests.

Since our tests have covered some 60 per cent of the total vocabulary of the ethical treatises, it is inconceivable that their results should be overturned by further study of the vocabulary. Since they have been restricted to vocabulary, they leave open the possibility that further information about the relationship of the *AE* to the *EE* and the *NE* may be obtained by the study of syntax: but it is in the highest degree improbable that the over-all picture, of a close resemblance between the *AE* and the *EE*, and a much more distant relationship between the *AE* and the *NE*, should be seriously disturbed by further stylistic investigation, however sophisticated.[1] The most plausible and economical explanation of

1. One stylistic test was carried out which does not depend on vocabulary counting: a test of the syntactic category of last words of sentences. Michaelson and Morton have suggested (1970, 192 ff.) that a study of the last words of sentences (defined as portions of text terminating with a period, colon, or question-mark) enables samples from different authors to be discriminated. (For a criticism of this view, see Johnson, 1973, 92 ff.) For this test, sentences in Aristotle were divided into three classes: those ending in a noun, those ending in a verb, and those ending in some other part of speech. Each book of each of the ethical treatises was then run off against each other to see whether the differences between them, as a whole and pairwise, were statistically significant, the chi-squared test being used to determine statistical significance. It turns out that Aristotle differs from other Greek authors who have been studied in this manner in that an unusually high proportion of his sentences end in parts of speech other than nouns or verbs. The application of the test to the ethical writings give the following results: Differences between individual books of the *EE* are non-significant (12·57 for 8 degrees of freedom). Differences between the books of the *AE* are non-significant at the 1-per-cent level (chi-squared 11·82 for 4 degrees). The differences between the *AE* taken as a whole and the *EE* taken as a whole are non-significant (0·73 for 2 degrees). The differences between the *AE* and the *NE* however are statistically highly significant: chi-squared is 30·25 for 2 degrees of freedom. It is difficult to know how to interpret these results, however, for it turns out that in respect of this feature the *NE* itself is highly inconsistent: taking the seven books of it together chi-squared for 12 degrees of freedom is 72·28. This inconsistency is caused by books 4 and 9: if these two books are removed the remainder of the *NE* is internally consistent and differs only in a statistically non-significant way from the *AE* and the *EE*. I know of no other reason for regarding books 4 and 9 as standing apart from the rest of the *NE*. Both books differ in this respect markedly from a test-block of 6687 sentences drawn from a number of Aristotelian works in various fields. For an account of the application of the last-word test to the entire Aristotelian corpus, see Kenny, 1977.

the evidence assembled in the last three chapters is that the common books of the *AE*, just as they now stand, belonged originally to the *Eudemian Ethics*. Having established this high probability on the grounds of statistical stylistics as well as of external historical evidence, we must now turn to the evidence provided on the topic by the philosophical content of the treatises.

CHAPTER 7

Wisdom in the
Aristotelian Ethics

In the half-century since the publication of Werner Jaeger's *Aristotle* it has been almost universally accepted by scholars that the *Eudemian Ethics* represents an early stage and the *Nicomachean Ethics* a late stage in the development of Aristotle's ethical theory. Jaeger's theory of development was based in large part on a change which he claimed to detect between the two ethics in Aristotle's use of the term *phronēsis*. In the *EE phronēsis* was used, he claimed, in the Platonic sense of a speculative, philosophical wisdom, uniting ethics and metaphysics; in the *NE* the term refers to practical wisdom, and is sharply and explicitly contrasted with *sophia* or philosophical wisdom. The difference between the two is explained by the development in Aristotle's thought from a Platonizing idealist ethic to a more empirical and pragmatic moral theory.

The contrast which Jaeger drew between *phronēsis* in the *EE* and in the *NE* was in reality a contrast between *phronēsis* in the *EE* and in the *AE*: his account of the nature of *phronēsis* in the *NE* rested almost entirely on the description of that virtue in the disputed book B. The theory of a development, so far as concerns the *phronēsis* argument, rests heavily on the assumption that the disputed books are Nicomachean: an assumption which Jaeger himself did almost nothing to defend, mentioning it only in an inadequate afterthought footnote. Given that we have shown that there are strong stylistic reasons for regarding the disputed books, as they stand, as belonging with the *Eudemian Ethics*, it would be possible to argue with as much justification as Jaeger that this *Ethics*, containing as it does the developed theory of *phronēsis*, must be the work of the later, mature Aristotle. Instead, we shall proceed more cautiously, and study separately the *phronēsis*-theory of each of the three treatises: we shall compare that of the *NE* and that of the *EE* in turn with that of the *AE*, and ask what contrasts can be drawn between the *NE* theory and the *EE* theory, and which of the two fits better with that of the *EE*. We shall not, in fact, attempt to draw from this comparison any positive conclusion about the relative chronology of the treatises: for rightly understood the data do not permit the drawing of any such conclusions.

Jaeger's contrast between the sense of *phronēsis* in the *EE* and *NE* has been severely criticized by scholars a number of times—notably by Margueritte, Gadamer, and Léonard. These criticisms have gained widespread acceptance, especially since being canonized in the commentary of Gauthier and Jolif.[1] None the less, it is worth while to look afresh at the concept of *phronēsis* in the ethics, since even those who have discarded Jaeger's view on this point frequently continue to accept his general theory of the development of ethical theory in Aristotle, and his assumption that the disputed book B is Nicomachean. Thus Rowe, in his monograph *The Eudemian and Nicomachean Ethics*, while admitting 'the kernel of Jaeger's discussion of the ethics, his account of the history of the term *phronēsis* . . . has been shown conclusively to rest on a misinterpretation of the texts', goes on to argue at length that

there is no sharp distinction between ethics and the theoretical sciences in *EE* . . . the practical and theoretical tend to merge into one another; and this is reflected in the close relation envisaged between speculative and practical thinking. But in *NE*, the distinction between the two spheres is complete. Ethics and the theoretical sciences no longer have anything in common, since their subject matters are now established as being totally different in kind. Correspondingly, the rational faculty is now divided into two; the *phronēsis* of *EE* becomes the *aretē* of one half, and *sophia* is appropriated for that of the other.

He goes on to conclude 'in principle, Jaeger's view of Aristotle's development was right' (op. cit. 11, 70–3).

Like Jaeger, Rowe regards the disputed book B as Nicomachean; he regards indeed all the disputed books as being Nicomachean as they stand: books A and C, he thinks, are based on and supersede lost Eudemian parallels, but B, he thinks, was cut from whole cloth for the *NE*. As with Jaeger, so with Rowe, there seems a certain

---

1. 'Une meilleure intelligence de la "*phronēsis*" de l'Ethique à Nicomaque . . . jointe à une meilleure compréhension de l'évolution doctrinale d'Aristote et à une connaissance plus exacte de la chronologie de son oeuvre . . . achève ainsi de ruiner l'hypothèse de Jaeger sur l'évolution du concept de *phronēsis* entre l'Ethique a Eudème et l'Éthique à Nicomaque : ici et là, c'est la même sagesse, pratique mais normative, que désigne le mot de *phronēsis*' (1959, ii, 469).

circularity in the argument for the Nicomachean context. First, a contrast between the *NE* and the *EE* is built up on the assumption that B belongs with the *NE*; then we are told that the original home of B must have been the *NE* because it fits the doctrine of the *NE* better than that of the *EE*.

The whole of VI is built up on the distinction between *phronēsis*, the *aretē* of the deliberative faculty, and *sophia*, the *aretē* of the contemplative; and since *EE* actually merges deliberative and contemplative thought, VI cannot have been intended for it, unless we suppose that Aristotle took up two opposing positions in the same work (p. 109).

Supposing we grant, for the moment, that the *EE* does not distinguish between deliberative and contemplative thought with the clarity that B does: even, so, before concluding that B belongs with the *NE*, ought not we to inquire whether the *NE*, *outside the disputed books*, makes the distinction made in B? Otherwise, may not the situation be that neither the *NE* nor the *EE* contains the fully worked out theory of *phronēsis*; and for the simple reason that in whichever of them B originally belonged, B was the place chosen for the full working out of the concept? The only sound procedure is to study the theory of *AE* in its own right and compare with *NE* and *EE* in turn. This we shall now do.

The doctrine of the *AE*, and in particular of book B, concerning *phronēsis* can be summed up under four heads. (1) *Phronēsis* is an intellectual virtue concerned with the truth about mutable matters and the whole good of man. (2) *Phronēsis* is the virtue of a particular part of the rational soul, and is distinguished from other intellectual virtues by being deliberative rather than intuitive and practical rather than theoretical. (3) *Phronēsis* is indissolubly wedded to moral virtue, providing the right reasoning necessary for the exercise of virtue, and dependent on virtue for the correctness of its own starting-points. (4) The union of *phronēsis* and moral virtue is dependent on the pre-existence of certain natural qualities, intellectual and affective. Let us develop each of these points in turn, and compare the *AE* doctrine with that of its competing contexts.

(1) Phronēsis *as an intellectual virtue.* 'In classifying the excellences of the mind,' we are told at the beginning of book B, 'we said that some were of the moral character, and others of the intellect. Moral excellences we have discussed at length; let us now

discuss the others' (1139^{a}1–2, trans. Greenwood). The nature of the *aretē* of anything depends on the *ergon* of that thing: the *ergon* of every intellectual part is the production of true and false judgements (1139^{a}29). That, at least, is its *ergon* in the sense of its characteristic activity, its *ergon* whether it is working well or ill; its activity when it is working well, its good activity, and therefore its *ergon* in another sense, is truth alone (1139^{b}12). The intellectual virtues are then excellences which make an intellectual part of the soul come out with truth. There are five states of mind which have this effect—*technē, epistēmē, phronēsis, sophia, nous*, which we may translate as skill, knowledge, wisdom, learning, and understanding—and so five candidates for being intellectual virtues. Being truth-productive is a necessary but not a sufficient condition for being an intellectual *aretē*: skill fails to pass some of the other tests for being an *aretē* (1140^{b}22–4); the other four qualities remain as virtues, though not all independent of each other (1141^{a}2–8, ^{b}3–5; 1142^{a}26–31). *Phronēsis* is defined as a ratiocinative, truth-attaining quality concerning what is good for human beings (1140^{b}5, ^{b}21). The fact that it is ratiocinative, and has the particular subject matter it has, distinguishes it, as we shall see, from the other three intellectual virtues. Thus far the *AE*.

In the *NE*, too, we find that *phronēsis* is an intellectual virtue: it is listed as a paradigm of such at 1103^{a}6 when the distinction between moral and intellectual virtues is introduced. The relation between having an *aretē* and doing one's *ergon* well is also familiar in the *NE* (1098^{a}8 ff.; 1106^{a}17 ff.); but we are not told the particular *ergon* of the intellectual part of the soul. We are, however, told implicitly that *phronēsis* is ratiocinative—is concerned with a *logos*—since moral virtue is defined as consisting in the observation of a mean 'which is defined by a *logos* such as a wise man would use to determine it' (1107^{a}2). Since we learn from here, and from the final book (1178^{a}10), that it is wisdom which sets the standard for the moral virtues, we might well conclude that the subject matter of wisdom is the whole good of man; but this is not spelt out in the *NE* as it is in the *AE*, though we are of course told, right from the beginning, that there is a discipline called *politikē* which has human good as its subject matter (1094^{a}27). But the relationship between this and *phronēsis* is left obscure.

Let us now turn from the *NE* to the *EE*. Here we find that *phronēsis* is not given as an example of the intellectual virtues when these are first introduced (at 1220ᵃ4–14) and indeed it appears at 1221ᵃ12 in what looks like a list of moral virtues. But in every other respect the doctrine of the *AE* is to be found more clearly in the *EE* than in the *NE*. From the last book of the *EE* it is clear that *phronēsis is* an intellectual virtue: it is a virtue (1246ᵇ35) which is in the *logistikon* or ratiocinative part of the soul (1246ᵇ23); it is in the ruling part of the soul (1246ᵇ12) and it gives commands (*epitattei*, 1249ᵇ15). All this accords with the description of intellectual virtues as belonging to the rational part which *qua* rational is in command of the soul (*tou logon echontos ho epitaktikon esti tēs psychēs hē logon echei*, 1220ᵃ9). As in the *AE* and the *NE*, an *aretē* makes the *ergon* of its possessor good: as in the *AE*, the *ergon* in question is the production of truth. We are told at 1221ᵇ29 that there are *aretai* corresponding to different parts of the soul: the *aretai* of the rational part are the intellectual virtues 'whose *ergon* is truth, either about how things are, or about bringing into existence'.[1] The distinction between these two kinds of truth fits perfectly the distinction between the subject matter of *phronēsis* and *sophia* in book B: *sophia*, we are there told, unlike *phronēsis*, is not concerned with bringing into existence (*oudemias esti geneseōs*, 1143ᵇ20). *Phronēsis* is ratiocinative in the *EE*: 'It is clear that [lucky people] do not succeed by means of wisdom, because wisdom is not unreasoning but can give reason why it acts as it does' (1247ᵃ14). Finally we are told in the first book that the good which is the end of human action is the subject matter of the supreme discipline of *politikē kai oikonomikē kai phronēsis*. These three *hexeis*, we are told, are alike in this respect: how they differ will be explained later (1218ᵇ15). The forward reference well fits a passage in B, 1141ᵇ24 ff. There we are told that *politikē* and *phronēsis* are the same *hexis* with a different *einai*: different applications, we might say, of the same mental quality. Wisdom applied to one's own affairs is *phronēsis* in the narrow sense; wisdom applied to the affairs of the *polis* or to the affairs of one's household is *phronēsis* in a broad sense. *Politikē*, too, has broader and narrower senses: in the broadest sense it includes the wisdom of the legislator, of the executive, and of the judiciary; more especially the word applies to the two latter, and *par excellence politikē* is wisdom in executive decision (1141ᵇ30).

(2) Phronēsis *and other intellectual virtues*. In the *AE* one of the

---

1. ὧν ἔργον ἀλήθεια, ἢ περὶ τοῦ πῶς ἔχει, ἢ περὶ γενέσεως.

main functions of *phronēsis*, one of the characteristic activities of the *phronimos*, is deliberation, *bouleusis*: this is said not only in the *endoxon* which introduces the principal treatment of *phronēsis* (1140ª25 ff.) but also in the passage contrasting *phronēsis* with *sophia* (1141ᵇ9 ff.) and in the discussion of *euboulia* (1142ᵇ32).

Wisdom is concerned with human affairs and with matters that can be objects of deliberation. We regard good deliberation as the pre-eminent characteristic of the wise man, and no one deliberates about things that cannot be other than they are, or that are not directed to an end, a good attainable by action (1141ᵇ9–13).

It is because wisdom is concerned with things that can be other than they are that it is the virtue of a different part of the soul from *sophia* or learning, which is concerned with unchanging and eternal matters. Book B began with a distinction between two parts of the rational soul, based on the principle that like is known by like: the *logon echon* which was previously distinguished from the *alogon* is now divided into the *logistikon* (named from the sense of *logizesthai* in which it is equivalent to *bouleuesthai*, deliberate) and the *epistēmonikon* which is concerned with the eternal truths. Repeatedly we are told that each of these parts has its proper *aretē*: *sophia*, apparently, for the *epistēmonikon*, and *phronēsis* for the *logistikon* now also called *doxastikon* (1139ª16; 1140ᵇ26; 1143ᵇ15–17; 1144ª2–3; 1145ª4). The other intellectual virtues turn out to be parts of either *sophia* or *phronēsis*, and to be thus located in one or other of the soul-parts mentioned: there is no need to go beyond a bipartition of the rational soul. Thus, *sophia* consists of *nous* (of one kind) plus *epistēmē* (1141ᵇ3–4): these two, then, will be, appropriately enough, in the *epistēmonikon*. Similarly, *gnōmē*, *synesis*, and *nous* (of another kind) share the same subject matter as *phronēsis* (1143ª25–ᵇ6) and therefore inhere in the same part of the soul as it and seem not to be separable from it as a distinct virtue (compare 1143ª25 with 1143ᵇ15 ff.).

The psychology of the *AE*, and especially of B, is easy to reconcile with that of either the *NE* or the *EE*. Both of these work regularly with a tripartite soul: a vegetable element, an appetitive element, and a rational element. The vegetable element, whose *ergon* is nourishment and growth, is called in the last chapter of *NE* I and in the first chapter of *EE* II the *threptikon* (1102ᵇ11; 1219ᵇ22 and 38); the name *phytikon* is also used (*NE* 1102ª32; *EE* 1219ᵇ38, accepting Victorius' emendation of the manuscripts). Both treatises call this an irrational part of the soul (*NE* 1102ª32: *tou alogou to men*; *EE* 1219ᵇ32: *heterōs alogon morion*), and both of them dismiss it as irrelevant to ethics. The irrational part of the soul that is of importance is one which, unlike the *threptikon*, is under the control of reason: in the *NE* it is described as participating in reason but distinct from reason, fighting reason in the incontinent man, obeying reason in the continent man, and harmonizing with reason in the virtuous man (1102ᵇ14–1103ª2); in the *EE* too it is said to participate in reason, having by nature the power to obey and listen and to follow the rational part (1219ᵇ28–30; 1220ª9–11). In the *NE* this is introduced as part of the irrational soul, but we are later told that you can if you like call it rational, in which case there will be two rational elements (1103ª2); in the *EE*, on the other hand, it is introduced as a part of the rational soul (1219ᵇ28), but is then later described as an irrational part (1220ª10); but it is clear that there is no real difference here between the doctrines of the two treatises. In the *NE* it is also called the *epithymētikon kai holōs orektikon*: the part of the soul for desire and appetite (1102ᵇ30); and similarly in the *EE* the part which is ruled by reasoning is the part concerned with *orexeis kai pathēmata*, appetites and passions (1220ª1) and it is called *aisthetikon kai orektikon* (1219ᵇ22)—an anticipation of the name the scholastics gave it when codifying Aristotelian psychology, the 'sensitive appetite'. It is 'the part of the soul that is capable of following in accordance with prescriptive reasoning' (1220ᵇ5). In each of the treatises the ethical virtues are virtues of this part of the soul: we gather this in the *NE* from being told that the distinction between ethical and intellectual virtue is based on this distinction of parts of the soul; in the *EE* we are told explicitly that an *ēthos* is a quality of this part of the soul (1220ᵇ26) and the connection of this with the notion of *ēthikē aretē* via the concept of *pathos* or passion is spelt out at great length (1220ᵇ8–1221ᵇ38). The Aristotelian *alogon metechon logou* corresponds to the two lower parts of the tripartite soul of Plato's republic: the *epithymetikon* and the *thymoeides*. A trace of this Platonic anatomy of the soul can be found in the *NE* 3, at 1117ᵇ24, where it is said that bravery and temperance 'seem to be the virtues of the irrational parts'; this probably also gives us a clue why this part of the soul is called the *epithymetikon kai holōs orektikon* in the *NE*—the other *orexis* which Aristotle has in mind is *thymos*. In the *EE*, on the other hand, *orexis* is divided into three species: *epithymia*, *thymos*, and *boulēsis* (1223ᵃ27). The first two are no doubt the *hormai*, or drives, of the irrational part spoken of at 1247ᵇ9; *boulēsis*, on the other hand, which involves a judgement that something is good, is no doubt the same as the *hormai apo logismou* of 1247ᵇ19. Here too is the germ of a later scholastic faculty: the intellectual appetite or will.

Neither the *NE* nor the *EE* makes a distinction between two parts of the rational faculty with the clarity of the *AE*, and indeed both of them, when distinguishing between the rational and irrational part of the soul, describe the rational part in terms appropriate to the *logistikon* of book B rather than to the whole bipartite *logon echon* of that book: the *EE* says that it participates in reason by prescribing (*tō(i) epitattein*, 1219ᵇ30), the *NE* introduces it as what 'exhorts to the best' (1102ᵇ16). However, it is not difficult to insert the divided rational soul of B into the slot provided by the rational soul in the framework of the early books of the *NE* and the *EE*. In these early books, whichever set of them is rightly taken as leading on to B, Aristotle would merely be refraining, wisely, from introducing a greater number of technical divisions than he needs at a given stage of exposition. Whether the *AE* is taken as belonging with the *NE* or the *EE* we have the same didactic procedure as in Plato's *Republic*: a division of the soul into parts in a provisional manner, followed by a further division of the topmost part into sub-elements geared to different subject matters. (Compare *Republic* 439 d and 478 a.)

In the early books of the *NE* *sophia* appears from time to time alongside *phronēsis* (1098ᵇ24; 1103ᵃ5): whether it is used as a quasi-synonym, or to mark a contrast, and if so on what basis, is not clear. In the early books of the *EE* there are two hints of the distinction between *logistikon* and *epistēmonikon* made explicitly in B. The first is the passage at 1221ᵇ29 already cited where we are told that the output of the intellectual virtues is truth 'either about how things are or about bringing into existence': in terms of the psychology of B, truth about how things necessarily are would be the output of the *epistēmonikon*, and truth about bringing into existence would be that of the *logistikon*. The *logistikon* also could very well be referred to in *EE* 1226ᵇ25 by the expression *to bouleutikon tēs psuchēs*, which we are told is the one which studies the final cause or wherefore (*hou eneka*) of such things as walking; for when the *logistikon* is introduced in B we are told that *logizesthai* is equivalent to *bouleuesthai*; the *logistikon* is called also the *dianoētikon kai praktikon* (1139ᵃ29) and this term in its turn appears in B to be synonymous with *dianoia heneka tou kai praktikē* (1139ᵃ36). The *logistikon* is in B also called the *doxastikon* (1140ᵇ26); in an *obiter dictum* in the *EE* treatment of friendship also we learn that there is a special part of the soul for *doxa* (1235ᵇ29).

It is, however, the final books of the *NE* and *EE* that it is most instructive to compare with book B in respect of psychological terminology and theory. In *NE* 10 happiness is identified with activity in accordance with *sophia* (1179ᵃ32), and *sophia* is described as something which is related to philosophy as knowing is related to seeking (1177ᵃ24–6). This fits well the *sophia* of book B, which is illustrated by famous philosophers and which has as its subject matter divine, honourable, and useless things. As in B there is a contrast between learning and wisdom as between theory and practice, so in *NE* 10 we are told that the *sophos* can act in isolation, while *phronēsis* appears along with moral virtue as a component of a second-rate type of happiness which is essentially social (1177ᵃ31; 1178ᵃ16–22). But there is in addition to this resemblance between *AE* B and *NE* 10 a great difference. Whereas in B *sophia* is the virtue of a particular part of the soul, and there is no suggestion that the *epistēmonikon* is transcendent or immortal, in 10 *sophia* resides not in the soul but in the *nous*, which is divine, or the divinest thing in us; the life of *nous* is superhuman and is contrasted with that of the *syntheton* or body-soul compound; the moral virtues and *phronēsis* are virtues of this compound, but the *aretē* of *nous* is capable of separate existence (1177ᵃ14, ᵇ26–9; 78ᵃ14–20). Moreover, it is in this *nous* that we must see the essential human being (1178ᵃ2 ff.): a contrast with B, where a human being is defined as essentially a chooser (1139ᵇ5).

With an effort, it is no doubt possible to regard the *nous* of *NE* 10 as being none other than the *epistēmonikon* of *AE* B; and certainly the tension between the conception of human nature dominant in 10 and that of B can be found within 10 itself (compare 1177ᵇ27 with 1178ᵃ7). The fact remains that though B uses *nous* in a variety of senses, it never uses it in a way resembling that of 10.

Nous in B is often used, like and sometimes with *dianoia*, as a general word for the whole human intellectual apparatus, for the cognitive as opposed to the affective half of the mind. Thus in the second chapter of B we are told that the three things controlling

truth and conduct are perception, *nous*, and *orexis*, and man is
defined as appetitive *nous* (1139^a17, $^b5$). But commonly *nous* is a
name for an intellectual *hexis*: and close inspection of the text of B
reveals that there are four different intellectual conditions which
bear the name.

First, and most explicitly, *nous* is the grasp of the first principles
of theoretical science; the understanding of unproven necessary
truths which is the basis of *epistēmē* ($1140^b31-1141^a9$). Together
with *epistēmē*, we are told, this *nous* constitutes *sophia* (1141^a19).
But there is also another theoretical *nous*, which is concerned with
individuals and is a kind of perception (1143^b6): this is the kind of
understanding which we must have of a particular instance if we are
to grasp it *as* an instance of something general; the kind of vision
whereby we *see* that a triangle is the simplest figure into which more
complicated figures can be analysed (1142^a29). What makes it
appropriate to use the same name for the grasp of very general and
abstract principles and for the appreciation of features of an
instance or diagram before one's eyes? It is appropriate, Aristotle
would say, because in each case we are dealing with something
immediate and intuitive: in each case there is a contrast with proof
and reasoning.

Corresponding to these two types of theoretical *nous* there are
two types of practical *nous*. Such, at least, I take to be the message of
one of the most difficult passages in the whole of the *Ethics*,
1143^a35-^b4:

Nous is concerned with extremes in both directions: it is *nous* and not
reasoning whose objects are primary terms and ultimate particulars. There
is one *nous* of the unchangeable and primary terms in the realm of
demonstration, and another of the ultimate and contingent element, and of
the other premiss, in practical reasoning; for these are the principles of the
wherefore; for universals come from particulars, and for these you have to
have a perception which is *nous*.

It is common ground among commentators that in this passage
Aristotle is teaching that there is a practical form of *nous* which
corresponds to the particular *nous* on the speculative side. But in
claiming that there are here two forms of practical *nous*—one
corresponding to the general abstract *nous* of the speculative
faculty, as well as one corresponding to the particular *nous*—I am
departing from the majority of commentators. When Aristotle says

that there is a *nous* dealing with 'the other premiss in practical reasoning' (*en tais praktikais . . . tēs heteras protaseōs*) I take it that he means a *nous* dealing with the major premiss of practical reasoning, the premiss which contains reference to the end: this will correspond to the intuitive understanding of speculative axioms, since axioms in mathematical reasoning, play the same role as the wherefore, or *hou heneka*, in practical reasoning (*AE* C, 1151ᵃ17). The phrase I render as 'the other premiss' is commonly rendered 'the second premiss': most commentators take it that there is just one practical *nous*, concerned with the changeable particulars which are the topic of the minor premiss of a practical syllogism. This makes irrelevant the introductory sentence '*Nous* is concerned with extremes *in both directions*' and renders unintelligible the feminine plural *hautai* in the sentence '*these* are principles of the wherefore'. If we take it that Aristotle is saying that *nous* is concerned with both extremes in both realms, practical and theoretical, then all becomes clear: we have universal speculative *nous* (the *nous* '*kata tas apodeixeis ton akinētōn horōn kai prōtōn*' of 1143ᵇ2 and 1140ᵇ31 ff.), particular speculative *nous* (the *nous* of particulars which is *aisthēsis*, of 1143ᵇ6 and 1142ᵃ29), particular practical *nous* (the *nous* which is '*en tais praktikais tou eschatou kai endechomenou*' of 1143ᵇ2), and universal practical *nous* (the *nous* of the *hetera protasis* of 1143ᵇ3). As in speculative matters, so in practical matters, *nous* provides the starting-point and the stopping-point for reasoning (1143ᵇ11). The practical reasoning which is the existence of *phronēsis* begins with a conception of an end, a *hypolēpsis* about the purpose of conduct (1140ᵇ17); this right conception of an end can itself be called *phronēsis* (1140ᵇ13; 1142ᵇ34). Practical reasoning ends with a judgement about what is to be done, a self-addressed command (1143ᵃ9) or a piece of advice to another (1143ᵃ15). This too can be called *nous* (1143ᵃ27) whether or not it is backed up in a particular case by a statement of reasons (1143ᵇ14).

There is thus a parallel between the structure of *phronēsis* in the *logistikon* and *sophia* in the *epistēmonikon* which can be illustrated as follows:

	epistēmonikon	*logistikon*	
sophia {	*nous* (of axioms) *logos* = *epistēmē* *nous* (of particulars)	*nous* (of end) *logos* = *euboulia* *nous* (of particulars)	} *phronēsis*

The pattern *nous-logos-nous* is common to both sides of the division. Just as *sophia* can be described as *epistēmē* plus *nous* ('knowledge with a head on it' 1141ᵃ19), so *phronēsis* could have been described as *euboulia* plus *nous*: instead, *euboulia* is described as *phronēsis* minus *nous*, as what you are left with if you discount that element of *phronēsis* which is the right conception of the end (1142ᵇ32-4). The particular *nous* is, in each case, the perception of an instance (of a term or a principle) *as an instance*: this may be either with a view to acquiring the general term or instance (e.g. 1143ᵇ5) or to applying it (e.g. 1143ᵇ15). Aristotle's fullest account of particular *nous* comes when he is contrasting *phronēsis* with *epistēmē*:

> That wisdom is not knowledge is clear: for as has been said it is concerned with particulars, since action is particular. It is something which perceives by *nous*; for *nous* is concerned with terms of which there is no deduction, and wisdom with particulars of which there is no science but only sense perception—not the perception of the proper sensibles, but that whereby we see in a mathematical case that a triangle is an ultimate element, another stopping-point. This wisdom is perhaps better called perception: it is a different kind from the wisdom we were talking about earlier. (1141ᵃ24-31)[1]

Aristotle nowhere gives an example in the *AE* of what is perceived by this *phronēsis-nous*: he relies on the analogy with the mathematical case of the analysis of a figure and with cases of the exercise of a skill such as medicine (1141ᵇ17 ff.). Presumably instances of the kind of thing he has in mind would be the perception that *A* needs cheering up, that *B* is being offensive, and that one is hurting *C*'s feelings: an awareness, we might say, of the morally relevant features of one's action and the situation in which one is acting. Someone who is blind to this kind of thing—who does not, as Aristotle puts it, have an eye for this kind of thing (1143ᵇ14, 1144ᵃ30)—will never be able either to acquire or to apply general principles about the good life or admirable action.

In all these passages *nous* is an acquired or natural condition of the soul or one of its parts: it is not a substance or faculty which can

---

1. Reading ἀντιληπτικὸν in 1142ᵃ25 with Kb, and understanding it in an active sense, as suggested by the correction in the manuscript O³ ἀντιληπτική; reading also at 1142ᵃ29-30 αὕτη μᾶλλον αἴσθησις ἢ φρόνησις with the majority of the best manuscripts and taking αὕτη with φρόνησις. So read, the text agrees with, rather than contradicts, the passage at 1143ᵃ35 ff.

be contrasted with and judged superior to the whole soul–body compound as it is in *NE* 10 at 1177^{b}28. But if we compare the *AE* use of *nous* with that of the *EE* we find no such difficult contrast as we find when we compare the *AE* and the *NE*. *Nous* is uncommon in the *EE* until the final book: in the earlier books it appears only in the popular phrase *noun echōn* (having common sense) and in conjunction with *theos* in the refutation of the Platonic Idea of the Good (1214^{b}31; 1237^{b}38; 1217^{b}31). In the final book, however, it appears a number of times, in senses which match those we have seen in the disputed book B.

Thus at 1246^{a}13–14 the incontinent man is described as an intemperate man with *nous* (*pōs akolastos . . . echōn noun*): this is no doubt a popular saying of some kind, but it suits very well the theory of B and C, according to which the incontinent man differs from the intemperate man by having a correct appreciation of the end—the *nous tēs heteras protaseos* of 1143^{b}3. At 1247^{a}30 *nous* appears along with nature and tutelage as a possible cause of successful action: here it must mean generic intellectual ability, including both *phronēsis* and *technē*. At 1246^{b}10 *epistēmē* and *nous* are linked together as they are in the account of *sophia* in B; at 1248^{a}17 ff. *nous* and *bouleusis*—the constituents of *phronēsis* according to our account of B—appear together as the conditions of right desire. At 1248^{a}29 we are told that (moral) virtue is the tool of *nous*, just as at 1246^{b}11 we were told that *phronēsis* was the employer rather than the employee of virtue. In all these passages in book VIII of the *EE nous* appears in senses familiar from B: either as the generic cognitive apparatus, or as the intuitive element in learning, or as the intuitive element in wisdom.

It is the final chapter of the *EE* that is the closest parallel to *NE* 10, and here the word *nous* is not used. Aristotle is looking for the criterion which the good man should use in his choice of the good things of nature and fortune. He says:

Here as elsewhere one should conduct one's life with reference to one's superior, and more specifically to the quality of one's superior's activity. A slave, for instance, should look to his master's, and everyone to the superior to whom he is subject. Now a human being is by nature a compound of superior and inferior, and everyone accordingly should conduct their lives with reference to the superior part of themselves. However, 'superior' is ambiguous: there is the sense in which medical science is superior, and the sense in which health is superior; the latter is the *raison d'être* of the former. It is thus, that matters stand in the case of our intellectual faculty. For God is not a superior who issues commands, but is the *raison d'être* of the commands that wisdom issues. But *'raison d'être'* is ambiguous, as has been explained elsewhere—this needs saying, since of course God is not in need of anything. To conclude: whatever choice or possession of natural goods—health and strength, wealth, friends, and the like—will most conduce to the contemplation of God is best: this is the finest criterion. But any standard of living which either through excess or defect hinders the service and contemplation of God is bad. (1249^b6-21)[1]

The word *'nous'*, as I have said, does not appear in Aristotle's text, but von Arnim proposed to insert it in place of each occurrence of the word 'God', whose presence he attributed to a Christian interpolator. The proposal has no support from any manuscript or version, and is implausible in itself—what Christian would assent to the proposition 'God is not a superior who issues commands'?—

---

1. My translation of this passage, like every other translation that has been offered, is controversial at a number of points. I follow Bekker's text exactly, even with respect to punctuation; with the exception of the misprint ἄρχοντες for ἄρχοντος in line 8. None of the emendations that have been proposed seems to me to be necessary to make the text intelligible, and few of them seem even to improve it. 'Superior' is not always the most natural translation of ἄρχων but seems the best English word to capture the two senses present in the Greek of 'higher in a scale of value' and 'higher in a chain of command' (as in 'superior officer'). There is no reason to emend πρὸς τὴν ἕξιν κατὰ τὴν ἐνέργειαν in line 7; what is meant is that the slave should help his master to do whatever his master is doing as well as it can be done: he should strive to see that his master's ἐνέργεια has the ἕξις of goodness. The most difficult clause to make sense of as it stands is ἕκαστον δὴ δέοι πρὸς τὴν ἑαυτῶν ἀρχὴν ζῆν. In this clause I think δή should not be emended: Aristotle is drawing a conclusion, not adding a second premiss. The genitive plural ἑαυτῶν is puzzling: Rackham's emendation ἐν αὑτῷ is attractive, and certainly expresses clearly what I take to be the sense. The plural is perhaps to be explained, as my translation suggests, as looking back to the implicit plural in ἕκαστον; or it may be due to the self being looked on in this passage as a plurality of parts. The genitive is as it were partitive: 'that part of themselves which is an ἀρχή'. I am unable to settle the parallel ambiguities of οὕτω and θεωρητικόν in the sentence οὕτω δ'ἔχει κατὰ τὸ θεωρητικόν. Does οὕτω mean 'like the foregoing (viz. "superior") in being twofold' or 'like the foregoing (viz. health) in being a *raison d'etre*'? Does θεωρητικόν mean the intellectual faculty in general, or the speculative faculty in particular? Elsewhere in the *EE* the use of the verb θεωρέω and its derivatives would support either reading: the wide sense is to be found at 1217^b26 ff.; 1226^b26; 1245^a23, and the narrow sense at 1214^a13; 1215^b13; 1216^b13; 1219^a17, $^b26$; 1221^b5; 1227^a9, $^b29$; other passages are themselves ambiguous or use the verb in the literal sense of 'see'. I incline to think that the faculty meant here is the theoretical intellect, the ἐπιστημονικόν of B: this fits the commoner use of the verb in the *EE*. But provided that the first sense of 'thus' is taken with the broader sense of 'intellectual faculty', or the second sense with the narrower sense, there is no difference in the over-all resulting significance of the passage. I owe to Professor D. J. Allan the neat translations of οὗ ἕνεκα as *raison d'etre* and of σώματος ἀγαθά as "health and strength".

so that it is not surprising that it has not been taken up by other commentators. Many distinguished scholars, however, while rejecting the proposal as an emendation have accepted it as an interpretation: the word 'God' here, they claim, does not refer to a transcendent God of the universe, but to the *nous* immanent in each of us, which is described in *NE* 10, at 1177ᵃ28–31, as something divine. If this interpretation is correct, then the expression I have translated 'the contemplation of God' must be translated as 'God's contemplation'—the genitive must be taken to mark the subject, not the object of the contemplation; and the phrase rendered 'the service and contemplation of God' needs to be taken accordingly as 'the service of God, and contemplation'. Thus there will be found in this passage a twofold division of the intellectual faculty: one part in which inheres prescriptive wisdom, the other which is called 'god' and issues in contemplation. The twofold division will correspond to the division between the *logistikon* and the *epistēmonikon* in B, while the divine status accorded to the contemplative *nous* gives the present passage a close resemblance to *NE* 10.[1]

Ingenious though it is, this interpretation is not in the end credible. The previous chapter of the *EE* contains several references to God, which are clear references to the cosmic God of the universe, who is not to be identified with, but is explicitly said to be more powerful than, *nous* and science. This God is contrasted with 'the divine in us', which in that context appears not to be any speculative faculty, but human reason in general.[2] It is hard to accept a quite unprepared switch to a use of 'God' to refer to the faculty of contemplation: this would be so even if there were any parallel for such a use, which there is not.[3] Bonitz offers no parallel either for the subjective genitive with *theōria*; and it can hardly be said of the speculative faculty that it 'is in need of nothing',

1. See D. Wagner, 1970, *passim*.

2. 1248ᵃ15–ᵇ4. The text is in part corrupt and is not easy to restore completely with confidence. Fortunately I do not need to discuss its emendation—other than to say that I accept Spengel's reading of ᵃ28, τί οὖν ἂν κρεῖττον καὶ ἐπιστήμης εἴη καὶ νοῦ πλὴν θεός, which is supported by the old Latin version of the *De Bona Fortuna*—for the points made above remain true on any of the proposed reconstructions including von Arnim's.

3. D. Wagner has devotedly combed classical literature for descriptions of *nous*, and other abstractions, as divine (op. cit. 128–39). But describing something as divine, or as a god, is quite different from using the word 'god' baldly to refer to it. Politicians and leader writers frequently say that inflation is a cancer; but if I read that someone has died of cancer, I do not take this to mean that his death was due to the depreciating value of money.

particularly in a context in which—on this view—wisdom is said to be issuing commands for its benefit. Finally, it is possible to make perfect sense of the passage without giving the word 'God' any such strained sense.

When Aristotle says that a human being is by nature compounded of superior and inferior, it is not the composition of soul and body that he has in mind, but the division between the irrational and the rational part of the soul. If we apply to this case the general rule that one should look to one's superior, we infer that a human being should govern his life in accordance with what is required by his rational soul. But there are two different kinds of *archē*: in matters concerning our body we need to take account of the requirements (i.e. prescriptions) of medical science; we also need to take account of the requirements (i.e. needs) of our health. Both medical science and health are *archai* in different ways: and the latter is the *raison d'être* of the former. We must apply this to the mind: there too there is an *archē* like medicine, and an *archē* like health. The *archē* corresponding to medicine is wisdom, which like medicine issues commands. So applying the rule about looking to one's superior, we must obey the commands of wisdom, and take account of the needs of that which is related to wisdom as health is related to medical science. So far—up to 1249^{b}14—all is reasonably clear. But now we naturally want to ask: well, what *is* it that stands in the same relation to wisdom as health does to medical science? Instead of giving us an immediate answer, Aristotle goes on 'For God is not a superior who issues commands. . . .' This sentence, and especially the 'for' is at first baffling in the context, and provides the principal reason which has made commentators want to change either the reading or the sense of 'God' so as to make Aristotle refer here to the speculative intellect.

The relevance of the sentence becomes clear if we connect it with the previous chapter. There we learnt that the cosmic God was the supreme *archē* in the soul, superior to *logos*, *epistēmē*, and *nous*. If, without further ado, we applied the rule that everyone should live according to the requirements of his superior as a slave lives according to the requirements of his master, we would most naturally conclude that in matters of the soul we must live in obedience to the commands of God. But this would be, in Aristotle's view, to make an erroneous move. We must first distinguish between senses of *archē*: *for God is not a ruler who issues commands.* We thus see the appropriateness of the 'for': it explains why the distinction just made had to be made. It is indeed true, even according to the final chapter of the *EE*, that God is the supreme *archē* of the soul: but not in the sense in which the analogy with slave and master would suggest.

Shall we say, then, that it is God who stands to wisdom in the relation that health stands to medical science? The rule about looking to one's superior would then be applied in this way: we must obey the commands of wisdom, and take account of the needs of God. But that in turn would be absurd: *since God of course is not in need of anything.* To prevent this absurd conclusion being drawn, Aristotle has to make a further distinction. Health was related to medical science, we said, as its *raison d'être* or *hou heneka*. But the *hou heneka* of an institution or activity may be either that which it seeks to attain, or that which it seeks to benefit. Aristotle often invokes the distinction, without offering a clear instance to illustrate it (*Phys.* II.2, 194^{a}35–6; *De An.* II.4, 415^{b}2–3, ^{b}20–1; *Met. Λ*, 1072^{b}2). Everyday examples of what he has in mind are easy to find: if I go into a toyshop to buy a toy railway for my young son, the railway is the *hou heneka* of my shopping trip in the one sense, the boy is the *hou heneka* in the other sense. *Met. Λ*, 1072^{b}1 applies the distinction to the First Mover: as Ross paraphrases the passage, 'A final cause in the sense of that whose good is aimed at cannot be found among unchangeable things, but a final cause in the sense of the good aimed at can; it moves by being loved' (Ross, 1924, 373). This is a close parallel to the present passage: Aristotle is here saying that God is not a *raison d'être* whose good is being aimed at, but a good whose attainment is the *raison d'être* of wisdom's commands.

Well, then, what *is* the *hou heneka* whose good is being aimed at, and what is it to attain God? Aristotle gives no explicit reply, but the answer is clear enough from the concluding passage: that which benefits from the commands of wisdom is that which serves and contemplates God; and this service and contemplation is itself the only kind of attainment of God which is possible. And what is it that serves and contemplates God? Either the soul as a whole, or its speculative part: which of the two is intended must depend on what is meant by 'service' here. And this, notoriously, is a very difficult problem.

The only other place in which Aristotle speaks of serving God, or the gods, is in *Pol. H*, 1329ᵃ30 ff., where the expression clearly means 'worship' in a literal, liturgical sense. Commentators have found it astonishing that in the last chapter of *EE* Aristotle should offer as a criterion for the goodness or badness of choices their effect on liturgical worship. Accordingly, they have preferred to take 'serving God' in the sense of 'cultivating the intellect', citing as parallels *NE* 10, 1179ᵃ23, where we are told that the *therapeia* of the *nous* endears us to the gods, and Plato, *Timaeus* 90 c 4 where the expression *therapeuonta to theion* will bear this sense. But if the bare *theos* in this context cannot mean *nous*, as we have argued, this interpretation is excluded.

If we are to look for Platonic parallels a much more appropriate one is provided by the *Euthyphro*. There a long section (12ᵉ24–14ᵃ1) is devoted to a discussion of *hē tōn theōn therapeia* in which Socrates argues against Euthyphro that the notion is unintelligible. There are a number of themes paralleling the present text: *therapeia* cannot be for the benefit of the gods, whose condition we cannot hope to alter for the better; *therapeia* is what slaves give to masters; but what slaves do for their masters depends on what their masters' *ergon* is: what then is the splendid achievement, the *pankalon ergon*, which is to be achieved by the gods with our service? '*Polla kai kala*' replies Euthyphro to Socrates, who promptly turns to some inconclusive teasing.

The service of the gods which Euthryphro has in mind includes prayer and sacrifice: but it includes also acts of justice such as Euthyphro's attempt to punish a murderer—the endeavour which gives the whole dialogue its framework. If Aristotle does have the *Euthyphro* in mind here, then the service of God could well include acts of moral virtue. These are the *kalai praxeis* of the *kalos kagathos* which are the subject of the first part of the same chapter; they could well be regarded as the *polla kai kala* which we, under the *archē* of God (1248ᵃ25 ff.) find our fulfilment in performing and by which we make our contribution to the splendour of the universe. This interpretation of '*therapeia*' is highly speculative: but given the excessively laconic style of the conclusion of the *EE*, no interpretation can be anything else. It is certainly not alien to Aristotle's manner in the *EE* to defend the moral opinions of the plain man against the paradoxes of Socrates.

It is with relief one turns from decoding the cryptogram of *EE* VIII to looking for a parallel in the *AE*. The search is not, of course, a difficult one. It has long been recognized that the final chapter of B is very close to the conclusion of the *EE*. Having established that wisdom and learning are the excellences of the two parts of the rational soul, at $1143^{b}18$ ff. Aristotle inquires what use each of these virtues is? Learning does not inquire how to make men happy, and the acquisition of wisdom is surely no more necessary in order to become happy than the acquisition of medical science is necessary in order to become healthy. 'Moreover, it would seem absurd if wisdom, being inferior to learning, should be put in authority over it: as seems to be implied by the fact that whatever produces something is superior to it and issues commands about it' ($1143^{b}33$–5). These *aporiai* are solved as follows. Learning does not produce happiness as medical science produces health: it is, rather, a constituent of happiness. Wisdom is not separable from virtuous activity as the possession of the science of medicine is separable from healthy activity. Finally

wisdom is not in authority over learning or the better part, any more than the science of medicine is in authority over health; it does not make use of it, but provides for its coming into being; the orders it issues are not issued to it but issued for its sake. To say it was in authority over learning would be like saying that political science was superior to the gods, because it issues commands about all the affairs of the state. ($1145^{a}6$–11)

Here, as in *EE*, wisdom is something which issues commands (*epitattei*: a word popular in the *EE*, but occurring only once in the *NE*). Here, as in the *EE*, the prescriptive role of wisdom is likened to that of medicine. Here, as in the *EE*, it is a function of wisdom to promote the contemplative activity of the soul: in the *EE* its function is to promote the contemplation of God, in the *AE* it is to promote the activity of the better part of the soul, whose objects are unchanging, eternal things, the most honourable things by nature, the divine constituents of the cosmos, and in general extraordinary, marvellous, mysterious, and superhuman things ($1139^{b}23$; $1141^{a}20$, $^{b}1$–7). In the *EE* there is stressed the relationship between wisdom and the *hou heneka* in the sense of *hou*: namely, God. In the *AE* there is stressed the relationship between wisdom and the *hou heneka* in the sense of *hō(i)*: namely, 'the better part of the soul'. But in substance the doctrine is the same.

The *nous* passage in *NE* 10 is the closest Nicomachean parallel to these two passages of the *AE* and *EE*, but it is much further from each of them than either is from the other. *Phronēsis* in *NE* does not appear as the handmaid of learning, but only as the yokemate of the moral virtues; the activity of contemplation is attributed not to an element of the soul, but to a separable *nous* contrasted with the human soul–body compound. In *AE* C, as in *EE* VIII, 2, there is a divine element in us: but as in *EE* VIII 2, it is not the theoretical *nous*: it is appetitive rather than speculative, the origin of the right sort of desire for pleasure (compare 1153^{b}32 with 1248^{a}17–29).

(3) *Phronēsis and Moral Virtue.* In *NE* 10 we are told: 'Wisdom is wedded to moral virtue, and moral virtue to wisdom, since the principles of wisdom are determined by the moral virtues, and rightness in morals is determined by wisdom' (1178^{a}16–18). This is a neat summary of the teaching of all three treatises. In both the *NE* and the *EE* a reference to wisdom is incorporated into the definition of moral virtue. In the preliminary general treatment of the subject in the *NE* virtue is defined as a state of character expressed in choice lying in a mean determined by reasoning in the way that the wise man would determine it (1106^{b}36)—a definition developed by Aristotle from the commonly accepted account of virtue as action 'in accordance with right reasoning' (1103^{b}32). In the *EE* virtue is defined as a state of character which makes people capable of performing the best actions and puts them in the best disposition with regard to the best and greatest good 'the best and greatest good being that which is in accordance with right reasoning, that is the mean' (1222^{a}9–10). After the treatment of magnanimity, Aristotle fills this out: 'the virtue concerned with each subject matter judges correctly what is the greater good and what is the less, just as the wise man and his virtue would command, so that all the virtues go with that virtue, or that virtue goes with all virtues' (1232^{a}25–38). In each *Ethics* there is a promise to expand, at a later point, the notion of 'right reasoning' (*NE* 2, 1103^{b}33; *EE* II, 1222^{b}8). The promise is not fulfilled in the *NE*, but both *AE* and *EE* contain passages which refer back to it. To say that the mean is in accordance with right reasoning, we are told in B (1138^{b}5 ff.), is true but uninformative: it is as if one were to prescribe the medicines 'that medical science, and the man who possesses it, would command' (1138^{b}31).[1] We must inquire, Aristotle says, what right reasoning is, and what is the standard or criterion which determines it (*horos*).

---

1. The similarity of language between *EE* III and *AE* B is striking. ἅπερ ὁ φρόνιμος ἂν κελεύσειε καὶ ἡ ἀρετή (1232^{a}3); ὅσα ἡ ἰατρικὴ κελεύει καὶ ὡς ὁ ταύτην ἔχων (1138^{b}32).

The first question is answered at some length in book B itself: right reasoning in these matters, we are told at 1144ᵇ23, is *phronēsis*; and *phronēsis* is the major topic of the book. But what of the question: what is the *horos* of right reasoning? There is no clear answer to this question in book B: some commentators take this as evidence that the book is in a fragmentary state, others that Aristotle though the question was misconceived, others that we are to look for the answer to book 10 of the *NE*.¹ The third answer seems to me more nearly correct than the other two, as becomes clear if we consider the analogy with medicine. What the Aristotelian doctor possesses and the rest of us lack is not so much a set of rules of thumb for prescribing, but a knowledge of the nature of health itself: he knows what the mechanism of the body is, how its humours are balanced when it is in good working order, what are the functions and interrelations of its parts. So in ethics, if we are to know the right action to do we must know the nature of a healthy—i.e. virtuous and happy—mind: we must know what the parts of the soul are, what their functions are, and how they are related to each other. This is why the *horos* can also be called the *skopos* (1138ᵇ23): it is a right understanding of the end of conduct, namely a good life, that is necessary for right reasoning in morals, just as it is a right understanding of health, which is the end of medical practice, that is necessary for right reasoning in medicine. In the *NE* it is in book 10 that we are given the fullest account of the nature of the good life—the contemplative activity of *nous*—and to this extent those who say that it is to *NE* 10 that we must look for the *horos* are correct. But of course in B itself in the concluding chapters the relationship of *phronēsis* to *sophia* is discussed and the relationship of both to happiness is sketched (1144ᵃ3–6; 1145ᵃ6–11). The relevance of this to the question of the *horos* is not however brought out either in *NE* 10 or in *AE* B. For that we have to turn to *EE* VIII.

   In *EE* VIII the question of the *horos* is taken up in language reminiscent of the beginning of B.

---

1. The first is the view of Allan (1970, 136) and the second of Rowe, who writes 'Within the limits of Aristotle's system, no detailed criterion is in fact possible . . . either the question "what is the standard" means what it says, and the answer is that there is no such thing; or else it is simply a misleading way of putting the more general question, how we apply the general rule to the particular case', in which case the answer is the intuition of the φρόνιμος (1971, 112–13). Both Allan and Rowe are mistaken, I believe, in thinking that Aristotle is here concerned with the formulation and application of rules. The third view is that of Dirlmeier (1969, 442) and other commentators.

The doctor has a standard by reference to which he distinguishes a healthy from an unhealthy body and the degree to which each activity is advisable and wholesome, and beyond which in either direction it ceases to be so. Similarly in regard to actions and choices of things which by nature are good but not praiseworthy, the good man should have a standard of possession, choice, and avoidance concerning abundance and scarcity of wealth and other gifts of fortune. Earlier we said "in accordance with reasoning"—but this, like saying in matters of diet "in accordance with medicine and medical reasoning", is true but uninformative. (1249^{a}21–6)[1]

Aristotle then goes on to give, as an answer to the question about the *horos*, the rule that everything should conduct its life with reference to its superior, which we considered in the previous section. The resemblances to B in the reference to the doctor, and in the use of the phrase 'true but uninformative' strike all commentators. The resemblance may seem *too* striking: if B belonged originally in the same context as *EE* VIII, would not this passage be a useless reduplication of the earlier one? But setting aside the fact that the undoubted *EE* and the *AE* itself contain a number of apparent doublets, a closer look at the text shows that it is not mere repetition of the B passage. Aristotle does not say here, as he does in B, that we must inquire what *is* the *orthos logos*: the answer he goes on to give is an answer to the question what is the *horos*—the *horos* of *kalokagathia* or perfect virtue, as is said in the concluding summary (1249^{b}24). Thus *EE* VIII can perfectly well follow *AE* B as part of the same treatise: a twofold question is raised at the beginning of B, and the first part of the question is there answered; the second half of the question is raised in VIII, in terms reminiscent of the twofold question of B, and the second half of the question is then answered.

Some have disputed that the final passage of *EE* VIII *is* an answer to the question raised in B. Rowe writes: '*EE* VIII, 3 severely restricts the application of its suggested *horos*: it is introduced as a standard for "actions in connection with and choices of things naturally good but not praiseworthy" . . . there is no justification in the text for supposing that *EE* is giving a standard for actions in general' (op. cit. 110). Like some other scholars, Rowe must be treating as an editorial addition the final statement that it has just been said what is the standard of perfect virtue. There is no

1. Reading, with Ross, ὑγιεινόν for εὖ ὑγιαινον in line 24, and φυγῆς περὶ for περὶ φυγῆς in line ^{b}3, after Allan and the Latin version.

reason for regarding this statement as spurious; but even if one does so, the discussion in *EE* VIII *does* give the general standard for the exercise of virtue. The 'things that are good by nature but not praiseworthy' are health, strength, honour, birth, wealth, and power (1248^{b}24, ^{b}28–30; 1249^{a}10–11). These are the subject matter of the virtues of magnanimity, magnificence, and liberality (*EE* III, 1231^{b}28 ff.). The subject matter of the virtues of courage, temperance, and meekness, on the other hand, are the passions of the irrational soul. For these too a standard is sketched in the last chapter of the *EE*: 'Thus it is, too, with the soul, and this is the best standard for the soul, to be as little as possible conscious of the irrational part of the soul *qua* irrational' (1249^{b}22–5).[1] Thus the last chapter of the *EE* does give a standard for the exercise of the six virtues which are discussed in the official treatment of the virtues in *EE* III and which together constitute the perfect virtue or *kalokagathia* of the first part of the final chapter. Other praise-worthy states, like dignity and candour and wit, are no doubt difficult to bring within the scope of the criterion offerred by *EE* VIII: but then according to the *EE* these states are not virtues (1234^{a}25) and since they do not involve *prohairesis* (1234^{a}26) they do not call for a *horos* to guide choice.

As has been said, it is ground common to all three treatises that wisdom and moral virtue are inseparably linked: but how and why this is so is spelt out at much greater length in the *EE* and the *AE* than it is in the brief quoted passage which is the *NE*'s only contribution to the topic. The *AE* has a long argument to the conclusion that 'it is impossible to be good in the strict sense without wisdom, or wise without moral virtue' (1144^{b}30–2). It is indeed possible to do good actions—the actions that a good man would do—without possessing either wisdom or moral virtue; but actions only express virtue if they are done out of *prohairesis* and for their own sake (1144^{a}13–20). Even good actions which are not the expression of virtue do of course call for some skill in planning: but this does not mean that there can be wisdom without virtue, for the planning is the expression not of wisdom, but merely of intelligence—intelligence which could be used for evil ends as well as good. Intelligence is a necessary, but not a sufficient, condition of wisdom: intelligence only becomes wisdom if accompanied by a

---

1. Reading οὕτω for τοῦτο, τὸ for τὰ, and ἀλόγου for ἄλλου (Fritzsche).

correct understanding of the supreme good for man (that 'right conception of the end' which is itself called 'wisdom' at 1142^{b}34). But only a morally good man has a correct understanding of the nature of the supreme good: wickedness perverts us and deludes us about the ultimate grounds of action (cf. 1140^{b}11–20). So wisdom is impossible without moral virtue (1144^{a}21–^{b}1).

Moral virtue, conversely, is impossible without wisdom. Without wisdom, and even in childhood, one can feel drawn to justice, temperance, courage; but such good tendencies, without wisdom, can be positively harmful, like the strength of a blind man. Only wisdom will turn these natural virtuous inclinations into genuine moral virtue. Socrates went too far when he said that each virtue was itself a branch of wisdom; but he was right in thinking that virtue was impossible without wisdom. Those on the other hand who say that virtue is determined by right reasoning (*kata ton orthon logon*) are understating the case: it is not enough to act in accordance with a man's instructions, as one might act in accordance with a doctor's instructions without oneself understanding medicine. The choices of the virtuous man must be determined by right reasoning in his own person 'Virtue is not just a state determined by right reasoning, but a state accompanied by right reasoning: and right reasoning about these matters is wisdom.' Thus virtue without wisdom is as impossible as wisdom without virtue (1144^{b}1–30).

It is noteworthy that in this passage Aristotle corrects as inadequate the formula which he himself gives in *NE* 10 to explain the way in which wisdom and the virtues are interlinked. Nowhere in the *NE* itself is it suggested that this formulation is a provisional or abbreviated one: in the treatment of virtue in the early books, no reason is given why the *phronimos* who defines the mean must be the same person as the virtuous man who is acting according to the mean.

The question whether wisdom and virtue are separable is discussed at length at the beginning of *EE* VIII in the form of an inquiry whether wisdom can be abused. Here, as in *AE* B, Aristotle is arguing against the Socratic identification of virtue and knowledge.[1] Some things, he says, can be used for their natural

---

1. The passage (1246^{a}26–36) is a difficult one, and like the final chapter of *EE* VIII it has suffered from the well-meant attentions of emendators who were unwilling to make a sufficiently patient effort to understand the text handed down. Undoubtedly it is corrupt in

purpose and also for other purposes; and they can be used for other purposes in two different ways, either *qua* the kind of thing they are, or quite *per accidens*. Thus an eye can be used for its natural purpose, to see straight; you can also (if you push on one eye in the way described in *Problems* 958ª5 ff.) use your eyes to see double: even this perverse use of them is a use of them *qua* eyes. Selling an eye, on the other hand, or eating one, counts as a *per accidens* use.[1] Knowledge, too, is capable of multiple use: you can use it correctly, or use it to make a deliberate mistake, e.g. in orthography—using it, as it were, like ignorance.[2] This is a sort of perverse use of one's hand in writing: there is the third kind of use of one's hand when it is used as a foot by dancers who dance on their hands and use their feet as hands.

Now if every virtue was a branch of knowledge, virtue could be misused like knowledge. You could use justice as if it were injustice: a man doing unjust things would then be acting unjustly out of justice, just as one can behave ignorantly out of knowledge.

places, but there is no need for such extensive reconstruction as is proposed, e.g. by Moraux in Moraux and Harlfinger (1971, 281–3).
In my paraphrase I follow Bekker's text with the following exceptions.
In line 26 I omit φίλῳ with P.
In line 27 I read ἤ ἤ αὖ for ἡδὺ following Jackson and Dirlmeier.
In line 30 I accept von Fragstein's neat emendation ὅτι ἤστην δ' ὀφθαλμώ for ὅτι δ' ὀφθαλμῷ.
In line 35 I accept Spengel's emendations εἰ δὴ for ἤδη and ἀρεταὶ for ἄρισται.
In line 36 I read εἴη ἂν for ἔπαν and in line 37 ἀδικήσει for εἰ δίκης εἰ with Spengel.
In line ᵇ4 I propose to read ἔτι εἰ instead of ἐπεί, which removes the inconsistency between 1246ᵇ4 and ᵇ35.
In line 8 I accept Victorius' reading.
In line 10 I omit ἔτι with P.
In line 15 I am attracted by von Fragstein's proposal to fill the blank in the manuscripts (η . . . . σφι . . . .) with ἤ ὁ νοῦς φρονεῖ.
In line 20 I read ἐν τῷ ἀλόγῳ for μὲν τῳ λογῳ following Susemihl.
In line 24 I accept Victorius' emendation of κόλασιν ἄν into ἀκολασίαν.
In line 25 I accept Spengel's proposal of ἔστι δὲ for ἐπί τε.
In line 28 I read οὐ for οὖν ὁ.
In line 29 I propose ἐάν ἐνῇ ἤ for ἐὰν ᾖ.
In line 31 I follow Jackson in inserting ἃ after γάρ.
In line 36 I read γνώσεως for γνως after Sylburg.
I also depart from time to time from Bekker's punctuation, as will be clear from the paraphrase.
   1. Commentators with a philological background find this bizarre, and hasten to emend the text. Philosophers greet the examples as instances of their familiar stock-in-trade.
   2. Several scholars (especially Allan) have drawn attention to the protracted parallel discussion of deliberate mistakes in the *Hippias Minor* (373 c ff.). There as here there is a discussion of a deliberate distortion of one's vision (374 d).

But if this is impossible, as it is, it is obvious that the virtues are not branches of knowledge. Even if you say that one is not strictly ignorant out of knowlege, but merely behaves incorrectly in the way that an ignorant man would, the argument still holds. For you cannot do, out of justice, the things you would do out of injustice.

But even if most virtues cannot be misused, perhaps *phronēsis* can. For if *phronēsis* is a branch of knowledge, a piece of truth, then it will perform in the same way as knowledge does. That is, it will be possible to act stupidly from wisdom, and go wrong in the same way as a stupid person. Doing stupid things out of wisdom might be called either acting wisely, or acting stupidly. If the former is the correct description (so that any action done out of wisdom is wisely done, so that the 'use' of wisdom is single and not multiple) then the first of the two descriptions just suggested is incorrect: doing stupid actions from wisdom will be acting wisely, not acting stupidly.

Let us take the two possible descriptions of this situation in turn.

Suppose that doing things out of wisdom is acting wisely. This would parallel the case where making deliberate mistakes in grammar or medicine expresses a knowledge of grammar or medicine. But the two cases are not parallel: the misuse of grammar and medicine is possible only because there is a superior branch of knowledge perversely employing the skill. But no branch of skill can thus boss wisdom, which is itself the boss of all; nor can science or understanding (presumably because they would not lend themselves to perversely employing anything.) Nor can moral virtue boss wisdom: wisdom, being the virtue of the superior part of the soul, makes use of the virtue of the inferior part: it is the employer, not the employee. What other candidate is there for the role?

Suppose on the other hand that doing stupid things out of wisdom is acting stupidly. Let us start from two popular dicta: incontinence is a vice of the irrational part of the soul; the incontinent man is almost an intemperate man—he is an intemperate man who still has sense. Incontinence, so conceived, might be thought to be a case of the misuse of wisdom. But this thought is mistaken. It is indeed true that strong desire can pervert the reason and cause it to make judgements opposite to those of *nous*. But in that case, of course, we have neither wisdom nor incontinence. What we have is a case of a bad state of the irrational part of the soul causing a change for the worse from a good state of the rational part. It is clear that we shall have a change the other way round if we have a good state of the irrational part, and stupidity in the rational part.[1] This will amount to our second possibility: justice will be capable of being used either justly (when the reason is in a good state) or unjustly (when there is stupidity in the rational part; and wisdom will be capable of being used stupidly (when there is evil desire in the irrational part). But this will not be all: there will also be the possibility of using injustice justly, and stupidity wisely, i.e. acting wisely out of stupidity. For (since surely virtue is stronger than vice) it would be absurd if vice in the irrational part could pervert the virtue in the rational part and turn it into ignorance, while virtue in the irrational part cannot turn stupidity in the rational part into wisdom, i.e. right judgement about what is to be done. After all—on this view—wisdom in the rational part makes intemperance in the irrational part act temperately: isn't that what continence is?

But all this is absurd: especially the idea of acting wisely out of ignorance. The very analogy on which our opponents rely tells against them here. Intemperance may pervert medical skill or grammar, but the opposite of intemperance does not convert ignorance into knowledge; because the opposite of intemperance does not contain the extra that would be needed to do so. It is virtue as a whole—moral *and* intellectual—that has this sort of superiority over vice: the just man can do all that the unjust man can, just as in general power ranges wider than impotence.[2] (Virtue, of course, is not itself a power: but it includes as necessary parts the powers of intelligence and natural goodness, as we shall see in the next section.)

So two conclusions emerge. First, wisdom and the *hexeis* of the irrational part of the soul[3] go hand in hand—to this extent Socrates was right that there is nothing stronger than wisdom, because there is no such thing as the misuse of wisdom by vice. Secondly, wisdom is not knowledge, because it is incapable of being misused: hence this second part of Socrates' thesis is wrong. Wisdom is not knowledge, but another type of cognition.

1. Commentators discuss whether the text here (^{b}16) and below (^{b}21) should read ἄγνοια or ἄνοια. The difference is immaterial to the sense: ἄγνοια about the subject matter of wisdom *is* ἄνοια.

2. Cf. the parallel text in *AE* A, 1137^{a}18.

3. Susemihl's emendation of αἱ ἄλλου ἕξεις into αἱ τοῦ ἀλόγου ἕξεις, though unnecessary, catches the sense exactly.

Thus, in *EE* VIII.1, the thesis that wisdom and moral virtue are inseparably linked is confirmed by a many-pronged *reductio ad absurdum* of the suggestion that one might occur without the other. Each theoretically possible such combination and permutation is examined in turn and shown to lead to absurd consequences. The doctrine is in perfect accord with, but in no way a mere duplication of, the closing chapters of *AE* B.

(4) *Phronēsis and Nature.* One of the more interesting theories of the *AE* is the account of the relationship between inborn and acquired virtue. According to 1144^{b}1 ff. there are both cognitive and affective natural qualities: in the cognitive faculty, corresponding to the acquired virtue of wisdom, there is the natural power of intelligence or *deinotēs*; there are also natural traits of character (*epi tou ēthikou*): 'We are just, capable of self-control, brave and so on from the moment of our birth' (1144^{b}5–6). These natural virtues, unlike the virtues strictly so called, can be possessed piecemeal (1144^{a}35): virtue strictly so called is only possible in conjunction with wisdom (1144^{b}16). Intelligence differs from wisdom in two ways: first, it is tactical rather than strategic, concerned not with the formation of a *prohairesis* but with its efficient execution (1144^{a}21); secondly, it is capable of misuse, and can help execute bad choices as well as good ones, whereas wisdom is impossible apart from virtue (1144^{a}30).

Readers of Aristotle are sometimes puzzled by this. If we have to acquire virtue in order to become wise, and we cannot become wise without virtue, how can we ever acquire either virtue or wisdom? Are we not trapped in a practical vicious circle? The difficulty is a spurious one. It is as if someone were to allege a difficulty about getting married. How can anyone ever become a husband? For to be a husband you need to have a wife; but a woman cannot be a wife unless she has a husband! As a single union simultaneously turns a man into a husband and a woman into a wife, so the wedding of wisdom and virtue makes what was *deinotēs* into *phronēsis* and what was *physikē aretē* into *kyriōs aretē*.

The distinction between wisdom and intelligence is drawn elsewhere in the *AE* (C, 1152^{a}10–11) but does not figure in the *NE*. Nor are the *physikai aretai* mentioned as such, though just possibly Aristotle has them in mind when at 1105^{b}23 he contrasts with *hexeis* the *dynameis* or capacities to be affected by various emotions. The need for a good natural grounding for virtue is stressed, as at

1179^{b}21 ff. But in the *NE* there is no close parallel to the *AE* teaching on natural virtue and inborn intelligence.

In the *EE*, however, the doctrine is clearly stated in the same terminology. At 1227^{b}29 ff. we are told that *prohairesis* is not concerned with ends but means; 'hitting on the things that must be done for the sake of the end belongs to another power'—the formula is that used to introduce *deinotēs* in B. At 1234^{a}28 we are introduced to the natural virtues. 'For every virtue, as will be explained later, exists both naturally and otherwise, that is, in conjunction with wisdom.' The natural virtues then listed are natural justice and natural temperance, just as in B at 1144^{b}5. The fit is perfect.

Aristotle's teaching on wisdom, then, so far from supporting Jaeger's theory of the evolution of his ethical theory, provides a number of arguments to confirm the conclusion that the disputed books belong with the *Eudemian* rather than the *Nicomachean Ethics*. A study of Aristotle on *phronēsis* destroys a large part of the basis on which Jaeger's theory was constructed.

CHAPTER 8

Happiness in the
Aristotelian Ethics

THE references to happiness in the *AE* are brief and sometimes cryptic: but they are of great importance in connection with the question of the original home of the disputed books. For, as we shall see, one of the most important differences between the *NE* and the *EE* lies in the different treatment of happiness offered by each of them. The difference is not simply one of presentation, but of substance also. The *NE* sees happiness as constituted essentially by the contemplative activity of *nous*: this is the only happiness really worthy of the name, and the life of wisdom and the moral virtues is a second-rate kind of happiness. In the *EE* on the other hand happiness consists in the ideal functioning of every part of the soul: the activity of contemplation is only one, admittedly the highest one, among a family of activities which constitute the happy life. This contrast, while it has been ignored or questioned by some commentators, seems to me capable of decisive demonstration. Less easy to settle is which of these two conceptions of happiness is the one to be found in the common books. I shall argue that in general the *AE* in this respect as in others resembles the *EE* more than the *NE*: but some of the evidence, it must be admitted, is ambiguous, and from one passage it is clear that while writing the common books their author was at least aware of the possibility of the Nicomachean conception. But before studying the texts of the *AE* it is necessary to examine at some length the relevant parts of the *EE* and the *NE*.

To institute a comparison between the *EE* and the *NE* is in many parts of the work very easy. The same topics are often treated in the same order, and one can tick off the arguments as they occur in each treatise, noticing occasional omissions and variations on one side or the other. The first books of the treaties are not so simple to compare. They deal, broadly speaking, with the same topic:

happiness. They follow, broadly speaking, the same method: they review important current opinions on the topic (with particular reference to Plato) and then use the notion of *ergon* to reach Aristotle's own definition of happiness. And the definitions reached in the end—in the case of the *EE* not until the first chapter of the second book—seem remarkably similar. For the *NE* 'activity of soul in accordance with virtue, and if there are more than one virtue, in accordance with the best and most complete' is given as the definition of human good (1.6, 1098ᵃ16); in the *EE* the concluding definition of happiness is 'activity of complete life in accordance with complete virtue' (2.1, 1219ᵃ39). In each work, having reached his own definition, Aristotle goes on to show how well it fits with received opinion (*NE* 1.8 ff., *EE* II.1), and takes as his next topic the distinction between parts of the soul as the basis of the division of virtues into moral and intellectual (*NE* 1.13, *EE* II.1). But behind this over-all similarity there is a great difference of plan, of style, of proportion and even, once one begins to examine it closely, in doctrine. There is nothing like the close paragraph by paragraph parallelism we can find in later books.

The first book of the *EE* is tightly structured: though the structure escaped some earlier commentators, it has been well brought out in a recent analysis by Rowe (1971, 15 ff.). We begin with a solemn literary introduction—unusual in Aristotle—which leaves us in no doubt that the subject of the work is happiness. Inquiries may be practical or theoretical: ours, it is implied, is practical, but theoretical considerations will be appropriate from time to time. The first point of inquiry is what is a good life and how is it to be acquired (I.1, 1214ᵃ15). Immediately we are presented with five candidate answers to the second question (by nature, by learning, by training, by grace and by luck) and three candidate answers to the first (wisdom, virtue, and pleasure).

So far all seems clear, but we may be brought up short by the beginning of the next chapter. It would be a mark of great folly, we are told, if one can choose one's own way of life, not to organize one's life in pursuit of some goal or end (*skopos* or *telos*), whether honour or reputation or riches or culture: so the first thing which must be done is to decide in one's own case (for oneself?) what are the constituents and the necessary conditions for a good life.

The relationship of this passage to what precedes is puzzling. Are honour, reputation, riches, and culture meant as alternative answers to the question of chapter one: what constitutes a good life? Or are they alternative descriptions of the three canonical lives: the life of culture being the same as the life of wisdom, the life of riches being perhaps the same as the life of pleasure, and 'honour' and 'reputation' being both meant as synonyms for the life of virtue? Neither answer seems very plausible: but the question arises from a misunderstanding of a passage near the beginning of the first chapter where we are told that theoretical questions are to be discussed as occasion arises. This is commonly understood as a reference to a fairly distant future discussion—either in undefined future works outside the *EE*, or later in the *EE* itself (for the latter view see Rowe, 1971, 15). But surely it is a reference to what immediately follows: though the treatise is a practical one, there will be occasion for discussing theoretical matters, and *right at the beginning* we have to discuss the question 'What is the good life and how is it caused?' The practical question 'What goal in life should I pursue?' is not introduced until the beginning of chapter 2. Obviously the two questions are intimately connected: as Aristotle says, in order to answer the practical question one needs to reflect on the theoretical one, and in particular to have an eye on the theoretical distinction between essential constituents and necessary conditions. But the two questions are not identical. For suppose that the answer to the second part of the theoretical question was: happiness is caused by luck or by unmerited divine favour. Or suppose that the answer to the first part was: happiness is an absence of all striving. In either case, it would be absurd to answer the question 'How should I organize my life?' by saying 'Pursue happiness'.

The working out of the relationship between the theoretical and the practical question is the key to many of the puzzling features of the prologue (I.1–6) of the *EE* and shows how a number of passages which have been thought to be repetitious are not so and need not be explained as survivals from earlier layers of composition. One purpose of the prologue is to show that in the subsequent discussion of happiness only the opinions listed in the first chapter need to be taken seriously. In the case of the opinions about the origin of happiness this is stated immediately: the five listed ones (provided that one takes 'learning' in an extended sense, so that any action originating in human thought can be said to be the result of learning) exhaust the types of causes there are ($1214^{a}30$); in the case of the opinions about the nature of happiness it takes longer to show, since everyone has something to say (1215^{b}16). We do not have to consider the opinions of the very young, the sick, and the mad; nor do we have to consider the opinions of the multitude (1214^{b}35). This may seem surprising, as Aristotle shortly afterwards devotes quite a long section (1.5) to a consideration of the multitude, and since in general, in the words of G.E.L. Owen, 'when Aristotle discusses the views of "the many and the wise" it is the second party that gets the shorter shrift' (1968, 154). But what Aristotle is rejecting are the theoretical opinions of the many about the nature and origin of happiness; what he treats with respect, as philosophical data are the everday choices and decisions (actual and hypothetical) of the ordinary man.

What we are to consider are the opinions which occur in the traditional *aporiai* about happiness, namely those listed in the first chapter. The practical importance of the question 'What is happiness?' is obvious; but Aristotle takes time to show the importance also of the other question, 'What is its origin?' If happiness originates by chance (which here includes grace) or nature, then it will be beyond most people's reach and they can do nothing about it (1215^{a}15). Aristotle adds a third theoretical question—whether happiness consists in a quality of a person or a quality of his action—which he says will be very useful in clearing up the philosophical problems, and therefore indirectly in answering the practical question. It will indeed: the distinction between *hexis* and *energeia*, I shall argue, is central to his own solution to the relationship between the traditional three lives and the nature of happiness. Moral virtue and wisdom, though different *hexeis*, are exercised inseparably in a single *energeia*, so that they are not competing but collaborating elements in happiness, and pleasure is identical with the unimpeded *energeia* of the appropriate *hexeis*: so that happiness, understood as *energeia kat' aretēn*, has the characteristics of the three philosophical opinions about the nature of happiness.

Chapters 4 and 5 offer two different proofs that only these three views need taking seriously. Chapter 4 starts from the different lives or professions, and shows that the only ones worth taking seriously are those chosen by people of means, which are the political, philosophical, and apolaustic life, corresponding to the three opinions; people's views on happiness depend on their walks of life, and Anaxagoras is quoted as an intimation of Aristotle's own eventual composite view. Chapter 5 starts from the objects of voluntary actions. If we ask what a worthwhile life is, we may go through the various things which occur in life, and ask which of them make life worth living (or, as Aristotle says, worth choosing). There are some occurrences, e.g. sickness and pain, which make people want to give up life: clearly these do not make life worth living. There are the events of childhood: these cannot be the most choiceworthy things in life since no one in his right mind would choose to go back to childhood. In adult life there are events which bring neither pain nor pleasure in themselves: all the things which we do choose in the sense that we do them voluntary, but only as means to another end and not for their own sakes; clearly these, in themselves, cannot be what makes life worth living, and no one would choose to live for the sake of them however long they were to continue.

If life is to be worth living it must surely be for something which is an end in itself. One such end is pleasure. Consider first the pleasures of food and drink and sex. Only a slavish person would choose to live a life consisting of these alone without any aesthetic or intellectual pleasures, for it would be a life no different from a beast's. Nor does the pleasure of sleep make life worth living, for continued sleep would be the life of a plant. We are left therefore with three possibilities for what makes life worth living: a combination of the pleasures of food and drink and sex with the other bodily pleasure of the senses, which is the apolaustic life of Sardanapalus or Smindyrides; the life of virtuous action (the life of the real politician, not like the false politicians who are only after money or power); and the life of scientific contemplation (represented, once again, by Anaxagoras).

The conclusion of both chapters 4 and 5—both the consideration of the kinds of life which people choose to live, and the consideration of the types of answer which they would give to the question 'what makes life worth living?' show that 'all connect happiness with one or other of three lives, the political, the philosophical, and the voluptuary' (I.5, 1216ᵃ27). The purpose of the prologue up to this point, then, has been to select the opinions on the nature of happiness which are to be taken as the starting-point of the inquiry. We have reached the same point by three different routes. First, we have noticed that philosophers regard happiness as consisting in one or other or some combination of the three goods of wisdom, virtue, and pleasure; and we have eliminated the views of non-philosophers in favour of these three which belong to the traditional *aporiai* on the topic (1214^{b}29–1215^{a}9). Secondly, we have started from an exhaustive division of the types of life men lead, and have decided that only three, those chosen by men of means, are worth considering, and have noted that these correspond to the three goods first listed (1215^{a}34). Thirdly, we have started from the answers to the question 'What makes life worth living?' and reached the conclusion that the choices made by men and the answers they would give to this question once again lead to the point that only three candidate answers need to be taken seriously.

These three answers provide the 'true but unclear statements' which are the starting-point for the inquiry. The inquiry will be devoted to sifting out the truth from the confusion in the views: a start is already made in the final statement of them in the prologue (1216^{a}11–26) when we are invited to distinguish the genuine politician, who values virtuous actions for their own sake, from the pseudo-politician who uses them as a means to an end; when we are told that it is pleasure itself rather than particular sensual pleasures that the voluptuary sees as happiness; when the philosophic life is specified as one of scientific knowledge rather than of wisdom. The importance of these nuances will become clear only after Aristotle has presented his own account of happiness. For happiness, according to him is the exercise, as an end in itself, of all the virtues, moral and intellectual; and according to him pleasure is the greatest good, but only because pleasure is identified with the exercise of all the virtues.

The traditional opinions about the three lives and the corresponding goods, besides providing the starting point of the inquiry, dictate the plan of the work, as Aristotle spells out immediately (1216^{a}28 ff.). To sort out the truth from the falsehood in the voluptuary's opinion there is no need to inquire into the nature of bodily pleasures and their causes; all that is obvious enough. What needs to be investigated is whether these are constituents of happiness, or only connected with it in some other way (perhaps as necessary conditions); and whether there are other pleasures which make the happy life a pleasant life. These inquiries are postponed: an answer to the questions is in fact to be found in C of the disputed books: bodily pleasures are necessary to prevent the obstruction of virtuous activity (1153^b18) and the pursuit of the right amount of them is itself an exercise of virtue (1154^a15-18; cf. 1231^a17 in III.2).

The inquiry immediately to be undertaken is that into virtue and wisdom. (I speak of 'the inquiry'; they cannot be regarded as two separate inquiries entirely, because the division between virtue and wisdom presupposed in the traditional trichotomy is something which Aristotle is going to correct, substituting for it the distinction between ethical and intellectual virtues.) The word 'wisdom', used in the traditional distinction to denote the goal of a philosophical career, will be reserved by Aristotle for the practical intellectual virtue which is the foundation of the 'political life' but which also subserves the theoretical contemplation characteristic of the philosopher. The way in which Aristotle concludes his inquiry into virtue and wisdom in the *EE* is something which cannot be described without settling the question whether the *EE* contains the disputed books of the *AE*. If the disputed books do belong here, then we can say that from I.7 until the end of disputed book B is devoted to answering the question raised in 1216^a38-^b2; but we cannot say without qualification that books II to IV of the inclusive *Eudemian Ethics* deal with virtue, and book V deals with wisdom, since that is to state Aristotle's definitive treatment in terms of a provisional one which is merely his traditional starting point.

That Aristotle was at this point well aware of the possibility of structuring the relationship between virtue and wisdom in various ways is immediately apparent: for he goes on to talk of Socrates, who like himself disagreed with the dichotomy between virtue and wisdom, but who unlike himself thought that the division contained not too few but too many members, since, on the Socratic view, virtue and wisdom were identical.

Socrates is introduced principally, however, to usher in the methodological considerations which end the prologue of the *EE*. The present inquiry, unlike theoretical sciences, has an essentially practical purpose: our aim is not merely to know what justice is, but to be just. On the other hand, it is a genuinely philosophical inquiry, concerned to discover not just what is to be done but why it is to be done, operating by means of argument, but with due respect for received opinions which contain a deal of truth however obscurely and confusedly expressed (1216^b26-27^a18).

After this prologue (1217ᵃ18) Aristotle takes his start from the generally accepted, but as yet unclarified, statement that happiness is the greatest and best of human goods (1217ᵃ21). 'Human' is first clarified: we are concerned with goods what are human both in the sense of being good *for* men (vs. goods for gods or animals) and attainable *by* men. It is of good which are human in both these senses that happiness is the best (1217ᵃ22, ᵃ40).

For the rest of *EE* I Aristotle devotes himself to elucidating the word 'best' in the popular account of happiness. People say that the best of all things is *auto to agathon*, the absolute good, whose goodness is not dependent on that of anything else (so that it can be called 'the first good') and which is the cause of goodness in every other good thing. Aristotle is prepared to agree that the best of all things is the absolute good, but there are three rival opinions as to what the absolute good itself is. First, there is the Platonic opinion that it is the Idea of Good (1217ᵇ6–16), against which Aristotle argues at length (1217ᵇ17–1218ᵃ38). Secondly, there is the view that the absolute good is a common, univocal universal *goodness*: this is briskly disposed of with the remark that no practical discipline—not to mention the highest practical discipline, ethics—is concerned to bring about the presence of so thin and ubiquitous an attribute in its subject matter (1218ᵇ1–6). Aristotle concludes by presenting the third possible opinion as his own view.

It is clear, then, that neither the Idea of Good nor the universal, *goodness*, is the absolute good that we are looking for: for the one is unchangeable and unattainable; the other, while it is changeable, is not an object of attainment. But the wherefore, in the sense of end (*to hou heneka hōs telos*) is the best: it is the cause of what leads up to it and the first of all. It is this, then, that is the absolute good: the end of everything achievable by man (*to telos tōn anthropō(i) praktōn*) (1218ᵇ7–13)

'Best', then, in the popular definition of happiness, is clarified with reference to the notion of purpose. When we ask for the why and wherefore of any human action, we can be told that it is to be done for the sake of something else; we can ask in turn for the why and wherefore of that something else; when we reach a point where there is no further answer to the question, we have reached the 'wherefore in the sense of end'. It is the worthwhileness of the end of an action which makes the actions leading to it themselves worth while: in this sense an end is the cause of the goodness of the means to it. The best of all human goods, then, would be a good which appeared at the top end of every chain of practical reasoning: that would be an absolute good, an independent good on which the goodness of every other human good depended, as the goodness of health-producing drugs or regimes depends on the goodness of health itself (1218^b17-21). This supreme good is the subject matter of the supreme science of ethics and the virtue of wisdom.

At this point the first book of the *EE* ends. Aristotle has reached this stage by reflection on the dictum that happiness is the best of human goods. Next, at the beginning of book II, he throws into the discussion two further premisses: first, what is common to the supporters of the three lives, that happiness is either wisdom or virtue or pleasure; and secondly an inductively established definition of *aretē*—'virtue' in its broadest sense of 'excellence'—as 'the best state or condition or power of anything that has a use or a function (*ergon*) (1218^b35; 1219^a1). With the help of these further assumptions (1218^b39) he then proceeds to a close-knit argument designed to elucidate further the nature of happiness as the best of human goods (1218^b32-19^a38).

On all three of the traditional views, the best goods are in the soul: so that best of all things that we are looking for will be something in the soul. Now the things in the soul fall into two classes: some are states (or powers), others are activities (or processes). So the best thing in the soul will be either the best state or the best activity. Consider first the best state. If a thing has an *ergon* (as the soul does) then its best state is *aretē*. So far, then, we can conclude that the best thing in the soul is either *aretē* or the best activity. So now consider the best activity ($^b32-^a6$, $^a29-31$). We have to approach this through a consideration of the value of an *ergon*. The best *ergon* must be the *ergon* of the best state: for in general an *ergon* takes the rank of the state whose output it is. But which of these two, the *ergon* or the state producing it, is better? Clearly the *ergon*: for an *ergon* is an end: and we saw in the final stage of *EE* I that an end is the cause of goodness in the things whose end it is. (It is a general Aristotelian principle that if X causes Y to be P, X must be P-er than Y: e.g. only if X is hotter than Y will X heat Y.)[1] *This principle about the relationship of ergon and hexis* applies to all kinds of *ergon*, and in particular to the case where

1. Later incapsulated in the scholastic dictum *propter quod unumquodque tale, et illud magis.*

the *ergon* is an *energeia* or activity (in the way that the *ergon* of sight is seeing) rather than a product of activity (such as the health produced by healing or the houses that are the output of architectural skill).

Applying these considerations about *ergon* to the activities of the soul, we can draw the interim conclusion that if the activity of the best state of the soul (i.e. *aretē*) is an activity which is also an *ergon*, rather than the production of an *ergon*, then it will be the best thing in the soul that we are looking for. For it will be better than any other activity (by the theorem that an activity takes its rank from the state producing it); and it will be better than the best state which produces it (by the theorem that an *ergon* is better than the state whose output it is); and that state was *ex hypothesi* the best state; and everything in the soul is either a state or an activity (1219^a9-18).

All that remains, then, to inquire is: what *is* the activity of *aretē*, and is it its *ergon* or not? To discover this, let us ask what is the *ergon* of the soul's *aretē*. The *ergon* of a good X, or of the goodness of an X, is a good *ergon*-of-an-X: thus the *ergon* of a shoemaker is a shoe, and the *ergon* of excellence in shoemaking, or of a good shoemaker, is a good shoe. Applying this to the case in point, the *ergon* of soul is life,[1] so the *ergon* of the *aretē* or excellence of a soul is a good life (1219^a26-8). But the life that is meant here is active, waking life, and this is identical with the activity of the soul. So the best thing in the soul which we are looking for as the essence of happiness turns out to be the activity of *aretē* or the activity of a good soul (1218^a35).[2] But *aretē* can be either complete or incomplete, according to whether we mean *aretē* as a whole, or a particular partial *aretē*; and life, whose active stage is the *energeia* of the soul, likewise can be complete or incomplete (in the sense of running its

---

1. ἔστω ψυχῆς ἔργον τὸ ζῆν ποιεῖν. It makes nonsense of the argument to translate this, as Solomon, Rackham, and Dirlmeier do, 'the work of the soul is to produce living'. ἔστω ποιεῖν is to be construed on the model of ἔστιν ἰδεῖν, with ποιεῖν to be taken in the third of the senses given in Bonitz s.v., namely 'to posit': 'Let us take leave, then, to posit that the *ergon* of soul is life.' There is no need, once this has been understood, to emend the following manuscript reading τοῦ δὲ χρῆσις καὶ ἐγρήγορσις: it means '. . . is life, and of life the active and waking part'.

2. The structure of the argument is simpler and clearer in the recapitulation ($^a29-34$): the best goods are in the soul; everything in the soul is ἕξις or ἐνέργεια; so the best is either the best ἕξις or the best ἐνέργεια; the best ἕξις as ἀρετή; the best ἐνέργεια is the ἐνέργεια of the best ἕξις, *and is better than the best* ἕξις: so happiness, the best good, is the ἐνέργεια of the ἀρετή of the soul, i.e. the ἐνέργεια of a good soul. In the full-fledged deployment the argument is complicated by the introduction of the notion of ἔργον.

proper course or not). So happiness—which is something perfect and complete—must finally be defined as 'activity of complete life in accordance with complete virtue' (1219ᵃ39). His definition thus completed, Aristotle goes on to confirm it by showing that it is in accord with universally received opinions (1219ᵃ39–ᵇ26).

Though the argument is always compressed, and sometimes sketchy, and though the style lapses at one point into mere jotting (1218ᵃ36), the discussion of happiness in the *EE* is clearly very carefully thought out and tightly structured. It is also in perfect accord with the philosophical method sketched in the prologue.[1]

When we turn from the first part of the *EE* to book 1 of the *NE* we find a different and far less organized structure. The *NE* starts not from the notion of *eudaimonia* but from that of goodness. The subject matter of ethics (*politikē*) is the good for man, the end of action for the sake of which all else is desired (an ultimate end whose existence is presented in a passage of notoriously suspect validity, 1094ᵃ18–22).[2] Most people would agree that this supreme good is happiness (however much they must disagree about what precisely happiness consists in) (1095ᵃ18–26); but some people, the Platonists, argue that the supreme good is an absolute good which is the cause of all other thing's goodness. Aristotle then goes on to expand the general view that the supreme good is happiness by outlining the three traditional lives (1095ᵇ14–96ᵃ10), and to criticize the Platonic view by providing a series of arguments to show the incoherence of the Idea of the Good (1096ᵃ12–97ᵃ4). Aristotle begins his own account by saying that the good we are looking for must be *teleion* by comparison with other ends—that is, it must be something sought always for its own sake and never for the sake of anything else; and it must be *autarkes* or self-sufficient—that is, it must be something which taken on its own

---

1. In recent years Allan (1961, 308–11) and Rowe (1971, 15–26) have done much to elucidate the structure of the *EE* discussion of happiness. Though I disagree with Allan on one or two points and with Rowe on many, my interpretation of the passage owes much to theirs.

2. In my paper 'Happiness' (1966) I attempted to defend the *NE* from the charge of committing a quantifier-shift fallacy at this point. Subsequent discussions with a number of people (in particular Mr. J. O. Urmson and Mrs. L. Brown) have made me less confident that the *NE* can be defended along the lines I suggested. But whatever the case with the *NE*, it is clear that the *EE* is guiltless on this point. For if Aristotle is guilty of the fallacy he is charged with, he must think it is a logical truth that, if there is choice at all, there is a single supreme end. But *EE* I, 1214ᵇ6 ff. admits it as a possibility—though a mark of folly—not to organize one's life in view of an end.

makes life worth while and lacking in nothing. *Eudaimonia* has both these properties ($1097^a15-{}^b21$). What, then *is eudaimonia?* To elucidate this, we must consider the *ergon* of man. Man must have an *ergon*, because particular types of men (e.g. sculptors) do, and parts and organs of human beings do. What is it? Not life, not at least the life of growth and nourishment, for this is shared by plants, nor the life of the senses, for this is shared by animals. It must be a life of reason concerned with action: the activity of soul in accordance with reason. So the good of man will be his good *ergon*: the activity of soul in accordance with virtue, and if there are several virtues, in accordance with the best and most perfect (*teleiotatēn*) virtue (1097^b22-98^a18).

Though on a superficial reading the accounts of happiness in the first books of the *NE* and *EE* appear rather similar, closer investigation reveals substantial differences in structure, in argument, and in doctrine. Even when the same technical terms appear—such as *ergon, teleion, auto to agathon*—they are put to very different use. And the concluding definitions of happiness enunciate radically different theories of its nature.

The structure of the *NE* treatment of happiness is much less neat than that of the *EE*. The flow of the argument is frequently broken by scattered and repetitive methodological remarks (1094^b11-95^a14; $1095^a30-{}^b14$; $1098^a26-{}^b9$). The connection between the discussion of the three lives and the refutation of the Idea of the Good is not brought out. The opinions of others on the topic, instead of being worked into the argument as they are in the *EE*, are presented in an enormous album of frequently disjointed remarks in chapters 8–12. There are a number of inconclusive passages where the argument comes back to its starting-point and a fresh beginning has to be made: sometimes this is even remarked upon in the text ('The argument has come around to the point where we were before', 1097^a23).

Rowe, who has detailed the incongruities of the *NE* text,[1] considers that they provide evidence that the *EE* represents an earlier stage of Aristotle's development. Having written the *EE*, he suggests, Aristotle changed his mind on a major point; he wrote the *NE* as a revision of the *EE*, but the revision was only partially

---

1. He even somewhat exaggerates them. There is no need, for instance, to attribute to the *NE* the suggestion that 'the Idea of the Good' might be an answer to the question 'what is happiness?' (Rowe, 1971, 27). In this section Rowe acknowledges his debt to Kapp (1912).

complete, leaving ugly traces of the original pattern. It seems a little curious to treat a more careful and polished treatment of a topic as prima-facie evidence of an earlier stage of composition: it would be at least as plausible to suggest that the *EE* represents a definitive ordering of material which had been only partially moulded into shape at the time of writing of the *NE*. The final scrapbook of received opinions, Rowe thinks, provides evidence against those who regard the *EE* as post-Aristotelian. 'If *EE* is spurious, and was constructed on the model of *EN*, then its Peripatetic author shows a remarkable ingenuity; he has evidently abstracted certain parts of the list presented by *EN*, worked them into the structure of I, 1–7, and still managed to construct a highly coordinated series of arguments.' The rewriting would certainly call for ingenuity. But a suggestion that the *EE* I is later than *NE* need not be a suggestion that *EE* I is non-Aristotelian; and it would surely be rash to assume that the ingenuity involved in turning *NE* 1 into *EE* I would be beyond the powers of an Aristotle.

The principal difference in structure between the *EE* and the *NE* is that whereas the *EE* begins with the concept of happiness, and goes on to discuss the nature of goodness in the course of commenting on the terms of a traditional definition of happiness, the *NE* begins with the supreme good as the subject matter of Ethics, and goes on to consider happiness as the most popular answer to the question 'what is the supreme good?' But the differences between the accounts, as has been said, go deeper than mere presentation. In the *EE*, unlike the *NE*, Aristotle is prepared to accept the notion of an absolute good (*auto to agathon*).[1] In both ethics in the construction of the definition of happiness use is made of the concept of *ergon*: but the *ergon* in question in the *EE* is the *ergon* of the soul, in the *NE* the *ergon* of man. The *EE* lays much more stress than the *NE* on the causal role of the supreme good: the final cause that is the first cause in the order of goodness-causation, the cause of the goodness of other goods.

1. D. J. Allan comments well on the significance of this. '[In the *NE*] he treats as equivalent the assertion of a Platonic Idea and the use of the expression "absolute". The search for the absolute good is consequently a wild goose chase. The author of the *EE* joins with enthusiasm in the search, and is in full agreement about the description of the bird that is being hunted. It would seem to me that the key to this difference in the style of criticism is not that the Eudemian version shows closer sympathy with Platonism . . . but that the passage is integral to the discourse on method which immediately precedes it. The Platonist is to be disabused of his errors by reasoning from the premises which he admits, and which are true, but not in the way in which he supposes' (1961, 309).

The question is often raised whether the *EE* is more Platonic than the *NE*. Most of those prepared to give an answer give one in the affirmative: but scholars in recent years have come more and more to realize that the question has too many facets to be given a simple yes–no reply.[1] In the present context of the discussions of happiness we can say that the *NE* resembles Platonic ethical theory more than the *EE* does in making the, good, rather than happiness, the primary ethical concept; on the other hand the *ergon* argument in the *EE* is closer than the *NE* one is to the parallel section in the *Republic* (352 e–354 a) in appealing to the notion of the *ergon* of the soul rather than to the philosophically more suspect notion of the *ergon* of man. The criticism of the Idea of the Good is more thoroughgoing, and conducted from a less sympathetic standpoint, in the *EE* than in the *NE*: in the words of D. J. Allan 'its manner of introducing the discussion, placed side by side with the Nicomachean equivalent, can only seem cool and abrupt'.[2] The discussion in the *EE*, as G. Verbeke has pointed out, is more closely linked than that in the *NE* to general Aristotelian theories of causation, potentiality, and actuality.[3]

The most important difference between the accounts of happiness in the *NE* 1 and in the *EE* I–II is that the former identifies happiness with a single dominant end, the activity of the highest virtue; whereas the latter views happiness as an inclusive end, the activity of all the virtues of the rational soul in the broadest sense. The *NE* says that the good for man is 'activity of soul in accordance with virtue, and if there is more than one virtue, in accordance with the best and most perfect (*teleia*)' (1098ª16). In the last chapter of the book we are told that there is indeed more than one virtue—there are, for instance, moral and intellectual virtues—and hence we conclude, unconditionally, that happiness is activity in accordance with the best and most perfect of these many virtues. (Compare 1102ª5–7 with 1103ª2–10.) In the *EE* we are told that happiness is activity 'of complete life in accordance with complete (*teleia*) virtue'; and the word 'complete' has just been unambiguously glossed when Aristotle has said that 'life is either complete or incomplete, and so also virtue—one being whole virtue, another a part (1219ª35–9). So that when in the *EE* Aristotle

1. This has been so especially since G. E. L. Owen's classic lecture 'The Platonism of Aristotle' (1965).
2. Op. cit. 309.
3. Verbeke, 1951, 83.

goes on to distinguish the parts of the soul and the virtues that correspond to them, and to list examples of moral and intellectual virtues, we know that their activities are all supposed to be part of happiness. The virtue of the soul that figures in the definition of the end of man—we learn at 1220ᵃ4—is a virtue which is constituted by the several virtues of the different parts of the soul.

The contrast I have just drawn has long been familiar to scholars.[1] It has recently been questioned by Professor J. L. Ackrill, who argues that it is a mistake to regard Aristotle's idea of *eudaimonia* in *NE* i as the idea of a 'dominant' end. The concluding clause of the *NE* definition 'if there are more than one virtue, in accordance with the best and most complete' should not be understood as referring to a particular supreme virtue, one of many, but rather to total and comprehensive virtue, the sum of all virtues (Ackrill, 1974, 15–18).

Ingenious though it is, this interpretation does not seem to me tenable. In the previous chapter of the *NE* Aristotle has already made clear that he does not regard happiness as an inclusive end, but as a dominant one, in the passage in which he says that when we are looking for happiness we are looking for something which, when not added to anything else, is most choiceworthy—clearly, if it is so added it is more choiceworthy with even the least additional good. If happiness were meant as an inclusive end, as the sum total of goods sought for their own sake, it would be absurd to speak of goods additional to happiness.[2] When Aristotle speaks of 'the best

1. e.g. Verbeke, 1951, 84: 'Le point de vue adopté dans l'*Ethique Eudémienne* est indéniablement plus large que la position prise dans l'*Éthique à Nicomaque*: dans ce dernier ouvrage Aristote cherche l'activité propre de l'homme, celle qui le distingue de tous les autres vivants, et pour y arriver, il procède par élimination progressive pour ne retenir que l'activité intellectuelle ou la contemplation; dans l'*Éthique Eudémienne* le Stagirite affirme simplement la supériorité des biens psychiques sur les biens extérieurs et il en conclut qua la perfection de l'homme se trouve dans l'activité de l'âme: mais il ne dit pas que cette activité serait purement intellectuelle ou contemplative: on ne voit pas qu'il exclut d'autres activités psychiques.'

2. This interpretation of 1097ᵇ f. was adopted in my paper 'Happiness' (1966). It is criticized by Ackrill, p. 12, who writes 'It is indeed only if one is willing, with Kenny, to treat "happiness" as a fair translation of the word *eudaimonia* that one can feel the slightest temptation to take the self-sufficiency passage as he does.' I agree that 'happiness' is an imperfect translation of *eudaimonia*, which means something more like 'worthwhile way of life'; I use it in preference to such a periphrasis on grounds of tradition and brevity. But my interpretation of this passage is a traditional one, which was adopted by Eustratius, Albertus Magnus, and Thomas Aquinas, who were comparatively free from the temptations presented by the distracting overtones of the English word. Thus Eustratius (*CAG* xx.65) γίνεται γὰρ τὸ προστιθέμενον ὑπεροχὴ τοῦ ἀγαθοῦ καὶ αὔξησις, ὡς μείζονα ἐκ τῆς προσθήκης τὴν εὐδαιμονίαν γινομένην αἱρετωτέραν εἶναι αὐτὴν μετ' αὐτοῦ, ἢ αἱρετή ἐστιν καὶ

and most *teleia* virtue' the word '*teleia*' admittedly has several
senses, one of which is 'complete';[1] but it is hard to take the word
for 'best' to mean 'comprehensive of many' rather than 'better than
the rest'. '*Aretē*', like the English word 'virtue', can be used as a
mass-noun (as in 'a man of great virtue') or as a count-noun (as in
'a man of many virtues'); but on Ackrill's view Aristotle is made to
switch from the mass-noun to the count-noun use and back again to
the mass-noun use within a space of ten words.

The traditional view sees the clause 'if there are more than one
virtue, in accordance with the best and most complete', as keeping
open a place for the eventual doctrine of *NE* 10 that happiness is the
activity of the supreme virtue of *sophia*. Even Ackrill does not try to
deny that in *NE* 10 a 'dominant' view of happiness is adopted. No
doubt we are wise not to take it for granted that *NE* 1 and *NE* 10
were written in a single stint: but there is evidence that when *NE* 1
was written Aristotle was thinking of the topic of *NE* 10 (1096ª5)
and that when he wrote *NE* 10 he had in mind *NE* 1 (1177ª11). 'If
happiness is activity in accordance with virtue, it is reasonable that
it should be activity in accordance with the most excellent virtue:
and this will be the one of the best part of us.' This is either *nous* or
something like it, so 'the activity of this in accordance with its
proper virtue will be perfect (*teleia*) happiness'. If *teleia* here means
'final' rather than complete, that suggests that it meant the same in
the *NE* 1 passage to which reference is made; if it means 'complete'
then again it implies that there is nothing else in happiness other
than the contemplative activity of *nous*. Aristotle then goes on to
show that theoretic contemplation possesses all the qualities which,
according to Book 1, were, in popular opinion and in truth,
properties of happiness. Thus: it is the highest activity, most
continuous and durable (1177ª21; cf. 1100ᵇ11–17); the pleasantest
(ª23 ff.; cf. 1099ª7 ff.); most self-sufficient (ª27; cf. 1097ᵇ6 ff.); it is
loved for its own sake (1177ᵇ1 ff.) and therefore *teleion* in the sense
explained at 1097ª30 ff. If Aristotle underwent a spectacular change
in his view of happiness between Book 1 and Book 10, as Ackrill's
view seems to imply, he wrote book 10 in such a way as to cover up
the change entirely. But even if Ackrill is right about *NE* 1, the

ἀπόντος αὐτοῦ. The traditional interpretation criticized by Ackrill is ably vindicated by
Clark (1975, 153–4).

1. In its immediately succeeding use, the word means 'complete' (1098ª18); the use
previously explained was 'always chosen for itself and never for the sake of something else'
(1097ª30).

contrast between the *EE* and the *NE* remains: for at no point does the *EE* adopt the view of happiness as identical with *theōria* which Ackrill agrees is presented in *NE* 10.

The complete virtue, whose exercise in a complete life constitutes *eudaimonia* according to *EE* I, is the sum total of the virtues discussed in the central books of the *EE*, and is treated again as a unified whole in the first part of the final chapter of *EE* VIII, under the description *kalokagathia* (1248^{b}8–16). Clearly, anyone who deserves the description *kalos kagathos* must have all the individual virtues, just as a body can only be healthy if all, or at least the main, parts of it are healthy. Aristotle then develops the theme that natural goods, like health, and wealth are beneficial only to a good man: to a bad man they may be positively harmful. But among good men we must distinguish between those of a utilitarian cast, who pursue virtue for the sake of non-moral goods, and the *kaloi kagathoi* who pursue the natural goods only for the sake of the virtuous actions for which they are useful. The two marks of the *kalos kagathos*—that he has all the virtues, and that he pursues the virtues for their own sake and other things for the sake of them—are not really distinct: already in the case of the particular virtues we were told that genuine virtue involves the choice of *to kalon* (1229^{a}2 ff.; 1230^{a}29–32). The new character introduced here is not the *kalos kagathos*, but the mere *agathos*, the 'Laconian' character who pursues virtue as a means to an end: he—like the continent and incontinent persons discussed in *AE* C and from time to time in the *EE*—occupies a position intermediate between the virtuous and vicious characters who are presented in an exaggeratedly well-defined trichotomy by the doctrine of the mean. This last distinction between the *agathos* and the *kalos kagathos* sets in final clarity the ideal of the happy life as one of complete virtue (1249^{a}18).

Though we are told that *kalokagathia* is complete virtue, we are not at this point explicitly reminded that happiness is the exercise of complete virtue. But Aristotle goes on immediately:

Pleasure has already been discussed: what kind of thing it is, and in what sense it is a good; and how things which are pleasant *simpliciter* are fine *simpliciter*, and things which are good *simpliciter* are also pleasant. But there cannot be pleasure except in action: and so the truly happy man will also have the most plesant life. This human quest is not an idle one. (1249^{a}18–21)

The first of the backward references in this passage is intelligible only if *AE* C, or something like it, preceded in the original *Eudemian Ethics*. The next points are both made in the book on Friendship: Things which are pleasant *simpliciter* are fine *simpliciter* because that most rightly deserves to be called pleasant which the wise man calls pleasant; and to him it is good and fine things that are pleasant (1235b36–36ᵃ7). Things which are good *simpliciter* are also pleasant, because it is natural goods which are good *simpliciter* and these are naturally pleasant: this natural pleasure is nature's road to virtue (1237ᵃ5–9).

Thus for the ideally virtuous man the concepts '*agathon*', '*hēdu*', '*kalon*' coincide in their application. If what is pleasant for a man differs from what is good for him, then he is not yet perfectly good but incontinent (1237ᵃ8–9); if what is good for him does not coincide with what is fine for him, then he is not yet *kalos kagathos* but only *agathos*: for the *kalos kagathos* the natural goods of health and wealth and power are not only beneficial but fine, since they subserve his virtuous activity (1249ᵃ9). So for him, goodness, fineness, and pleasantness coincide. The bringing about of this coincidence is the task of ethics (1247ᵃ3). But whereas something can be *kalon* or *agathon* whether it is a *hexis* or an *energeia* (1248ᵇ35–7, ᵇ23–4) it is only an *energeia* or *prāxis* that can be pleasant. So it is in the fine activities of the good man that the highest pleasure is to be found and that pleasure, goodness, and fineness meet. But the fine activities of the good man are the activities of perfect virtue with which happiness was identified in book one. So the treatise has reached completion: Aristotle has carried out the promise of his first paragraph to show that happiness combined the three superlatives—finest, best, and pleasantest—of the Deliac inscription (1214ᵃ7–8).

The quotation just given is not, however, the last paragraph of the *EE*. It is followed by the passage already discussed concerning the *horos* of *kalokagathia*. For at 1249ᵃ21 Aristotle has yet to finish showing the truth contained in the true but unclarified premiss that happiness belongs to one of the three traditional lines.[1] The discussion of virtue and of pleasure and of *kalokagathia* has shown that what the seekers of pleasure and the pursuers of virtue seek is to be found in Aristotelian ideal. But what of the Anaxagorean life of

---

1. I think Jaeger was well inspired to regard Aristotle's ideal as a synthesis of the three lives (235–8). John Cooper says 'The study of the three lives no more provides the structure of the *Eudemian Ethics* than it does that of the *Nicomachean*; Jaeger was grasping at straws here with which to prop up his theory of Aristotle's development' (Cooper, 1975, 145). This seems to me imperceptive.

philosophic contemplation? Are the values of that life too
incorporated in the inclusive programme of *eudaimonia*?

Let us continue to leave aside, for the moment, the *AE*, and try to
answer the question from the *EE* context alone. If *kalokagathia* is a
synthesis of the virtues of parts of the soul in the way that health is a
synthesis of the health of various parts of the body, then it must
include the virtues of the intellectual parts of the soul as well as of
the passional part. Wisdom is alluded to as a necessary part of
kalokagathia at 1248^{b}31: but is the healthy functioning of the
speculative part of the soul part of the complete virtue which is
happiness? The final section about the criterion of *kalokagathia* is
there to tell us not only that is it part of happiness itself but that it
sets the standard to which the activities of the other virtues must
conform if they are to remain within the realm of virtue and
happiness. Not, of course, that reference to the contemplation and
service of God settles *how much* of the other virtues one should
have; that would be absurd, since virtue is something of which
there cannot be too much. But virtuous action consists in executing
choices about the right amount of other things—the passions and
external goods which are the field of operation of the moral
virtues—and it is reference to the *horos* which is necessary to decide
what *is* the right amount of such things. This does not conflict with
the doctrine that virtue must be chosen for its own sake, because it is
kalon; the *horos* provides the measure, not the motive, of virtuous
action. Brave, temperate, and generous living is an end in itself,
chosen for its own sake, and as part of happiness in its own right.
But what particular behaviour in concrete circumstances counts as
virtuous living cannot be settled without consideration of the
contemplation and service of God. Aristotle's favourite analogy
between spiritual and physical health may help us here. The
healthy man has a good appetite for the right sort and the right
amount of food. The right sort and the right amount of food means:
the sort and amount of food that conduces to health. But the healthy
man, unlike the hypochondriac, does not eat his food *because* it
conduces to health; he eats it because he has a good appetite and he
enjoys his food.

The contrast, then, between the inclusive, organic view of
happiness in the *EE*, and the dominant, intellectualist one of the
NE is clear and profound, Instead of a single life offering us all the
values sought by the promoters of the three traditional lives, the
concluding section of the *NE* offers us a first-class, perfect

happiness consisting of the exercise of *sophia*, and an alternative, second-class career consisting in the exercise of *phronēsis* and the moral virtues. [1] Now which of these conceptions of happiness matches better the remarks about happiness in the disputed books?

In *AE* A we are told that 'we call those acts just that tend to produce and preserve happiness and its parts for the political community' (1129^b19). This seems to presuppose the *EE* view of happiness as a whole with parts, rather than the *NE* view of happiness as a single dominant activity—and one which at its best can be pursued outside a community (1177^a33). In B we are told that wisdom studies 'the things which will make a man happy': the plural perhaps fits the *EE* conception better than the *NE* one, but it is hard to be certain whether the Greek expression (*ex hōn estai eudaimōn anthrōpos*) refers to means towards happiness or actual constituents of happiness (cf. *EE* 1214^b12 ff. and 1216^b21). The crucial passage in B for our concerns is the following answer to the objection that learning and wisdom are superfluous because unproductive: 'They are indeed productive: not like medical skill in relation to health, but like health itself; it is thus that learning is productive of happiness: for being a part of virtue entire by being possessed and being operative it is productive of happiness' (1143^a3–6). [2] The passage is difficult enough to deserve five pages of discussion in Gauthier and Jolif's commentary. The difficulties are these. (1) The passage begins with a plural verb ('they are productive') and then we are offered a single subject ('learning'): how much of the passage is about both learning and wisdom, and

---

1. I agree with Cooper (1975, 157–60) against Gauthier–Jolif (1959, 893–6) that this is the only possible interpretation of 1176^b26–$^a22$, and Aristotle's doctrine cannot be taken to be that there is a single happy life consisting primarily of the exercise of learning and secondarily of the exercise of the other virtues. Cooper shows convincingly that this is not a possible reading of the crucial sentences: καὶ τῷ ἀνθρώπῳ δὴ ὁ κατὰ τὸν νοῦν βίος, εἴπερ τοῦτο μάλιστα ἄνθρωπος. οὗτος ἄρα καὶ εὐδαιμονέστατος. δευτέρως δ' ὁ κατὰ τὴν ἄλλην ἀρετήν. But Cooper's own view, that the second-rate life of *NE* 10 is the same as the mixed life of *EE*, seems as untenable as Gauthier's. The only positive argument he offers for it as that it would be strange if the mixed life championed in the *EE* were not so much as mentioned in the *NE*. That is so, only if the *NE* is later than the *EE*. And for this we need an independent argument—which, of course, Cooper believes he has: the psychology of *NE* 10, he says, is closer to the *de Anima*, which he assumes is late (pp. 175 ff.). Devereux (1977, 8), who shares Cooper's faith in the lateness of *NE* 10, has shown how little support the *NE* text gives to Cooper's interpretation of the two types of happiness.

2. ἔπειτα καὶ ποιοῦσι μέν, οὐχ ὡς ἡ ἰατρικὴ δὲ ὑγίειαν, ἀλλ' ὡς ἡ ὑγίεια, οὕτως ἡ σοφία εὐδαιμονίαν. μέρος γὰρ οὖσα τῆς ὅλης ἀρετῆς τῷ ἔχεσθαι ποιεῖ καὶ τῷ ἐνεργεῖν εὐδαιμονίαν. Like von Fragstein (1974, 247) I prefer to read εὐδαιμονίαν with Pap. Oxyrhync. 2402, Lb and Ob and Eustratius; but if one reads εὐδαίμονα with Mb ('makes a man happy') the sense is much the same.

how much about learning alone? (2) What is it that health is supposed to be productive of? (3) What is meant by saying that learning, as part of virtue entire, is productive of happiness?

I answer the difficulties as follows. (1) It is true of both wisdom and learning that they are productive of happiness in the way that health is productive: but it is true only of learning, and not also of wisdom, that it is *not* productive in the way that medical skill is. For both learning and wisdom are constituents of happiness; but wisdom contributes to happiness not only in being a constituent of it, but in prescribing for the sake of another constituent, namely learning (1145^a9). (2) What health produces is neither happiness (as some commentators have thought in contradiction to *EE* 1219^b20-2) nor health (as others have thought, in spite of the relation between health and health being manifestly one of tautologous equivalence rather than efficient causality) but the activities of a healthy body. Health is a *hexis* which produces, causally, the *energeiai* characteristic of it. Ross caught the sense exactly in his note on his translation: 'I.e., as health, as an inner state, produces the activities which we know as constituting health.' It is in this way that wisdom and learning produce happiness: they are the *hexeis* whose activities constitute happiness, as is spelt out in the final part of the passage. (3) Learning is only a *part* of virtue entire; it would be pointless of Aristotle to remind us of this here if he intended to say, as many commentators make him say, that it is the *whole* of happiness. It is because it is *part* of virtue entire, and because the activity of virtue entire (the 'complete virtue' of *EE* I) is happiness, that the possession plus exercise of learning is productive of happiness: learning is one of the *hexeis* which causally produce *energeiai* which in their totality are happiness.

Thus understood—and this way of understanding it, I would contend, is the natural way of understanding it even on grounds of its internal structure alone[1]—the passage is in perfect accord with the doctrine of *EE* I and *EE* VIII, but in flagrant contradiction with that of *NE* 10 and more muffled contradiction with that of *NE* 1. It

---

1. No one has taken more pains to square this passage with *NE* 10 than Gauthier and Jolif, and even they admit that the most obvious way of taking the passage 'bouleverse tout l'édifice de la morale aristotélicienne en faisant entrer la sagesse pratique,—et avec elle la vertu morale qui en est inséparable,—dans la constitution même de la fin suprême, qui partout ailleurs[!] consiste dans la seule contemplation' (1959, 543). Their own interpretation, which on the basis of comparison with fr. 6 W of the *Protrepticus* makes Aristotle say that learning is an improper part (i.e. the whole) of happiness, is rightly found unwarranted and fanciful by Cooper (1975, 112–13).

clearly envisages an inclusive, not a dominant conception of happiness.

There remains one further passage on happiness in the disputed books. It is a long passage in the discussion of pleasure in *AE* C, which I shall first quote and divide into numbered sections to facilitate further discussion.

(1) If certain pleasures are bad, that does not prevent the chief good from being some pleasure, just as the chief good may be some form of knowledge though certain kinds of knowledge are bad. Perhaps it is even necessary, if each disposition has unimpeded activities, that, whether the activity (if unimpeded) of all of our dispositions or that of some one of them is happiness, this should be the thing most worthy of our choice; and this activity is pleasure. Thus the chief good would be some pleasure, though most pleasures might perhaps be bad without qualification. (2) And for this reason all men think that the happy life is pleasant and weave pleasure into their ideal of happiness—and reasonably too; for no activity is perfect when it is impeded, and happiness is a perfect thing; this is why the happy man needs the goods of the body and the external goods, i.e. those of fortune, viz. in order that he may not be impeded in these ways. (3) Those who say that the victim on the rack or the man who falls into great misfortunes is happy if he is good are, whether they mean to or not, talking nonsense. (4) Now because we need fortune as well as other things, some people think good fortune the same thing as happiness; but it is not that, for even good fortune itself when in excess is an impediment, and perhaps should then be no longer called good fortune; for its limit is fixed by reference to happiness. ($1153^{b}7$–24, trs. Ross)

(1) In the first section of this passage, it is very striking that Aristotle appears to leave open the question whether virtue is the activity of *all* the virtues (for the 'dispositions' he has in mind are clearly virtues) or of some one of them. This is the only place in the *EE* or the *AE* where this is done, and it cannot but remind the reader of the definition of the human good in *NE* 1 as 'activity of soul in accordance with virtue, and if there are more than one virtue, in accordance with the best and most complete'. If any passage of the *AE* has the ring of a Nicomachean interpolation, it is surely this one. Yet the style, in other respects, is not more Nicomachean than Eudemean; and it would be ironic to regard this passage as evidence of a Nicomachean origin for the disputed books when it was the very same passage which—because of its identification of the supreme good with a pleasure—seemed to Aspasius (*CAG* xix.151) to provide evidence that the context was

not by Aristotle but by Eudemus. In fact a closer reading of the passage shows that there is a crucial difference from the Nicomachean parallel. In *NE* 1 the disjunctive definition of happiness appeared in a conclusion of Aristotle's own argument, and had as its purpose to keep open an unobvious alternative he was later to argue to be the correct one. Here, it appears as an *ad hominem* argument against those who refuse to identify pleasure with the supreme good—whoever they may be, whether Plato, Speusippus, or other Platonists perhaps even including an earlier Aristotle. The disjunction can very well be understood as intended to allow, *dato non concesso*, a premiss which Aristotle rejects: 'Whether happiness is (as argued in the present work) the unimpeded activity of all human virtues or (as our opponents allege) the unimpeded activity of one particular human virtue, either way happiness is unimpeded activity and therefore pleasure.' Certainly this passage allows assumptions to which Aristotle, on his own account, would never have assented at the time when he wrote either the *NE* or the *EE*: as that the majority of pleasure are bad *haplōs*.

(2) That the happy life is rightly thought to be pleasant is common ground in the *NE* (1177^{a}22) and the *EE* (1249^{a}20). Both treatises also allow that happiness may be impeded by lack of external goods (*NE* 1178^{b}33 f.; *EE* 1249^{b}20); but of course the way in which lack of money 'impedes' liberality is more intimate than that in which it impedes contemplation. The present passage would fit either type of prevention.

(3) That a virtuous man is happy in the midst of suffering and misfortune is a view which is criticized both in the *NE* (1096^{a}2) and by implication in the *EE* (1214^{b}14): it was, as Burnet and Gauthier showed, a view dear to Plato and the author of the *Protrepticus* (Gauthier–Jolif, 1959, 32).

(4) In both ethics the mistaken identification of happiness with good fortune is mentioned (*NE* 1, 2099^{b}8; *EE* 1215^{a}12 ff.); in both we are warned that excessive good fortune may make virtue and happiness difficult (*NE* 1124^{a}30 ff.; *EE* 1249^{b}20). The language of the warning in the *EE*, like the one here, makes use of the technical term *horos*.

We have now considered all the references to happiness in the *AE*. We can see that, despite the difficulties in interpretation of two of the most crucial passages, they add up, on balance, to a theory of happiness and its parts and its relation to virtue and fortune which is closer in both substance and terminology to that of the *EE* than to that of the *NE*. This impression is confirmed when we consider that the *Eudemian Ethics* itself makes a much more coherent whole when the *AE* is included in it than if it is omitted. The intellectual virtues are then dealt with at a length proportionate to that devoted to the moral virtues; the relation of the Aristotelian ideal of happiness to the Anaxagorean contemplative life is spelt out by the discussion of *sophia* and its relation to *eudaimonia*; the promise in *EE* I to discuss the value of pleasure and its relation to human goodness is kept in *AE* C. If the *AE* belongs with the *EE* then there is consistently presented a view which combines an inclusive conception of happiness as the exercise of all the virtues with an insistence on the primacy and supreme value of philosophical contemplation. On this view, wisdom and the moral virtues find expression in actions which are both parts of happiness in themselves and also promote the contemplation which is the supreme element in happiness. Acts of the moral virtues contribute to happiness in the way that good breathing contributes to good singing and not in the way in which (say) being early to bed and early to rise may do so. They are things which a happy man does *qua* happy, as the good singer's good breathing is an inseparable and essential part of his good singing. Finally, the summary in *EE* VIII.3 of the whole course of the discussion fits admirably a *Eudemian Ethics* which contains the *AE* and displays to the careful reader the elegant structure of the work as a whole.[1]

The contrast that we have drawn between the *NE* view of happiness and the *EE* view of happiness, and the comparison we have made between each and the observations on happiness in the *AE*, once more confirms the hypothesis that the disputed books originally belong with the *EE*. In conclusion, we may note that our discussion also enables us to throw light on a crux in the *EE*. In the discussion (1120^b35-21^a10) of the doctrine of the mean in *EE* 2 Aristotle presents a list of triads of which the final member is 'cunning–stupidity–wisdom'. As many of the triads in the list are

---

1. This is well brought out by Dirlmeier in his excellent note on 1249^a17: 'VIII 3 ist überhaupt ein Kap. de Rückbeziehungen: am Anfang der Verweis auf *EE* III; sodann ist die Existenz von *EE* Iv (= *NE* 5, verteilende Gerechtigkeit) vorausgesetzt, ferner die von *EE* V (= *NE* 6, *Phronēsis*) une eben auch *EE* VI (= *EN* 7, Lust).' This note is the more impressive because Dirlmeier believes that the original *EE* middle books are lost.

names of moral virtues and vices, this passage has seemed to many to be in such flagrant contradition with *AE* B that the paradox could be resolved only by excising the offending triad, or by denying the *EE* to Aristotle, or at the very least by denying B to the *EE*. Now in fact the triad contains many entries which are not moral virtues and vices (the most obvious being 'gain–loss–just'). Aristotle's aim is not to show that wisdom is a moral virtue, but to show that here too there can be an application of the mean to the case of wisdom. Aristotle, at 1221^{a}36 shows how it applies in the case of the choice of means. But the contrast between the inclusive and the dominant notion of happiness shows us how the doctrine of the mean applies also to the choice of ends. The parameter to which the mean is to be applied is given by the question: how many values does a man pursue? The stupid man pursues *too many*: he follows one little project after another: he is guilty of the folly we were warned against in *EE* I, 1214^{b}9. The wise man pursues the right number: he follows the Aristotelian ideal which combines the values of the contemplative, political, and hedonic lives. The cunning man pursues a single dominant goal and is ruthless about other values. An intemperate man who pursued pleasure, come what may, would, provided he was intelligent, provide an obvious example of a cunning man (cf. *AE* 1142^{b}18; 1144^{a}28). But so, if I am right, would the man who gave himself to the single hearted and unrelenting pursuit of philosphy without regard for the moral virtues. A person who organized his life entirely with a view to the promotion of philosphical speculation would be not wise but cunning, not *phronimos* but *panourgos*. The type of person whom many regard as the hero of the *Nicomachean Ethics* turns out, by the standards of the *Eudemian Ethics*, to be a vicious and ignoble character.[1]

1. Cooper (1975, 164) says 'Aristotle in the *NE* conspicuously avoids saying that his theorizer will be a virtuous person. . . . He will not possess the social virtues or any other virtues, because he will lack the kind of commitment to this kind of activity that is an essential characteristic of the virtuous person.' Devereux points out on Cooper's interpretation, there is nothing to prevent the contemplative from being quite ruthless in pursuing his goal. For example, he may by betraying a friend gain a large sum of money and thereby assure himself years of leisure for philosophizing. What would hold him back?' (1978). I am not sure that Cooper's interpretation of *NE* 10 is correct, on this point; but if it is, the contemplative surely deserves the condemnation which the *EE*, by my conjecture, would wish to pass on him.

CHAPTER 9

The Dating of the
Aristotelian Ethical Treatises

IT is the almost universal opinion of Aristotelian scholars that the *EE* was composed earlier in Aristotle's career than the *NE*. As to the *Magna Moralia*, scholars do not agree whether to view it as a genuine work of Aristotle: but those who treat it as authentic are unanimous in regarding it as the earliest of the ethical treatises. Scholars are far less united about the absolute chronology of Aristotle's ethical works than they are about the relative chronology. This is because the opinions concerning the order of the treatises are based rather upon *a priori* theories of Aristotle's philosphical development than upon the historical data to be found in the treatises themselves. This is particularly true in the case of the *Magna Moralia*, which is unusually rich in topical allusions permitting a fairly precise dating: the dating which the allusions suggest is quite other than the one which is accepted by the scholars who regard it as genuine. But it is also true in the case of the *EE* and the *NE*, where the rather sparser historical data lend no support to the view that the *EE* is earlier in date. This is particularly the case if the *AE* is located in its rightful context in the *EE*, so that the historical allusions in the *AE* can be drawn on in order to give a *terminus post quem* for the date of the *EE*. The present chapter will examine the evidence for dating the ethical treatises which can be drawn from their texts. It will not attempt to present an overall theory of Aristotle's ethical development, much less of the progress of his philosophy as a whole.

Before examining the textual evidence in detail, let us look briefly at the chronologies for the ethical treatises which scholars have proposed within the framework of the known dates of Aristotle's life. We know that he was born in the year 384; he came to Athens in 367 and remained there in the Academy until approximately the time of Plato's death in 347. For the next three years or so he was at

Assos under the patronage of his friend and future in-law, Hermeias the tyrant of Atarneus. In 343/2 he was summoned to Mieza by Philip of Macedon to act as tutor to his son Alexander. After Philip's death and Alexander's accession Aristotle returned to Athens in 335/4, and taught there some thirteen years until just before his own death in 322.[1]

W. Jaeger, who regarded the *MM* as inauthentic, assigned the *EE* to the middle forties, during Aristotle's stay in Asia Minor; the *NE* belonged, he believed, to the final Athens sojourn. Gauthier and Jolif, in both editions of their massive and authoritative commentary on the *NE*, accept this chronology, dating the *EE* shortly after 348/7 and the *NE* between 335 and 330.[2] Some more recent scholars, while accepting Jaeger's order for the *EE* and the *NE*, have argued for the authenticity of the *MM* as an early work of Aristotle's: thus Dirlmeier proposed that they date from his period in the Academy.[3] The chronology put forward by Düring in his article in *RE* Supplement-Band xi.331 ff. dates the *Magna Moralia* before 360, the *Eudemian Ethics* between 355 and Plato's death, the *NE* and the existing *AE* to the period between 334 and 332.

To date the *Magna Moralia* as it stands to a period before Plato's death is quite impossible, for the following reasons.

(1) At 1197[b]21, to illustrate the distinction between *deinotēs* and *phronēsis*, the author says 'Even a bad man may be called intelligent: for instance Mentor was generally thought intelligent, but he was not a wise man.' Commentators are unanimous in seeing here a reference to Mentor the Rhodian, who in 341/0, by ingenious and treacherous means, entrapped Hermeias and sent him to the court of the Persian King where he was crucified. The imperfect tense is often, though not always, taken to indicate that the sentence was written after Mentor's death (*c.* 337/6).[4] The allusion would be clear to Aristotle's own circle; Aristotle himself was deeply moved by Hermeias' death and wrote a paean in his praise which later led to his own prosecution for impiety. This tells, as supporters of the authenticity of the *MM* have insisted, against the theory that the work was written long after Aristotle's death, when the memory of

---

1. See Düring, 1957, 249 ff. The crucial dates are given by Dionysius of Halicarnassus in his letter to Ammaeus: see Chroust, 1973, 16–24.
2. Gauthier, 1970, 61–2.
3. Dirlmeier, 1958, *passim*.
4. So von Arnim, 1924, 10.

Mentor was less vivid:[1] but it tells even more strongly against those who wish to place the *MM* in the 360s.

(2) At 1203ᵃ23 the writer gives a list of evildoers on the grand scale. Along with Phalaris, he names Dionysius and Clearchus. It is not clear whether the first or the second Dionysius was meant: either of them, by their ill treatment of Plato as well as their other misdeeds, could deserve to figure in such a list. Clearchus is most likely the tyrant of Heraclea in Pontus, once a pupil of Plato, whose sanguinary reign lasted from 364/3 to 353/2.[2] The reference would perhaps be more natural after his death; at the very earliest it cannot be much before 360.

(3) At 1205ᵃ19–23 the writer illustrates a point about the individuation of dispositions by a reference to the knowledge of grammar 'in Lampros and in Neleus'.[3] No likely Lampros is known; but Neleus is now universally taken to be Neleus of Skepsis, the son of Coriscus and nephew of Theophrastus, who inherited the latter's library at his death *c.* 285 (Strabo, xiii.608). Neleus, Strabo tells us, was a pupil of Aristotle. Unless he inherited the library at an improbably advanced age, he can hardly have been old enough to know grammar during the 360s.[4]

(4) At 1212ᵃ4 the writer is discussing the difference between being well-disposed to someone and being their friend. 'If there were people as perhaps there were, well disposed to Darius far away in Persia, it does not follow that they were friends of his.'[5] The reference is almost certainly to Darius Codomannus, who certainly

1. I agree with Düring (1966) 'Der Sinn von Namen wie Alkibiades oder Lysander war zu jeder Zeit verständlich. Mentor kann nicht zu dieser Kategorie von Persönlichkeiten gerechnet werden. Nur wenn dieser "heimtückische Mann" noch in aller Gedächtnis war, hatte es einen Sinn, ihn als Beispiel hinzustellen.'

2. *RE*, s.v. 'Klearchos'. One manuscript adds to the list the name Εὐμάνθης. No such name is known. Εὐμάθης was one of the Thirty Tyrants, but there seems no reason to single him out (Xenophon, *Hell.* 11.32; *RE* vi.1075). Perhaps the text should read 'Εριάνθης. Erianthes, the commander who wished on his own authority to destroy Athens after Aegospotami, might well have lived in Athenian memory as an arch-evildoer. No other credible name ending in ανθης is given in Hansen.

3. The reading Νηλεῖ of the manuscript M, though not accepted by Bekker and Susemihl, has been universally read since the article by Wilamowitz (1927).

4. Von Arnim, who was anxious to place the date of Neleus' birth as early as he plausibly could, concluded that he was probably born in the fifties, and would be about eighteen in 334, the date which at that time von Arnim favoured for the *MM*. He argues convincingly that the knowledge of grammar in question is not that of the professional philologist, but of a schoolboy (von Arnim, 1928).

5. οὐ γὰρ εἴ τις ἦν Δαρείῳ εὔνους ἐν πέρσαις ὄντι, ὥσπερ ἴσως ἦν, εὐθέως καὶ φιλία ἦν αὐτῷ πρὸς Δαρεῖον.

had well-wishers among the anti-Macedonian party in Athens. Whether or not the imperfect tense indicates composition after Darius' death in 330, the reference cannot be earlier than his accession in 336 and is most likely after his great battles against Alexander at the Granicus in 334 and Issus in 333.

(5) The *MM*, when discussing deliberation, says that no one has to deliberate how to spell the name 'Archicles'. The reference may of course be to some member of the immediate circle of the author of the *MM* who has, like Lampros, been forgotten. Certainly it is not easy to find an Archicles whose name would be on everyone's lips: but the best known of those who have come down to us was a trierarch in a battle fought in 334/3 (*CIA* ii.804ᵃ18).

Taken together these references make impossible a date for the *MM* in the sixties, and make most likely a *terminus post quem* for the work of about 335. This fact is, of course, well known to the partisans of the view that the *MM* is an authentic work of Aristotle's and the earliest of his ethical treatises. Von Arnim, who was the first and most candid of the twentieth-century champions of the authenticity of the *MM*, accepted that the references proved that the *MM* could not be earlier than 334, and concluded that it, and consequently the two later treatises the *EE* and the *NE*, belonged to Aristotle's final years of teaching in Athens (1924, 10–12; 1928, 1 ff.).[1]

Later partisans of an Aristotelian *MM* have been reluctant to follow von Arnim here. In the opinion of all those who have compared the works in the last century and a half,[2] the *MM* is philosophically naïve and crude by comparison with the *EE* and the *NE*. If we are to attribute it to Aristotle himself, then, it seems that we must assign it to his apprentice years in the Academy rather than to his magisterial period in the Lyceum. We shall have to postulate, therefore, to explain the historical allusions, a revision of the work, or updating of the course, in the late thirties. Moreover, the stylistic differences between the *MM* and the Aristotelian ethical treatises

---

1. At the time of writing the later monograph, von Arnim believed he had found confirmatory evidence for this date for the *MM*. *Rhetoric* B must be later than 338, since it refers to the speech of Demades after the battle of Chaeronea (1401ᵇ32). But the treatment of several passions in chapter 9 of that work shows that Aristotle had not yet worked out the doctrine of the mean, which is clearly to be found in the *MM*. This therefore must be some years after 338 (loc. cit).

2. The qualification is necessary because Schleiermacher, writing in 1817, regarded the *MM* as the *only* authentic Aristotelian ethical treatise (1835, 123).

have impressed other scholars more deeply than they impressed von Arnim. Consequently, it has been postulated that this updated juvenile Aristotelian treatise has reached us through another hand—whether, as Düring supposes, the updating itself was entrusted to someone else, or whether, as Cooper suggests, the updated course given by Aristotle has been preserved only in the lecture notes of one of the members of its audience.[1]

Now of course every scholar is at liberty to postulate as many juvenile treatises by Aristotle as he wishes, and as many revisions as he thinks necessary to explain the present state of the manuscripts of the corpus. Moreover, if he is prepared to regard as detachable from the postulated treatise all chronologically locatable references and all quantifiable features of style, his hypothesis will be conveniently secure against any possibility of objective falsification. But even safeguarded with this protective covering, a hypothesis such as that of Cooper can hardly escape the charge of superfluity. If we are to postulate, in order to explain the un-Aristotelian style of the *MM*, that what we have is the published notes of a student who attended his course, we do not need to postulate further a juvenile version of the course in order to explain the crudity of the philosphical discussion. For the crudity to be explained is not a lack of overall philosophical vision or comprehensive organizing design: it is a constant botching of the details of a philosophical argument. And this kind of incompetence can perfectly adequately be explained by the mediocrity of the note-taker who has already been postulated to account for the style. The present state of the *MM* is overdetermined if we explain it both by the immaturity of Aristotle and by the imperfect accuracy of his recording disciple.

In itself, the hypothesis that the *MM* is a student's presentation of his lecture notes of a course given by Aristotle in his final Athenian period is an attractive one. It explains, first of all, the appearance of the work in the Aristotelian corpus better than the still most popular hypothesis of totally post-Aristotelian origin. It explains why the historical introduction to the work ends with Plato: something difficult to explain if the work was written by a later peripatetic (1182^a30). It explains how the author can refer to Aristotle's doctrine of the syllogism as his own (1201^b25). The crabbed syllogistic manner of much of the work, so well brought out

---

1. Cooper, 1973, 327–49.

in Brink's monograph,[1] sorts better with the diligence of a student polishing up his lecture notes than with Aristotle's ubiquitous and lordly contempt for the technical terms and methodological devices of his own invention. If not associated with the hypothesis of an effectively vanished juvenile treatise, the theory does justice in an unforced way to the topical allusions which forbid the assignment of the treatise to a period earlier than the middle thirties. Indeed, it almost reconciles the parties to the traditional debate. For there is not a very great difference between a scholar who says that the *MM* is not authentic Aristotle, but is the product of a Theophrastean peripatetic, and a scholar who says that the *MM* is an authentic work, but has reached us through the hand of Theophrastus or another of Aristotle's disciples. The difference between them, rather, is not so much a difference about the historical probabilities, as a difference in the rigour of their standards of authenticity.[2]

If the *MM* is a student's version of a course given by Aristotle, there is no reason why the course it records should not be a course for which we have Aristotle's own lecture notes: i.e. either the *EE* or the *NE*. In fact, as we have seen, the *MM* follows the *EE* slavishly, in the order of topics and the manner of their treatment, for almost the whole of its length. By far the simplest hypothesis to explain the present state of the *MM* is that it is a student's published notes of the course which we have in its authentic form as the *EE*. With the exception of a few brief passages, which will receive special consideration shortly, there are no differences between the content of the *EE* and that of the *MM* which cannot be explained by a combination of a pardonable degree of incompetence in understanding, and a modest talent for editorial revision, on the part of a disciple of Aristotle present at the lectures.

Scholars have failed to see this obvious and attractive explanation of the evidence largely because of their conviction that the *EE* is an early work. If the *MM* is based on notes taken at a course given during Aristotle's final Athenian sojourn, then it cannot be a record of the *EE* if that belongs to the period in the Academy under Plato or in Assos with Hermeias. But we must ask ourselves what

1. Brink, 1933.
2. To take a modern parallel: students of Wittgenstein differ in the amount of authority they ascribe to G. E. Moore's notes of his lectures in the early thirties, or Barrett's reconstruction of his lectures on aesthetics.

really solid evidence there is for assigning an early date of this kind to the *EE*. Von Arnim, as has been remarked, thought that the *EE* belonged to the final Athenian sojourn. An examination of the evidence will show that there is nothing to prevent, and much to commend, such a chronology.

The *EE*, like the *MM*, contains a number of references to contemporary persons and events. The mention of Coriscus at 1220ª19 and 1240ᵇ25 has been thought to confirm a dating for the *EE* in the early forties: for Coriscus was probably among the group around Aristotle in Assos. But Coriscus, whether or not he listened to lectures in Assos, occurs as a John Doe figure in so many of Aristotle's writings, assigned by scholars to so many different periods of Aristotle's life, that it is impossible to base any chronological hypothesis on the use of his name. Other references are prima facie more useful for establishing a *terminus post quem* for the *EE*.

(1) 'Gourmands pray', we are told at 1231ª16, 'not to have a long tongue but to have a crane's gullet: like Philoxenus son of Eryxis.' Several gourmands seem to have borne the name: Philoxenus son of Eryxis is possibly identical with the dithyrambic poet Philoxenus of Cythera (*c.* 435–380) who seduced Dionysius I's mistress Galatea. At all events he must have been old enough to be active during the first part of the fourth century, for Athenaeus tells us (5.220) that Aeschines mocked Anaxagoras for having so disgusting a pupil as Philoxenus son of Eryxis. His being mentioned, therefore, is no help in assigning a date to the *EE*.

(2) 'A man who is in love endures many dangers,' says Aristotle at 1229ª23, 'like the man at Metapontum who murdered the tyrant, and the person in Crete in the story.' 'Die beiden Beispiele sind nicht zu verifizieren' says Dirlmeier, commenting on the passage (1969, 315). The second reference is indeed too vague; but it is not difficult to find a story to fit the first. Plutarch (*Moralia* 760 c) refers to Antileon of Metapontum, along with Harmodius and Aristogeiton, as instances of tyrannicides motivated by love. The story of Antileon is told in detail by Parthenius in a passage drawn from the peripatetic historian Phanias of Eresus (*FHG* II.298). In love with the young Hipparinus, he carried out various dangerous exploits to gratify his beloved's whim. He met his death after assassinating the tyrant Archelaus of Heraclea in order to rescue the young man from his attentions. A monument was erected to him

when, shortly after, the city of Heraclea regained its former democratic constitution.

This allusion would assist in dating the *EE* if only we knew the date of the death of Archelaus. Heraclea was not founded until 432, so that the story cannot belong to the sixth century, as some commentators, misled by Plutarch's coupling of Antileon with Harmodius and Aristogeiton, have suggested. The time at which the cities of Magna Grecia, and Sicily, one after the other, were reverting from tyranny to democracy was during Timoleon's march down the Italian coast and his expedition to dethrone Dionysius II of Syracuse in 344 (see Hackforth, 1927, 288 ff.). But I have been unable to find confirmation for the conjecture that Archelaus' assassination is to be assigned to this period.

(3) In the tenth chapter of book VII Aristotle is discussing friendships in which what is given and what is taken differ. These often lead to trouble, he says.

This is how it happens in love affairs, since in them one party pursues the other as a pleasant person to live with, but sometimes the other the one as useful, and when the lover ceases to love, he having changed the other changes, and then they calculate the *quid pro quo*, and quarrel as Python and Pammenes used, and as teacher and pupil do in general (for knowledge and money have no common measure) and as Prodicus the doctor did with the patient who offerred to pay his fee with a discount and as the harpist and the king fell out. (1243ᵇ17–25, trs. Rackham)[1]

The passage is rich in historical allusions. From the Greek it is clear that Python and Pammenes were in the relationship of teacher to pupil.[2] There is no difficulty in finding a famous teacher of the name of Python: the Byzantine rhetorician, who came to Athens in 343 as an ambassador from Philip of Macedon, and who may indeed have conveyed the monarch's invitation to Aristotle to undertake

---

1. οἷον συμβαίνει ἐπὶ τῶν ἐρωτικῶν. ὃ μὲν γὰρ διώκει ὡς [τὸν] ἡδὺν ἐπὶ τὸ συζῆν, ὃ δ' ἐκεῖνον ἐνίοτε ὡς χρήσιμον· ὅταν δὲ παύσηται τοῦ ἐρᾶν, ἄλλου γινομένου ἄλλος γίνεται, καὶ τότε λογίζονται τί ἀντὶ τινος, καὶ ὡς Πύθων καὶ Παμμένης διεφέροντο καὶ ὡς διδάσκαλος καὶ μαθητής (ἐπιστήμη γὰρ καὶ χρήματα οὐχ ἑνὶ μετρεῖται), καί ὡς ʽΠρόδικος ὁ ἰατρὸς πρὸς τὸν ἀποδιδόντα μικρὸν τὸν μισθόν, καὶ ὡς ὁ κιθαρῳδὸς καί ὁ. Like Rackham I accept Jackson's emendation τί ἀντὶ τίνος; but I reject ʽΗρόδικος.

2. Jackson is surely correct in drawing this conclusion from the ὅλως in the manuscripts (1900, 42). Whether Dirlmeier is correct in concluding that Python and Pammenes were also lovers seems to me more doubtful: though a stormy affair with a male pupil is of course not ruled out by the rollicking heterosexual domesticity attributed to Python in Athenaeus, 5.499.

the education of his son.[1] But if so, the Pammenes mentioned can hardly be the well-known Theban general, though the name is not a common one. Prodicus of Selymbria appears in Pliny's apostolic succession of Hippocratic doctors between Hippocrates and Chrysippus, the teacher of Aristotle's medical grandson Erasistratus.[2] This would place him in roughly the same generation as Aristotle, but does not enable us to fix his date with any precision. As for the story of the harpist and the king, Michael of Ephesus tells us that some scholars thought it was Alexander while others thought it did not suit that monarch's character.[3] Modern scholars on the basis of a similar story in Plutarch have thought the allusion is to Dionysius of Syracuse.[4] But would Aristotle have referred to either Dionysius as *basileus*? Despite its rich allusiveness the passage leaves us in total uncertainty about its date.

(4) At 1231ª11 Aristotle quotes an elegant remark of the musician Stratonicus. No one knows for certain the dates of this wit, whose principal stock-in-trade appears to have been the kind of joke that New Yorkers like to make about Philadelphia. A survey of all the witticisms attributed to him—a depressingly unhilarious experience—shows that they cannot all have been made by the same person, unless he lived from about the time of Alcibiades' return to Athens in 407 until Ptolemy Soter declared himself king in 304.[5]

Altogether, the undisputed books of the *EE* offer us tantalizingly little help to anchor their date. The various allusions can be made to fit with, but in no way enforce, a dating of the *EE* during Aristotle's second Athenian period.

The matter is altered if we restore the disputed books to their rightful place as part of the *EE*. For in the disputed book C there is a reference which is universally taken by commentators to be a reminiscence of the court of Alexander. At 1150ᵇ13 we are told of a Xenophantus who was unable to restrain his laughter on some

---

1. If Aristotle was in Athens at the time of receiving the summons, as seems to be implied by his best-known joke (fr. 619, Rose): ἐγὼ ἐκ μὲν Ἀθηνῶν εἰς Στάγειρα ἦλθον διὰ τὸν βασιλέα τὸν μέγαν, ἐκ δὲ Σταγείρων εἰς Ἀθήνας διὰ τὸν χειμῶνα τὸν μέγαν.

2. Pliny, *N.H.* 29.2. Editors emend both Pliny and Aristotle to read 'Herodicus'. But this involves gratuitously attributing to Pliny not only a confusion between master and pupil but also a muddle about birthplaces.

3. *CAG* xx.464.

4. Plutarch, *Moralia* 33 f.

5. *RE* ivA.1.326 gives the dates of his activity as 410–360. See Gow, 1968, 70.

solemn occasion and broke into a guffaw. We know from Seneca
(*De Ira* ii.2) that Xenophantus was a musician in the service of
Alexander. Moreover, his period at Alexander's court must have
been the very beginning of his career, since he was still active
enough to play for the funeral of Demetrius Poliorcetes in 283.[1] As
long as book C was thought to belong to the *NE*, or to a post-
Aristotelian *Eudemian Ethics*, this passage excited no remark: but if
it is indeed an allusion to the Macedonian court musician, and the
AE belongs with the *EE*, then we must date the *EE* well after Plato's
death, well after the period in Assos, and most probably therefore
during the final Athenian period: the same period, in fact, to which
we were led by the historical allusions to date the *Magna Moralia*.[2]

   If we turn to the *NE*, we find a very solid *terminus post quem* for
the work in the allusion, in the discussion of courage, to a battle 'At
the temple of Hermes', 1116^b19. Thanks to the well-informed
second-century scholiast (*CAG* xx.165) this can be identified with
an event during the Sacred War in 353 at Coronea in Boeotia.[3] We
know therefore that at least this part of the *NE* cannot have been
written earlier than the period just before Plato's death. We cannot
assume from the casual nature of the allusion that the battle was still
news at the time of writing: a little later, at 1117^a27, there is an
equally off-hand reference to a battle at the Long Walls of Corinth
in 392. The reference to the splendid character of Eudoxus in *NE*
10.2 (1172^b15) has seemed to many to betray the tones of the
obituarist. According to the most usual chronology, Eudoxus died
about 355.[4] From the tensing of the reference to Speusippus in

---

   1. See Berve, 1926, s.v., citing Plutarch, *Demetrius* 53.
   2. In the same passage there is a reference to a play of Theodectes, whom Plutarch
(*Alexander* 17) tells was a pupil of Aristotle along with Alexander. This confirms the
identification of Xenophantus: but the exact dating of Theodectes' dramatic career is
uncertain. Susemihl (*Rh. Mus.* liv.631 ff.) dates his first tragedy to 353, and Pickard-
Cambridge placed his death (which we know occurred when he was forty-one, Plutarch, *X
Orat.* 837 d), in 334. This dating fits the ancient literary evidence best; but on the basis of the
Didaskaliai other scholars (Webster, 1954, Diehl, *RE* vA.1722) place his career six or more
years earlier. Of Carcinus, the other dramatist mentioned here by Aristotle, all we know is
that he attended the court of Dionysius II. It would assist us to date the *AE* if we could be
certain of the identity of Σάτυρος ὁ φιλοπάτωρ in 1148^a34, the son of Sostrates according
to *CAG* xx.426. More than one Pontic king bore his name in the fourth century (Gauthier–
Jolif, 1959, 624).
   3. See *RE*, s.v. *Onomarchos*.
   4. So Heath, 1921, 322–34. Merlan, 1960 (like von Fritz, 1930), has argued for a redating
of Eudoxus' lifespan to 395–342, making him survive Plato.

1196^b7 it is impossible to tell whether he was alive or dead at the time of writing, which may therefore be before or after 339. Plato is twice quoted in the present tense (1104^b12; 1172^b28): no conclusion can be drawn from this, for so is Homer (1116^a22 etc.). Nothing in the *NE* forces us to a date much later than 353; but equally, nothing disproves the traditional assignment of it to Aristotle's last years. Certainly he cannot have been a young man when he introduced his course with the remark that a youth was no fit student of ethics (1095^a2).[1]

The historical data, then, are perfectly consistent with our hypothesis that the *MM*, while incorporating a small amount of material from an already existing *NE*, is essentially based on a course given by Aristotle during his last years at Athens which corresponds in substance with our text of the *EE*. But we must examine more closely the cases in which the text of the *MM* diverges from the structure and content of the *EE*.

No great difficulty is presented by the fact that the *MM* begins with a summary of the thought of previous ethical thinkers which does not appear in the *EE*. The content of the *MM* introduction (1182^a10–30) would not be beyond the ability of a moderately talented student to construct for himself. On the other hand, Aristotle no doubt gave the course which we possess as the *EE* on more than one occasion: and most of us rewrite the beginning of our lecture courses more frequently than we rewrite the rest of them. There is evidence in the text of the *EE* that the first chapters have been more carefully revised than the rest of the work: they and they alone are at pains to avoid hiatus.

The incorporation of the Nicomachean material presents more of a problem. The two most substantial Nicomachean portions of the *MM* are the amalgam of quotations identified by Allan, introduced with the words 'this can be seen from the *Ethics*' (1185^b15),[2] and the section on self-love in chapters 13 and 14 of book 2 (1212^a38–13^b2).

---

1. To illustrate the point that we do not deliberate about what is beyond our control *EE* 1226^a29 says 'We do not deliberate about affairs in India'; *NE* 1112^a28 says 'No Spartan deliberates about what form of government would be best for the Scythians.' If we are to attach any importance to this difference, we might say that the Scythians became a poor example of things beyond our ken with Philip's intervention in Scythia in 339, while the Indians remained a good example until Alexander's invasion of India in 327. By the end of Aristotle's life both examples must have looked a little *passé*.

2. See above, p. 10.

Now it is a startling coincidence that at each of the points where the *MM* draws extensively on the *NE*, there occurs in the text of the *EE* an allusion by Aristotle to an earlier work of his—allusions which scholars, blinkered by the dogma of the priority of the *EE*, have universally found baffling.

At 1220[b]11 in the *EE*, during the discussion of the way in which moral virtue concerns pleasure and pain, we read 'After this comes the classification of passions, powers, and dispositions made *en tois apēllagmenois*'.[1] The three Greek words have often been found puzzling and various emendations have been proposed. D. J. Allan has suggested two possible translations of the manuscript reading: 'in the cancelled version' or 'in the separate section'.[2] In either case, Aristotle is referring here to an appendix. Rackham's comment on the passage is interesting: it is, he says, 'perhaps a reference to *NE* 1105[b]20, inserted in the belief that the *EE* is the later work' (1935, 247). Certainly, except for very slight variations, the *EE* text and the *NE* text are here very similar.[3] The corresponding passage in the *MM* (1186[a]9 ff.) comes right in the middle of the Nicomachean cento introduced with a reference to the *Ethics*.[4] If, as the words *en tois apēllagmenois* suggest, the *EE* contained (or the *EE* lectures appealed to) an appendix of superseded material at this point, and if the superseded material was in fact the *NE* or part of it, then we would have a full explanation of why the *MM* in this area apparently deserts its usual model, the *EE*, for verbatim copying of the *NE*.

1220[b]11 is not the only place in the *EE* where Aristotle refers to his own earlier work. In the discussion of self-sufficiency in the

---

1. μετὰ ταῦτα ἡ διαίρεσις ἐν τοῖς ἀπηλλαγμένοις τῶν παθημάτων καὶ τῶν δυνάμεων καὶ τῶν ἔξεων.

2. Allan, 1961, 312; 1966, 148. In support of the first sense of ἀπαλλάττομαι Allan appeals to Plato, *Rep.* viii.559 b and ix.571 b.

3. The *EE*, as is its wont, is a little conciser and more precise, specifying passion by its accompaniment with *sensory* pleasure and pain, and explaining that ἕξεις are defined by being κατὰ λόγον ἢ ἐναντίως.

4. *MM* 1185[b]14 reads: ὅτι δὲ ἡ ἔνδεια καὶ ἡ ὑπερβολὴ φθείρει τοῦτ' ἰδεῖν ἔστιν ἐκ τῶν ἠθικῶν· δεῖ δ' ὑπὲρ τῶν ἀφανῶν τοῖς φανεροῖς μαρτυρίοις. Allan comments: 'The attempts of scholars to emend ἐκ τῶν ἠθικῶν (see Susemihl) show that they failed to recognize the words from δεῖ to χρῆσθαι as a verbatim quotation of *EN* 1104[a]12. . . . With this commences a passage of about five Teubner pages in which phrases from the *NE* are cited with some embroidery and expansion; that we find nothing similar outside these pages of *MM*; and that in view of this it is only reasonable to translate ἰδεῖν ἔστιν ἐκ τῶν ἠθικῶν 'it can be seen from the *Ethics*' (Allan, 1966, 142; see allan, 1957, 7).

treatise on friendship, Aristotle makes an obscure critical reference to a book in which the same topic has been treated.

If therefore one abstracted and treated knowledge as absolute and independent and did not . . . (but this is obscure in the way it is written in the book, though in fact it need not be obscure) in that case there would be no difference between knowing oneself and knowing another instead of oneself, and likewise no difference between another living instead of oneself: whereas patently to be conscious and aware of oneself is more desirable. Two of the things in the book have to be put together: life is desirable, but so is goodness. (1244^b29-45^a)[1]

Here a book—presumably one by Aristotle, else the author would have to be mentioned[2]—is being criticized for being obscure, and for excessively separating knowledge from goodness and regarding life, identified with this knowledge, as the only desirable thing. Can we locate an earlier work of Aristotle which is criticisable on these grounds?

Most authors treat the reference as being to a lost work, and are therefore at liberty to invent for it a text suitable to be a peg for these criticism.[3] But if we turn to the parallel passage in *NE* 9, we can find an extant argument of Aristotle's which passably fits the *EE*'s strictures. First, the passage (1170^a25-^b9) is intolerably obscure: it contains a sprawling sentence of 112 words whose construction is impermeable even with the aid of the five braces of brackets thoughtfully provided in Bywater's edition.[4] The argument goes approximately thus: life consists essentially in perception and thought, both of which are accompanied by self-consciousness: it is

---

1. εἰ οὖν τις ἀποτέμοι καὶ ποιήσειε τὸ γινώσκειν αὐτὸ καθ' αὑτὸ καὶ μὴ . . . (ἀλλὰ τοῦτο μὲν λανθάνει, ὥσπερ ἐν τῷ λόγῳ γέγραπται, τῷ μέντοι πράγματι ἔστι μὴ λανθάνειν), οὐθὲν ἂν διαφέροι ἢ τὸ γινώσκειν ἄλλον ἀνθ' αὑτοῦ· τὸ δ' ὅμοιον τοῦ ζῆν ἀνθ' αὑτοῦ ἄλλου. εὐλόγως δὲ τὸ ἑαυτοῦ αἰσθάνεσθαι καὶ γνωρίζειν αἱρετώτερον. δεῖ γὰρ ἅμα συνθεῖναι δύο ἐν τῷ λόγῳ, ὅτι τε τὸ ζῆν [καὶ] αἱρετόν, καὶ ὅτι τὸ ἀγαθόν. The text is corrupt in places, and I do not know how to emend it; but the general sense is clear.

2. So Dirlmeier (1969, 461): 'wir haben wieder jenes in Corpus Ar. einzigartige, auf *EE* und *Poetik* 1454^b18 beschränkte, Sich-berufen auf ein geschriebenes Werk, ein Buch.'

3. The most promising attempt hitherto to locate a source in the lost works of Aristotle for the quotation is that of Gaiser (1967) who thinks that the *logos* referred to is the *Protrepticus* (see also Widmann, 1967). The two passages which Gaiser cites as parallels from modern reconstructions of the *Protrepticus*—*frs. B 71-7, 97-103* Düring—are far less close to the allusions in the *EE* than the texts in *NE* 9 and *NE* 10 discussed below.

4. According to the figures given by Wake, 1957, and Morton and Winspear, 1971, this must be one of the longest sentences in Aristotle. Wake, indeed, does not record any sentence in the *NE*, *EE*, or *AE* longer than 115 words.

indeed the consciousness of one's own existence that makes life
pleasant. But a good man looks on his friend just as he looks on
himself: therefore consciousness of his friend's existence will be
just as desirable to him as consciousness of his own. Hence, a good
man must have friends, or he will lack something desirable and will
not be truly happy.

There seems something very strange about this derivation of the
desirability of friends from the value of self-consciousness. The
argument in the *EE* shares some of the strangeness, but it does
criticize one thing which seems a feature of the *NE* argument: the
exaggerated value placed on the abstract awareness of one's own or
other's existence. No doubt it is nice for the good man to know he is
good (1170^b5); but he has to *be* good, to exercise his virtues, and not
just to contemplate his goodness with self-satisfaction. It is in the
exercise of the virtues—in the performance of good and worthwhile
actions—and not just in the contemplation of them that we should
surely look for the value of friendship. It seems to be along these
lines that the *EE* develops its own argument. Looking at life simply
in terms of the possession and communication of knowledge leads
to the conclusion that the society of others is superfluous (1245^a1-
19); but it is obvious that we all want to share things with our
friends, whether bodily pleasure, or artistic culture, or philosophical inquiry. Hence there must be something wrong with an
argument[1] leading to an opposite conclusion. (1245^a20-8) The
knowledge of one's friends who resemble one in various ways is
indeed a way of knowing oneself; and because a friend is an *alter ego*
one can look on his good as on one's own. But the value of so doing
will depend fundamentally on the value of the good shared.

To share even common pleasures and ordinary life with a friend is
obviously pleasant (for it is always accompanied by consciousness of him);
but it is even more pleasant to share the more divine pleasures. This is
because it is always pleasanter to see oneself enjoying a superior good: and
this may be now an emotion, now an action, and now something different
from either. If it is pleasant to live well for oneself and a friend, and if
living together involves working together, their sharing will be above all in
the things which make up the end of life. (1245^a38-^b4)[2]

---

1. It is not clear whether *logos* in line 27 means 'argument' or is another reference to the
book criticized in lines 31 and 35 above.
2. ὥστε καὶ τὰ φορτικὰ μὲν συνήδεσθαι καί συζῆν τῷ φίλῳ ἡδὺ εὐλόγως
(συμβαίνει γὰρ ἐκείνου ἅμα αἴσθησις ἀεί). μᾶλλον δὲ τὰς θειοτέρας ἡδονάς. αἴτιον δ'

So we must study together and feast together and share the best things in life so far as we can attain them. The contrary view[1] which made the solitary life seem as valuable as life in the society of friends was based on a false comparison between man and god. If men were like gods they would not need friends; but if they were like gods they would not have any thoughts either, except of themselves. 'For us, our well-being has reference to something other than ourselves; in his case he is himself his own well-being'. ($1245^{b}18-19$)

Both in the *NE* and in the *EE* Aristotle, then, Aristotle argues to the value of friendship from the value of self-consciousness and the role of the friend as an *alter ego*. But the *EE* is anxious to criticize a presentation of this argument which divorces knowledge too much from other values, which treats human beings as if they were pure godlike intellects, and which does not sufficiently stress the need for friends to share in all the elements of the good life. It is striking that all these points of criticism are the very points in which, in the previous chapter, we identified the differences between the *EE* and the *NE* with regard to the nature and constituents of happiness.[2] There is no need to look elsewhere than to the *NE* for the *logos* which is here being subjected to critical commentary.[3]

Once again, the conjecture that the *EE* here refers to the *NE* is confirmed by a comparison with the *MM*. The second large Nicomachean borrowing in the *MM* occurs at $1212^{a}28-^{b}24$, in the section on self-love which in the *NE* immediately precedes the passage corresponding to the *EE* criticism of the *logos*, and which first introduces the identification of a human being with his *nous* ($1168^{b}29-69^{a}3$) which is developed in the *NE* 10 account of contemplative happiness. The *MM* then goes on, like the *EE*, to criticize the excessive assimilation of man with God which is to be found *en tois logois*.[4] Once again, the presence of the unusual

---

ὅτι ἀεὶ ἥδιον ἑαυτὸν θεωρεῖν ἐν τῷ βελτίονι ἀγαθῷ. τοῦτο δ' ἐστὶν ὁτὲ μὲν πάθος, ὁτὲ δὲ πρᾶξις, ὁτὲ δὲ ἕτερόν τι. εἰ δ'αὐτὸν ἒ ζῆν καὶ οὕτω καὶ τὸν φίλον, ἐν δὲ τῷ συζῆν συνεργεῖν, ἡ κοινωνία τῶν ἐν τέλει μάλιστά γε.

1. λόγος is again ambiguous at $1245^{b}12$.

2. *NE* 10, $1178^{b}20-24$, provides an example of the excessive assimilation of man with God which exactly fits the complaint of *EE* $1244^{b}23$ and $1245^{b}13-19$.

3. Several particular passages in the course of the argument suggest that *EE* is commenting on *NE*: thus *EE* $1245^{a}2-9$ expands and modifies—admittedly not in a very perspicuous manner—the brief allusion to what is ὡρισμένον at $1170^{a}20$; and *EE* $1245^{a}15-16$ corrects $1170^{b}12$.

4. The plural may mean that *MM* has other texts too in view, perhaps including ones in which the comparison with God was made more explicit. *MM* differs from *EE* here in that

Nicomachean material in the *MM* would be simply explained by the presence in the *EE* of a Nicomachean appendix: in this case, chapters 8 and 9 of *NE* 9.[1]

Most scholars will reject these conjectures out of hand as presupposing the existence of at least parts of the *NE* at the time when the *EE* was written or delivered as a course of lectures. Certainly it is difficult to find a scholar who will seriously consider the possibility that the *NE* antedates the *EE*: but the time has come to look at the evidence for the priority of the *EE*.

Probably the commonest ground for assigning the *EE* to an earlier date has been the belief that it is more Platonic than the *NE*. In so far as this claim rests on the actual doctrines of the ethical treatises the claim seems unfounded: as we have shown, the *EE* is no more Platonic than the *NE* in its treatment of wisdom, and considerably less Platonic than the *NE* in its refusal to identify happiness with the activity of the separable *nous*. If the claim rests on the constant allusions to Platonic themes and terminology, then it must be admitted that the *EE* is highly Platonic: it is shot through with reminiscences of Plato's ethical dialogues from the *Euthyphro* to the *Philebus*. But so too is the *NE*. I do not know that anyone has undertaken a count to see which of the two treatises contains the more explicit and implicit allusions to Platonic texts. The exercise would no doubt be futile: but it might well be that there are more clearly identifiable Platonic citations in the *EE*. This would merely be an instance of a general feature of the style of the *EE* remarked on long ago by Grant, a more copious and explicit manner of quotation. This stylistic feature may merely indicate that the *EE* is

instead of using the theory of divine self-contemplation of *Metaphysics* as part of a *reductio ad absurdum* of the comparison between man and god, it introduces (whether or not it endorses) a comparison between man and god as part of a criticism of the *Metaphysics* Λ view: if a man spends all this time gazing at his own navel we regard him as a dunce; how can we accept a self-contemplating God? (1212ᵃ36–13ᵃ8)

1. In one other place *EE* refers to a *logos*, in the criticism of Plato's Ideas. ἔτι καὶ τὸ ἐν τῷ λόγῳ γεγραμμένον. ἢ γὰρ οὐδεμιᾷ χρήσιμον αὐτὸ τὸ τοῦ ἀγαθοῦ εἶδος ἢ πάσαις ὁμοίως· ἔτι οὐ πρακτόν. This too would fit the *NE* well: after the arguments which are common to both treatises the *NE* then goes on to an argument which depends on the disjunction: either the definition of good applies only to the idea, in which case μάταιον ἔσται τὸ εἶδος; or else we have to suppose the same definition in goods of diverse kinds which are related only analogically (1096ᵇ8–31); he then goes on to object that the idea οὐκ ἂν εἴη πρακτὸν οὐδὲ κτητὸν ἀνθρώπῳ (ᵇ31–5). The note again is easily explained as a reference to an appendix, or hand-out, of Nicomachean material.

further on the way to publishable form than the *NE* ever was.[1] But scholars are coming more and more to agree that Aristotle's works cannot be ordered on a scale of deviation from Plato: his philosophy was a lifelong development of Platonic themes and a lifelong confrontation with Platonic problems.[2]

To be sure, there is evidence that at different times in his career Aristotle's attitude to the Platonic theory of Ideas varied between different degrees of sympathy and harshness. But it is unwise to conclude that the sympathetic criticisms are early and the harsh criticisms are late;[3] it is equally imprudent to draw the opposite conclusion, imagining a pupil growing gradually more tolerant of his teacher's doctrines under the mellowing influence of age. If we compare the criticism of the theory of Ideas in *NE* 1.6 with that in *EE* I.8 I think it is undeniable that the criticism of the *EE* is made from a greater distance. In the *NE* Aristotle introduces his attack with an apology and an admission that the inventors of the theory are dear and close to him: 'amicus Plato sed magis amica veritas'— an apology which tactfully echoes Plato's own remarks on Homer (1096^a11-17). In the *EE* he begins: 'the existence of a Form not only of good but of anything else is an idle abstraction: this has been considered in multifarious ways both in popular and philosophical writings' (1247^b20 f.). The arguments in the *NE* share more Platonic premises than those in the *EE*, and are less sharply and crisply developed.[4] If the differences between the two treatments were to be settled by assigning a temporal order between them, it is undoubtedly the *EE* that an open-minded reader would regard as the later. But the reason for the differences may well be quite other than a lapse of time.

When nineteenth-century scholars sought to show that the *EE* was post-Aristotelian they pointed to the fact that there are some virtues for which Aristotle tells us in the *NE* he has to coin a name,

---

1. Grant, 1885, 30: 'The Eudemian writer . . . shows indeed a proclivity to indulge in abundance of literary quotations, and he quotes more fully and explicitly than Aristotle.'

2. For Dirlmeier, Aristotle's development is 'Reifen, in Verbindung mit Plato, bis zuletzt' (1969, 568).

3. The best treatment of the *EE* and *NE* criticism of the Ideas is Flashar, in *Festschrift Schadewalt*, 223–37. Flashar notes that the *EE* contains two arguments not to be found in the *NE*, and thinks that while all the *NE* arguments are directed against Plato the *EE* arguments are against Xenocrates—though not necessarily after Plato's death.

4. Flashar's own explanation—that the *NE* is more exoteric than the *EE* and therefore more apology to Plato seemed called for—hardly seems plausible in view of the generally more finished and polished form of the *EE*.

but which are alluded to by that name without hesitation in the *EE* and the *MM*. Thus, at 1108ª4–9 we read:

In regard to anger also there exists an excess, a deficiency and a mean. Although there are really no names for them we might call the mean *praotēs* (gentleness) since we call a man who occupies the middle position gentle. Of the extremes, let the man who exceeds be called *orgilos* (short-tempered) and his vice *orgilotēs*, and the deficient man *aorgētos* (apathetic) and his vice *aorgēsia*.

Again in book 4 Aristotle says that the middle here is nameless, and the extremes almost so (1125ᵇ26 ff.). But in the *EE praotēs* is used without apology at 1220ᵇ38, as is *orgilotēs* (the corresponding defect is here called *analgēsia*); *praotēs* is again used without hesitation in III.3, 1231ᵇ5 ff., where various names are offered for the corresponding defects, including *orgilos*. *Anaisthēsia* is listed at 1221ª2 as the contrary vice to intemperance: at 1230ᵇ14 we are told that some people call those uninfluenced by pleasures *anaisthetoi* and others give them other names. In *NE* at 1107ᵇ8 Aristotle says that such rare birds are nameless, and offers *anaisthētos* as a coinage. Again, at 1126ᵇ11 a virtue of sociability is introduced which is described as having no name (cf. 1108ª17): Aristotle settles for calling it *philia*. The name is used without embarrassment at 1221ª7 and 1233ᵇ30 in the *EE*. Such examples do not show that the *EE* is post-Aristotelian: but the nineteenth-century scholars may well have been right to see them as an indication that the *EE* postdates the *NE*.[1]

It is not only differences in nomenclature which distinguish the treatments of the virtues in the *NE* (3–4) and in the *EE* (III). The ampler and more vivid treatment of the particular traits of character is one of the features which contributes to making the *NE* longer than the *EE*. In particular the virtues of magnificence and magnanimity are given longer and more loving treatment in the *NE* (six and a half Bekker columns) than in the *EE* (less than three columns).[2] Gentleness, on the other hand, while treated like all the virtues at greater length in the *NE*, is upgraded in the *EE* to third place among the virtues. The lists in the two *Ethics* agree in their content, though not in their ordering, with one exception. The *NE* has a place for a nameless virtue of proper ambition, a satellite

1. See Spengel, 1841, 457.
2. See D. Rees, 1971, for a detailed comparison between the treatments.

virtue to magnanimity ($1125^{b}1$–25)—it may be called *philotimia* without the pejorative overtones of that word. The *EE* knows no such virtue. Instead, in its list of good passional means ($1234^{a}24$) it has the quality of *semnotēs* (dignity), a mean between obsequiousness and self-will. No doubt it is rash to draw any conclusions from these variations in emphasis. But it is perhaps worth pondering the following question. Who is the younger man, and who is the older man: the author of the *NE* who prizes highly proper ambition, magnificence, and magnanimity, or the author of the *EE* who is more attracted by dignity and gentleness?[1]

We come finally to an argument which probably most scholars today would regard as the strongest for dating the *EE* early, or at least earlier than the *NE*: the treatments of pleasure in *AE* C and *NE* 10. Most scholars are convinced that the treatment in *AE* C is Eudemian, even if they are prepared to regard most of the *AE* as Nicomachean: for as part of the *NE* it makes such a puzzling doublet with *NE* 10 which makes no reference to it. Most scholars are also convinced that the treatment of *NE* 10 is philosophically more sophisticated than that in *AE* C: consequently, they say, since *AE* C belongs with the *EE* and *NE* 10 with the *NE*, and *NE* must be later than the *EE*.[2]

Recently, G. E. L. Owen has argued that the two treatments are not doublets because they are not about the same topic. The *AE* treatment offers to tell us what our real pleasures are; the *NE* discussion is designed to tell us the nature of enjoying by reviewing the logical characteristics of pleasure-verbs.[3] It is a mistake, he thinks, to draw a contrast, as many scholars do, between a treatment which identifies pleasure with unimpeded activity and a treatment which regards pleasure as an epiphenomenon supervenient on activity.[4]

1. My colleague, Mr. J. Griffin of Balliol College, has suggested that if the *EE* is later than the *NE* the difference between the two treatments could be explained by disillusionment with the career of Alexander.

2. See Festugière, 1946; Lieberg, 1958; Gautheir–Jolif, 1958, 778 ff. Our stylistic criteria support the common view that *AE* C's treatment of pleasure is Eudemian and *NE* 10's is Nicomachean: Table 9.1 shows the result of comparing the two treatments with expectations drawn from the *EE* and from the remainder of the *NE*. The comparison would hardly have been worth making, for the point is so generally accepted, were it not for the attempt of Webb (*Phronesis* 1977, 236) to show that it is the C treatment that is the Nicomachean one.

3. Owen, 1972.

4. Thus Anscombe says that pleasure 'astonishingly, reduced Aristotle to babble, since for good reasons he both wanted pleasure to be identical with and to be different from the activity that it is pleasure in' (1957, 76).

TABLE 9.1 *Nicomachean and Eudemian Favourite Expressions in the Two Treatments of Pleasure*

Group	Total in NE less 10·1–5	Expectation in NE 10·1–5	Actual in NE 10·1 5	Expectation in AE C 11–14	Actual in AE C 11–14
N-favourites					
N I	542	42·38	45	24·48	18
N II	453	35·42	29	20·11	7
N III	385	30·11	33	17·44	6
N IV	373	29·17	31	16·86	12
N V	377	29·48	30	16·98	6
N VI	403	31·46	14	17·39	7
	2533	198·02	182	113·27	56

Group	Total in EE	Expectation in NE 10·1–5	Actual in NE 10·1–5	Expectation in AE C 11–14	Actual in AE C 11–14
E-favourites					
E I	311	33·90	14	19·47	25
E II	263	28·67	16	16·46	24
E III	279	30·41	11	17·46	25
E IV	256	27·90	12	16·02	25
E V	267	29·10	12	16·71	13
E VI9	380	41·42	39	23·79	18
	1756	190·88	104	109·98	130

I agree with Owen that the traditional contrast is mistaken, but I find his own contrast unconvincing.[1] The doctrine of the *AE* and the *NE* seem to me to be identical with respect to the classification of pleasures, the nature of pleasure and its relation to activity, and the moral value of pleasure.

First, the classification of pleasure. There are five different types of pleasure, or pseudo-pleasure, considered by Aristotle, and all of

1. Owen has been criticized by Gosling, 1973.

them appear both in the *AE* and in the *NE*. At the bottom of the scale there are the pleasures of the sick (sick either in body or soul) which are not really pleasures at all: these appear in *AE* at $1153^{b}33$ and $1154^{a}32$, and in B at $1173^{b}22$ and $1176^{a}19$. Next up the scale come the *per accidens* pleasures of food and drink and sex as enjoyed by the gourmand and the lecher: these appear in *AE* at $1152^{b}35$ ff., $1154^{a}17$, $^{a}35-^{b}3$ where they are distinguished from the lower class of false pleasures.[1] These pleasures appear in *NE* at $1173^{b}8-15$. Next up the hierarchy come the aesthetic pleasures of the senses. These are divided into two classes—the pleasures of the inferior sense of touch and taste, and the pleasures of the superior senses of sight, hearing, and smell. These are mentioned in *AE* at $1153^{a}26$ and in *NE* especially at $1174^{b}14-75^{a}10$ and $1175^{b}36-76^{a}2$. Finally there are the pleasures of mind mentioned in *AE* at $1153^{a}1$ and 20, and in *NE* at $1173^{b}17$, $1174^{b}21$, and $^{b}34$ and elsewhere.

Secondly, the nature of pleasure and its relation to activity. The passage in the *NE* which is usually thought to distinguish pleasure from activity in a way which is incompatible with the *AE* is $1174^{b}23-32$:

Each sense has a corresponding pleasure as also have thought and speculation, and its activity is pleasantest when it is most perfect, and most perfect when the organ is in good condition and when it is directed to the most excellent of its objects; and the pleasure perfects the activity. The pleasure does not however perfect the activity in the same way as the object perceived and the sensory faculty, if good, perfect it; just as health and the physician are not in the same way the cause of being healthy. . . . The pleasure perfects the activity, not as the fixed disposition does, by being already present in the agent, but as a supervening perfection, like the bloom of health in the young and vigorous. (trs Rackham)

How can this statement be reconciled, scholars have wondered, with the definition of pleasure in *AE* ($1153^{a}14$) as the unimpeded activity of a disposition in accordance with nature? The reconciliation is not difficult, and the way to undertake it is briskly indicated in Owen's article:

The activities of the natural states which served as [*AE*]'s paradigms of pleasure need not be enjoyable at all. Smith is exercising his wits on an argument; but his wits are blunt, he is tired, the argument is tangled. So

---

1. There is a difficulty at $1154^{b}17$ where the two types of pleasure distinguished above seem to be confused.

[*NE*] is spelling out the further conditions that are requisite for pleasure—sharp wits, impeccable object. (1972, 146)

Such conditions are precisely what is covered by Aristotle's requirement in *AE* that an activity, to be pleasant, must proceed unimpeded. You are at a wine-tasting; you are free from colds or distracting flute-playing; then if you do not enjoy the wine either it is a bad wine or you have a bad palate; there is no third alternative. The language of *NE* is an expansion of what is brusquely said at 1154^{b}20: those things are naturally pleasant which bring a healthy nature into action (*physei d'hēdea, ha poiei praxin tēs toiasde physeōs*). Pleasure 'perfects' activity: that is to say, it causes the activity to be a good one of its kind. The faculty and the object, between them, are the efficient cause of the activity; if they are both good, they will be the efficient cause of a good activity, and therefore they too will 'perfect' activity, i.e. make it be a good specimen of such activity. But pleasure causes activity not as efficient cause, but as final cause: like health, not like the doctor.[1] The *physis* of *AE* is the good *hexis* of *NE*, the *praxis* of *AE* is the *energeia* of *NE*, and the *poiei* of *AE* and the *teleioi* of *NE* both refer to the agency of a final cause.

It is true that Aristotle prefers to speak of the activity as *being* a pleasure in *AE* and of the pleasure *arising from* the activity in *NE*: but this does not mark a difference of doctrine. It simply means that when he talks of 'activity' in *NE* he is often talking of impeded activities as well as unimpeded ones. The pleasure supervenes on the activity to the extent that if you say an activity is pleasant you are saying more than that it is an activity of a specific kind: but you are not saying anything more than that it is a good, unimpeded, activity of that specific kind. It is no more something that could exist in isolation from the activity than the *hōra* could be peeled off those in their prime.[2]

---

1. So, convincingly, Gauthier–Jolif, 1959, 839.
2. Gosling's comment on this passage is excellent: 'Perfect activity is not a condition for the occurrence of pleasure. Perfect activity is what pleasure is. But activity is not what pleasure is, since activity needs the addition of perfection to be pleasure, which perfects activity not as a condition already present, but in the way in which any perfection added to something makes it perfect (1174^{b}31–33). The point is repeated in the remark so unfortunately translated in terms of the bloom on the cheek of youth. It is, indeed, difficult to get a non-redundant translation, but the sense is that pleasure perfects in the way their prime perfects those of full age. Similarly, validity makes an argument perfect, humour a joke and so

Finally, the relation between pleasure and goodness. Both *AE* and *NE* regard the question 'is pleasure good or bad?' as too simple. Both regard the question as only answerable after pleasures have been distinguished and classified in the manner just discussed. Pleasure in a good activity is good, and pleasure in a bad activity is bad: this doctrine of the *NE* (1175^b27) leaves it open—as only the *AE* says explicitly—for the pleasure of the best activity to be the best of all human goods.

If we are to seek, then, to settle the temporal relationship between the *EE* and the *NE* by a comparison between the two treatments of pleasure, it must be to features of composition rather than to matters of philosophical substance that we shall have to appeal in awarding the palm to one text rather than the other. Festugière is the only author to have really argued a case for the superiority of the *NE* treatment: and recently Webb has shown that in the great majority of cases Festugière has simply argued from the greater length of the *NE* treatment to its being the more mature one (Webb, 1977). Apart from this, Festugière's principal argument is that the *AE* treatment is largely a refutation of Speusippus, while the *NE* treatment puts forward a positive view of Aristotle's own. But Festugière is mistaken both about the doctrine of Speusippus (which he identifies with the theory in *NE* 10 that pleasure is absolutely bad, 1172^a28, despite Aristotle's denial that Speusippus held this view at 1153^b8) and about the method of Aristotle (in *AE* C 7–10 Aristotle is practising the policy recommended at the beginning of *EE*, and carried out throughout that work and the *AE*, of squeezing the truth out of a discussion of received opinions). There is no denying that *NE* 10 contains much that is of the highest philosophical interest concerning the nature of states, processes, and activities;[1] but it cannot be said that either the study of these metaphysical questions, or the discussion of philosophical opinions on the morality of pleasure, has been worked into Aristotle's own ethical argument with anything resembling the density and economy of the treatment in *AE* C. Worst of all, the treatise in *NE*

---

on.' The passage most difficult to reconcile with *AE* is not 1174^b24 ff., but 1175^b33 οὐ μὴν ἐοικέ γε ἡ ἡδονὴ διάνοια εἶναι οὐδ' αἴσθησις (ἄτοπον γάρ), ἀλλὰ διὰ τὸ μὴ χωρίζεσθαι φαίνεται τισι ταὐτόν. But this is consistent with the *AE* view if διάνοια and αἴσθησις are taken, as throughout the previous discussion, to refer to a faculty and not to a particular exercise of a faculty.

1. I have studied some of the philosophical lessons to be learnt from *NE* 10, 4–5, in Kenny, 1963, ch. 6.

10 leaves the reader unclear about Aristotle's own views on the crucial points of the relationships between pleasure, activity, and goodness. A charitable student can tease out of the text a doctrine consistent in itself and consistent with the theory of *AE* C: but patient and learned readers have been left in doubt whether Aristotle in *NE* 10 did or did not identify pleasure with the relevant activity, did or did not reject the identification of the supreme pleasure with the supreme good. No one has been left in similar doubt by the brief and lucid arguments of *AE* C.

In my view, it is as impossible to settle the chronological relationship between the *EE* and the *NE* by comparing the treatments of pleasure as it is to do so by comparing the criticisms of the Ideal theory. All I have tried to do, in each case, is to show that the arguments which claim to prove by these means that the *EE* is early and immature are built upon sand. No doubt, when finally pressed, most scholars would say that their belief in the priority of the *EE* to the *NE* rests not upon any particular argument but upon their over-all impression of the respective philosophical merits of the works. Such judgements are, of course, partly a function of variations in the fashionableness of criteria for judging philosophical merit: they are also very much a function of how closely a text has been read, analysed, and meditated upon. It will only be when the *EE* has been for some time as carefully and widely studied as the *NE* has been for centuries that we shall be able to make an unclouded judgement about their comparative worth.

The contribution of the present work has been, I hope, to show that such a study can only be fairly undertaken if the disputed books are replaced within the Eudemian framework. I have presented a succession of arguments, historical, philological, and philosophical, to prove that they fit within that framework very much better than they fit within the Nicomachean framework in which they have been so long read. In addition, I have tried to show that the historical and philosophical arguments for the comparative lateness of the *NE* and the comparative earliness of the *EE* are inadequate and should never have secured the almost unanimous assent of the learned world. I have put forward a hypothesis concerning the dating and origin of the *EE* and the *MM* which, I flatter myself, explains the phenomena no worse than those current in the commentaries and in the periodicals. But I do not attach to these conjectures the weight which I believe should be attached to my arguments for a Eudemian origin for the common books. In particular, I have no strong convictions about the original date of the *NE*: indeed, given the lack of evidence for the existence of our *Nicomachean Ethics* until the second century A.D. it may well be misleading to speak of *the* date of the *NE* at any point in Aristotle's career. Loosely connected as its books are internally, and uncertainly evidenced as it is by external testimony, it could well be a collection of material from various periods of Aristotle's life which did not exist in a collected form until the time of Aspasius. Such a conjecture, however, could be supported, if at all, only by further close work on the style of individual Nicomachean books as part of an over-all investigation of the stylistic features of the Aristotelian corpus. Only such a study could produce a general scholarly consensus about the chronology of Aristotle's writings resembling that which, since the work of Campbell and Lutoslawski, it has been the good fortune of Platonic scholars to possess.

BIBLIOGRAPHY

ACKRILL, J. L., *Aristotle on Eudaimonia*, London, 1974.

ALLAN, D. J., *The Philosophy of Aristotle*, Oxford, 1952.

——, 'Magna Moralia and Nicomachean Ethics', *Journal of Hellenic Studies* 77 (1957).

——, 'Quasi-mathematical Method in the Eudemian Ethics', in Mansion, 1961.

——, 'Aristotle's Criticism of Platonic Doctrine Concerning Goodness and the Good', *Proceedings of the Aristotelian Society* 64 (1963-4).

——, 'Review of Dirlmeier 1962', *Gnomon* (1966).

——, 'The fine and the good in the Eudemian Ethics', in Harlfinger and Moraux, 1971.

ANSCOMBE, G. E. M., *Intention*, Oxford 1957.

ARBERRY, A. J., 'The Nicomachean Ethics in Arabic', *Bulletin of the School of African and Oriental Studies* 17 (1955).

ARKIN, H., and COLTON, R. R., *Statistical Methods*, New York, 1970.

ARNIM, H. von, 'Die drei Aristotelischen Ethiken', *SB Wien* 202 (1924).

——, 'Arius Didymus' Abriss der peripatetischen Ethik', *SB Wien* 204 (1926).

——, 'Die Echtheit der Grossen Ethik des Aristoteles', *Rheinisches Museum* 76 (1927).

——, 'Eudemische Ethik und Metaphysik', *SB Wien* 207 (1928).

——, 'Neleus von Skepsis', *Hermes* 63 (1928).

——, 'Nochmals die Aristotelischen Ethiken', *SB Wien* 209 (1929).

——, 'Der neueste Versuch, die Magna Moralia als unecht zu erweisen', *SB Wien* 209 (1929).

ARY. D. and JACOBS, L. C., *Introduction to Statistics*, New York, 1976.

BENDIXEN, J., 'Bemerkungen zum siebenten Buch der Nik. Ethik.', *Philologus* 10 (1885).

——, 'Übersicht über die neueste des Aristoteles Ethik und Politik betreffende Literatur', *Philologus* 11 (1856).

BERVE, H., *Das Alexanderreich auf prosopographischer Grundlage*, Munich, 1926.

BIGNONE, E., *L'Aristotele perduto e la formazione filosofica di Epicuro*, Florence, 1936.

BLOCK, I., 'The order of Aristotle's Psychological Writing', *American Journal of Philosophy*, 1961.

BODEUS, R., 'Histoire des oeuvres morales d'Aristote', *Revue philosophique de Louvain*, 1973.

BRINK, K. O., *Stil und Form der pseudaristotelischen Magna Moralia*, Ohlau, 1933.

BYWATER, I., *Contributions to the Textual Criticism of Aristotle's Nicomachean Ethics*, Oxford 1892.

CAULCOTT, E., *Significance Tests*, London, 1973.

CHROUST, A-H., *Aristotle*, London, 1973.

CLARK, S. R. L., *Aristotle's Man*, Oxford, 1975.

COOK WILSON, J., *On the Structure of the Seventh Book of the Nicomachean Ethics*, Chs. 1–10, Oxford, 1879.

COOPER, J. M., 'The *Magna Moralia* and Aristotle's Moral Philosophy', *American Journal of Philology* 94 (1973).

——, *Reason and Human Good in Aristotle*, London, 1975.

DEVEREUX, D., Review of Cooper, 1975, forthcoming, 1978.

DIELS, H., *Doxographi Greeci*, Berlin, 1879.

——, 'Zu Aristoteles' Protreptikos und Cicero's Hortensius', *Archiv für Geschichte der Philosophie* 1 (1888).

DIRLMEIER, F., *Aristoteles, Magna Moralia, übersetzt und erläutert*, Berlin, 1958.

——, *Aristoteles, Nikomakische Ethik, übersetzt und kommentiert*, Berlin, 1959.

——, *Merkwürdige Zitate in der EE*, Heidelberg, 1962.

——, *Aristoteles, Eudemische Ethik, übersetzt und kommentiert*, Berlin, 1969.

DROSSART-LULOFS., J., *Nicolaus Damascenus: On the Philosophy of Aristotle*, Leiden, 1965.

DÜRING, I., 'Ariston or Hermippus', *Classica et Medievalia* 17 (1956), 11–21.

——, *Aristotle in the Ancient Biographical Tradition*, Goteborg, 1957.

——, *Aristoteles*, Heidelberg, 1966.

——, *Aristoteles* (Sonderausgaben der Paulyschen Realencyclopädie), Stuttgart, 1968.

ELLEGÅRD, A., *A Statistical Method for Determining Authorship*, Gothenburg, 1962.

EUCKEN, R., *De Aristotelis Dicendi Ratione. Pars Prima*, Göttingen, 1866.

——, *Über den Sprachgebrauch des Aristoteles*, Berlin, 1868.

FESTUGIÈRE, A. J., *Aristote, Le Plaisir*, Paris, 1936.

FISCHER, A. M., *De Ethicis Nicomacheis et Eudemiis*, Bonn, 1847.

FLASHAR, H., 'Ideenkritik in der Ethik des Aristoteles', in *Synusia, Festschrift Schadewalt*, Pfulling, 1965.

FORTENBAUGH, W. W., *Aristotle on Emotion*, London, 1975.

FRAGSTEIN, A. von, *Studien zur Ethik des Aristoteles*, Amsterdam, 1974.

FRITZSCHE, A. T. H., *Eudemi Rhodi Ethica* (*Aristotelis Ethica Eudemia*), Regensburg, 1851.

FRITZ, K. von, 'Eudoxos von Knidos', *Philologus* lxxxv (1930), 478–81.

FURLEY, D., *Two Studies in the Greek Atomists*, Princeton, 1968.

GADAMER, H.-G., 'Der aristotelische Protreptikos und die entwicklungsgeschichtliche Betrachtung der aristotelischen Ethik', *Hermes* 63 (1928).

GAISER, K. 'Zwei Protreptikos-Zitate in der E. E. des Aristoteles', *Rheinisches Museum* N.F. 110, 4 (1967).

GAUTHIER, R. A., Introduction to Second Edition of *l'Éthique à Nicomaque*, Louvain, 1970.

GAUTHIER, R. A. and JOLIF, J. Y., *L'Éthique à Nicomaque*, Louvain, 1958 and 1959.

GOHLKE, P., 'Die Entstehung der aristotelischen Ethik, Politik, Rhetorik', *SB Wien* 223 (1944).

GOSLING, J. C. B., 'More Aristotelian Pleasures', *Proceedings of the Aristotelian Society* (1973) 15 ff.

GOW, A. S. F., *Machon*, Cambridge, 1965.

GRANT, A., *The Ethics of Aristotle*, London, 1857.

GREENWOOD, L. H. G., *Aristotle, Nicomachean Ethics Book VI*, Cambridge, 1909.

GRIFFIN, M. T., *Seneca, a philosopher in politics*, Oxford, 1976.

HACKFORTH, R., 'Sicily, 367 to 330 B.C.' in *The Cambridge Ancient History*, VI, Cambridge, 1927.

HALL, R., 'The Special Vocabulary of the Eudemian Ethics', *Classical Quarterly* N.S. 9 (1959).

HANSEN, B., *Rückläufiger Wörterbuch der griechischen Eigennamen*, Berlin, 1957.

HARDY, W. F. R., *Aristotle's Ethical Theory*, Oxford, 1968.

HARLFINGER, D., 'Die handschriftliche Überlieferung der Eudemischen Ethik' in Harlfinger and Moraux, 1971.

—— and MORAUX, P., *Untersuchungen zur Eudemischen Ethik*, Berlin, 1971.

HEATH, T., *A History of Greek Mathematics*, Oxford, 1921.

HICKS, R. D., *Diogenes Laertius* (Loeb edn.), Harvard, 1925.

JACKSON, H., *The Fifth book of the Nicomachean Ethics of Aristotle*, Cambridge, 1879.

——, 'On some passages in the seventh book of the Eudemian Ethics, Cambridge, 1900.

JAEGER, W., *Aristotle: Fundamentals of the History of his Development* (trs. Robinson), Oxford, 1948.

——, 'Aristotle's use of medicine as a model of method in the *Ethics*', *Journal of Hellenic Studies* 1957, 58 ff.

JOHNSON, H., 'The use of Statistics in the Analysis of the characteristics of Pauline Writing', *New Testament Studies*, 1973.

KAPP, E., *Das Verhältniss der Eud. zur Nik. Ethik*, Berlin, 1912.

KEARNEY, J. J., 'Two notes on the Tradition of Aristotle's Writings', *American Journal of Philology* 84 (1963), 52–63.

KENNY, A., *Action Emotion and Will*, London, 1963.

——, 'Happiness', *Proceedings of the Aristotelian Society* 66 (1965–6).

——, 'A stylometric study of the Aristotelian Corpus' CIRPHO, autumn 1976.

LEONARD, J., *Le Bonheur chez Aristote*, Brussels, 1948.

LIEBERG, G., *Die Lehre von der Lust*, Munich, 1958.

MANSION, A., 'La génèse de l'oeuvre d'Aristote d'apres les travaux récents', *Revue néoscolastique de la philosophie* 29 (1927).

MANSION, S., *Aristote et les Problèmes de Méthode*, Louvain, 1961.

MARGUERITTE, H., Review of Jaeger, 'Über Ursprung und Kreislauf des philosophischen Lebensideals', *Revue d'histoire de la philosophie* 4 (1930).

MASELLIS, V., 'Traduzione e cataloghi delle opere aristoteliche', *Rivista di filologia e d'istruzione classica* 34 (1956).

MAURUS, Silvester, *Collected Works*, ed. F. Ehrle, ii, Regensburg, 1885–6.

MEINECKE, A., 'Zu Stobaeus', *Zeitschrift f.d. Gymnasialwesen* 13 (1859).

MERCKEN, H. P. F., *The Greek Commentaries of the Nicomachean Ethics of Aristotle in the Latin Translation of Robert Grosseteste*, i, Leiden, 1973.

MERLAN, P., *Studies in Epicurus and Aristotle*, Wiesbaden, 1960.

MICHAELSON, M. and MORTON, A. Q., 'The Authorship and Integrity of the *Athenaion Politeia*', Proceedings of the Royal Society of Edinburgh, 1973.

MINGAY, J., 'Coniunctio inter Homines Hominum' in Stern, Hourani, and Brown, 1972.

MONAN, J. D., *Moral Knowledge and its Methodology in Aristotle*, Oxford, 1968.

MORAUX, P., 'L'exposé de la philosophie d'Aristote chez Diogène Laerce', *Revue philosophique de Louvain* (1949).

——, 'Das Fragment θ, 1' in Harlfinger and Moraux, 1971.

——, *Les Listes anciennes des ouvrages d'Aristote*, Louvain, 1951.

——, *Der Aristotelismus bei den Griechen*, i, Berlin, 1973.

MORTON, A. Q. and WINSPEAR, A. D., *It's Greek to the Computer*, Montreal, 1971.

MORTON, A. Q. and McLEMAN, J. J., *Paul, the Man and the Myth*, London, 1966.

MUHLL, P. von der, *De Aristotelis Ethica Eudemea*, Göttingen, 1909.

MULLER, A., *Die griechischen Philosophen in der arabischen Überlieferung*, Halle, 1873.

MUNRO, H. A. J., '*Nicomachean Ethics*, Book V: *Eudemian Ethics*, Book IV', *Journal of Classical and Sacred Philology* 2 (1855).

MURRAY, O., 'Philodemus and the good King', *Journal of Roman Studies* 55 (1965).

NEWMAN, W. L., *Aristotle's Politics*, Oxford, 1887–1902.

NUYENS, F., *L'Évolution de la psychologie d'Aristote*, Louvain, 1948.

OWEN, G. E. L., 'Logic and Metaphysics in Some Earlier Works of Aristotle' in *Aristotle and Plato in the Mid-Fourth Century*, Goteborg, 1960.

——, *Tithenai ta phainomena* in Mansion, 1961.

——, *The Platonism of Aristotle*, London, 1965.

——, 'Aristotelian Pleasures', *Proceedings of the Aristotelian Society* 72 (1971–2).

PARET, R., 'Notes bibliographiques sur quelques travaux récents', *Byzantion* 29/30 (1959/60).

PETERS, F. E., *Aristotle and the Arabs*, New York, 1968.

RABINOWITZ, W. G., *Aristotle's Protrepticus and the Sources of its Reconstruction*, Berkeley, 1957.

RACKHAM, H., *The Eudemian Ethics* (Loeb edn.), London, 1935.

REES, D., 'Magnanimity in the EE and NE', in Harlfinger and Moraux, 1971.

RIST, J. N., *Epicurus, an Introduction*, Cambridge, 1972.

ROSE, V., *De Aristotelis librorum ordine et auctoritate*, Berlin, 1854.

——, 'Uber die griechische Kommentar zur *Ethik* des Aristoteles', *Hermes* 5 (1871).

ROSS, W. D., *Aristotle*, London, 1923.

——, *The works of Aristotle* (Oxford translation), vol. ix, Oxford, 1925.

——, *Aristotle's Metaphysics*, Oxford, 1924.

ROWE, C. J., *The Eudemian and Nicomachean Ethics: A study in the development of Aristotle's Thought*, Cambridge, 1971.

SCHACHER, E. J., *Studien zu den Ethiken des Corpus Aristotelicum*, Paderborn, 1940.

SCHLEIERMACHER, F., *Über die ethischen Werks des Aristoteles*, =*Samtliche Werke*, iii.3, Berlin, 1835.

SOLOMON, J., 'Translation of the Eudemian Ethics', *The Oxford Aristotle*, ix, Oxford, 1925.

SPENGEL, L., 'Über die unter den Namen des Aristoteles erhaltenen ethischen Schriften', *Abhandl. der Bayer. Akademie* 3 (1841 and 1843).

——, 'Aristotelische Studien', *Abhandl. d. Bayer. Akademie*, Munich, 10 (1864) and (1866).

STERN, S. M., HOURANI, A. and BROWN, V., *Islamic Philosophy and the Classical Tradition*, London, 1972.

STEWART, J. A., *Notes on the Nicomachean Ethics of Aristotle*, Oxford, 1892.

STOCK, St. G., Introduction in Ross, 1925.

SUSEMIHL, F., *Eudemii Rhodii Ethica (Aristotelis Ethica Eudemia)*, Leipzig, 1884 (Amsterdam, 1967).

——, 'Die Lebenszeit des Theodektes,' *Rhenisches Museum*, LIV.

THEILER, W., 'Die Grosse Ethik und die Ethiken des Aristoteles', *Hermes*, 69 (1934).

TITZE, F. N., *De Aristotelis Operum serie et distinctione*, Leipzig, 1826.

VERBEKE, G., 'L'idéal de la perfection humaine chez Aristote et l'évolution de sa noétique', *Fontes Ambrosiani*, 25 (1951).

WAGNER, D., *Das Problem einer theonomen Ethik bei Aristoteles*, Heidelberg, 1970.

WAKE, E., 'Sentence-length Distributions of Greek Authors', *Journal of the Royal Statistical Society*, 1960.

WEBB, P., 'The relative Dating of the Accounts of Pleasure in the *Nicomachean Ethics*', *Phronesis*, 1977.

WEBSTER, C., 'Fourth Century Tragedy and the *Poetics*', *Hermes* 82 (1954).

WALZER, R., *Greek into Arabic*, London, 1984.

——, *Magna Moralia und Aristotelische Ethik*, Berlin, 1929.

WEHRLI, F., *Die Schule des Aristoteles*, Basel, 1959-.

WIDMANN, G. *Autarkie und Philia in den Aristotelischen Ethiken*, Tübingen, 1967.

WILAMOWITZ-MOELLENDORFF, U. von, 'Neleus von Skepsis', *Hermes* 62 (1927).

INDEX